£450

C000225742

Swan Island

Caribbean Sea

tuca
Caratasca Lagoon
Cape Gracias a Dios
ejmus
Miskito Cays
PUERTO CABEZAS
Rio Grande Bar
Providence Island
Rama Cay
Little Corn
Great Corn
BLUEFIELDS
Monkey Point
San Juan del Norte

LIMÓN
Changuinola
Colón
Portobello
Panama City
Panama Canal
COL.

TEKKIN A WAALK

TEKKIN A WAALK

Along the Miskito Coast

PETER FORD

HarperCollins*Publishers*

HarperCollins*Publishers*,
77–85 Fulham Palace Road,
Hammersmith, London W6 8JB

Published by HarperCollins*Publishers* 1992
1 3 5 7 9 10 8 6 4 2

First published by
Viking US Publishers 1991

A catalogue record for this book is
available from the British Library

ISBN 0 00 255002 4

Set in Garamond

Printed in Great Britain by
HarperCollinsManufacturing Glasgow

To Edith,
and to the people
of the coast

. . . that he should kindly use and relieve such straggling Englishmen as should chance to come that way with plantains, fish and turtle.

—Commission entrusted to the first king of the Miskitos, circa 1660, by the English Crown.

ACKNOWLEDGMENTS

I do not have room to thank all those who helped me write this book. I would like to offer special gratitude, though, to Professor Richard Adams and the staff of the Latin American library at the University of Texas; German Romero and his colleagues at the Atlantic Coast Research and Documentation Centre (CIDCA) in Managua; and John Holms, who all suggested valuable lines of research. Bob Foster, Linda Nance, Peggy Westwell, Laura Zabeo, Marie Claude Picard and her brother Jean Paul offered vital practical assistance. Thank you.

I could not have travelled along the Nicaraguan coast in time of war without permission from both Sandinista Interior Minister Tomas Borge and rebel guerrilla chief Brooklyn Rivera. Each was open-minded enough to give his blessing to my journey knowing that the other approved it, too.

I would also like to thank the captains and owners of the *Stuart Little, Terry, Mamy Joan, Guatemala, Mely, Tona C., Utila Tom, Alpha 1, Nitu Tita, Diadira Wan, Kisan, Yang Taikras, Miss Aneeth, Maria Bella, Yecenia, Carinito, RS-17, Ru de Chobra* and all the other—unnamed—vessels of varying sizes and seaworthiness that carried me down the coast from Belize to Panama.

TEKKIN A WAALK

ONE

"You're sooo fockin handsome."
I had been afraid of an approach like this ever
since I had spotted her, at the edge of the crowd
around the finish line, dancing by herself in the blazing
sun, beckoning to me with a bottle of rice wine.

"Tek a drink," she offered, sitting down heavily beside
me on the bench, throwing her free arm around my neck
and giving me a glazed-eye smile. *"Tek a likkle drink."*

I had come to the Burrell Boom racetrack outside Belize
City to watch the horses, not to get drunk. But I didn't
seem to have much choice; Yolanda, bursting out of her
bright red dress, was relying on me to help keep her upright. I decided to get into the spirit of the afternoon. A
few swigs of the pale gingery wine, still fizzing as it fermented, gave me the proper perspective. Horse racing was
clearly a secondary attraction at this meeting, an excuse to
"tek a likkle drink." But if I kept the rice wine up for the
rest of the afternoon, I was going to be in trouble: It had
been brewed with enough sugar to give it the strength of
sherry.

Above us in the stands, a dreadlocked youth twiddled some dials on a complicated-looking piece of electronic machinery that I had innocently thought was connected to a camera used for photo-finishes. Instead, Bob Marley and the Wailers belted out a song from a pair of loudspeakers.

I pulled Yolanda to her feet, draped her arms over my shoulders, and shuffled a few steps to the reggae music before catching the eye of a bystander who seemed eager for a dance. Yolanda scarcely noticed she had a new partner as I sidled off to see what else was happening.

I found myself at Ascot, forced through a tropical mincer and reconstituted in the Caribbean. The smart Rangerovers had turned into beat-up Chevrolet station wagons, their lowered tailgates laden not with bottles of *blanc de blanc* but with coolers full of rum. The refreshment stands and snack bars had become a row of wide-hipped, foulmouthed women shaded by their makeshift stalls of plastic sheeting and serving platefuls of rice and beans and river-turtle stew from greasy tureens.

The racegoers themselves had no use for binoculars or form sheets. Their Easter Monday race-day gear comprised a pair of mirror shades and a plastic cup from which they drank rum mixed with evaporated milk.

The turtle stew was rich and pungent, as if nature had crossed a fish with a well-hung pheasant, and well worth the effort of swallowing my compunctions about eating an endangered species. The rum and evaporated milk, on the other hand, was best left alone. It was like getting legless on baby food.

The racecourse was a broad swathe of parched savannah grass cut from the surrounding scrub. The track itself, a mile around, was worn down in parts to sandy earth and set off by irregular termite-ridden posts. Some stands had been erected under a canvas awning, but they were empty, except for the sound crew and a tangle of cables.

The paddock was marked by a line of pickup trucks and horse boxes surrounding a patch of rough grass. There I found the men who had come for the racing as well as for the party. Arguing fiercely amongst themselves about the talents of the various jockeys, the accuracy of the bathroom scales on which the riders weighed in and the length of time since it had last rained, they paid curiously little attention to the horses themselves.

On inspection, I realised why. Lined up under a palm-thatched shelter was the most pitiful collection of knock-kneed, cross-eyed nags I had ever seen. There was nothing to choose among any of them, save one sleek chestnut stallion with black forelegs. He was a three-year-old named "The Baron," I was told, and I decided that he would carry my afternoon's one bet.

It was not easy, however, to place a bet. During the prelude to the first couple of races, in which The Baron was not running, I studied the apparently random manner in which money changed hands between the handful of men who were betting. It soon became apparent that there were no bookmakers, nor was anyone fixing any odds, which left me at sea.

Uncertain how to proceed, I went back to The Baron, to admire his mane plaited into Rastafarian dreadlocks, and to see if I could glean any hints, without betraying my ignorance, as to how one went about laying money on a horse.

The Baron's jockey, a slight youth with the coppery skin of a Maya indian and hair tied back in a pigtail, was tightening a girth strap as I approached, and then busied himself polishing up his riding boots. They were decorated with

Rasta decals portraying a roaring Lion of Judah against a red, yellow, black and green flag. I asked him for a little advice.

"Bettin, mon? I doan bet. Go aask dem fellers over dere," he suggested.

"Dem fellers" were the same crowd of argumentative rowdies I had not dared interrupt before, but I buttonholed one who had turned away to pee into the undergrowth. He explained that it was actually all very simple. You merely chose a horse, sought out somebody who had chosen another one and then bet dollar for dollar that your horse would beat his.

As The Baron pranced around the paddock, putting the other three horses in the race to shame, I set about trying to win some money with him.

"Anybody bet against The Baron?" I called, pressing my way into the knot of men around the weighing scales. They looked at me as if I was mad. I looked from face to face, a ten-dollar Belizean bill in my hand. "Who'll bet against The Baron?" No response. I felt extremely foolish.

Eventually an old man with a broken nose and watery eyes came to my rescue. *"Dere's a feller dat side who's bettin any amount of money,"* he said, pointing towards the stands. *"Try him."*

I found the man in question without difficulty, the biggest mouth on the track, wearing outsized reflecting sunglasses, a violent yellow shirt and loudly checkered trousers, waving fistfuls of bills about. He agreed to bet against The Baron if I "gave him the field." That, he explained, meant that I was betting on The Baron and he was betting on all the other horses in the race. Given the pathetic air of the competition, I did not think I was risking too much. I proffered my ten-dollar bill.

"I not here to fock aroun, mon. I doan tek a bet dat smaal," he said. *"I gotta mek money or lose money."*

I persuaded him, though, that I wanted only an interest in the race—that I was there only to *"fock aroun"*— and he accepted my bet. I moved away as the horses went into the starting gate, and asked the watery-eyed old man what he reckoned on the race.

"I doan bet on haarses miself," he said. *"Haarse races are fonny tings."*

Down the track the gates opened. The Baron came out last and he stayed there all the way round. He had not even been in the running. Forlornly, I handed my ten dollars to the man in the yellow shirt, along with the ten-dollar bet he had given me to hold. He was jumping up and down with glee; I went over to the paddock to talk to the jockey. I felt that my lost bet had given me a proprietorial right to find out what had gone wrong.

"Dey fly de gate when I in de air," he told me. *"I had me foot out de stirrup an I tell de mon wait, bot he still fly de gate."*

I lost my enthusiasm for the races after that, and as the sun set I made my way down the sandy track through thorny bushes and stunted trees that led to the road to Belize. I passed Yolanda, curled up and asleep in the shade of a parked car, and hoped she would not wake up. I need not have worried. The next morning, as I emerged from my hotel room, I stepped aside at the top of the narrow stairs to let the maid come by. It was Yolanda. She did not recognise me.

I had arrived in Belize by sea, as I intended to continue my journey down the coast. But I did not intend to continue in such style.

In the Mexican resort of Cozumel, I had come across Alan Dawson, a lanky sun-bleached South African sailor who had spent the past three years captaining a rich American's seventy-five-foot racing yacht around the world. After three weeks in port taking care of some repairs, he was sick and tired of Cozumel, and I sympathised with him. The town was a tawdry mock-up of a tourist brochure's make-believe Mexico, full of gaudy gold-threaded sombreros, over-iced margaritas and reheated tacos. To make matters worse, it was Spring Break for American universities, and the resort was packed. Alan was anxious to sail his yacht down to Belize, and was looking for crew. I had found the ride I was looking for.

The designer of the *Stuart Little* had not sacrificed much in the way of comfort to the owner's lust for speed, but he had given small thought to the safety of inexperienced hands such as myself. The length of her sleek white deck offered precious little to hang onto: a wire railing ran around the edge at knee height, which was ideal for catching your legs on and tipping you overboard, but not much use as a guardrail; a few halyards by the mast and innumerable winches offered some hope, but to make use of them I found I had to clamber around on all fours.

When I went on board the first night, just before we set sail, I stayed safely close to the well of the cockpit. Alan asked me to take the wheel, which I was glad to do if only because it gave me something to hold onto in the heaving swell, but I was soon in trouble. Staring fixedly at the luminous compass dial, I found, made me unbearably nauseous. Alan gave me a couple of pills, and I slunk down the hatch to my cabin. I fell asleep slowly, since the conversation above my head between Alan and the other crewman, Robert, centred on how badly the rudder had come loose, and how any sudden wave or pull on the wheel could snap it off and leave us out of control.

With the seasickness tablets fogging my mind, I wondered whether this adventure down the Central American coast was a good idea after all. I had been at sea on a small boat only once before in my life and was now planning to spend three months on boats a good deal smaller than this one. The thought made me feel even worse.

I tried to console myself with encouraging recollections of all the stories I had read about the weather at this time of year. I was starting my journey in the middle of March. Until July, according to accounts ancient and modern of French privateers, English merchants and the US Meteorological Service, the trade winds should blow steadily from the east, and they ought not to be carrying much rain. If I lagged, however, I was in danger of being caught by the rainy season, which comes on fast in this part of the world. And if anything held me up until September I was in real trouble, because that is when the hurricanes start blowing.

Pulling out of Cozumel harbour, though, I was happy to confirm the experience of seafarers through the years— the trade winds were blowing firmly, from the right direction. At least something of what I had read in books over the previous six weeks of preparation for the trip would stand me in good stead.

Comforted, I fell asleep.

It took thirty-six hours for us to reach Belize, and I spent the time seeking some sort of understanding with the sea. This I contrived to do by screwing my face into a mask of concentration as I communed to the choppy, purplish waves that I would be around for the next twelve weeks and would appreciate some cooperation. At the same time, I learned how to keep my balance by developing an exaggerated seadog gait that was no more dignified than crawling on all fours, but had the advantage of keeping my hands free.

We arrived off San Pedro, the only village on Ambergris Cay, soon after dawn, as the sun caught white curls of foam seething on the coral reef and threw long coconut palm shadows over the gleaming beach beyond. Standing on the deck of a million dollars' worth of *Stuart Little* as she eased through a cut in the reef, I felt embarrassingly like something out of a Martini advertisement. This was not at all how I had pictured myself battling down the unexplored coast, rediscovering a forgotten world. That would come later, I told myself. Meanwhile, this would do for a start.

The police constable who doubled as immigration officer on Ambergris Cay came out onto the porch of his stilted clapboard house as we walked up the beach, and told us to fill out our landing cards. As we did so, he sat behind a cluttered desk reading a simplified edition of *The Wind in the Willows.*

I tried to imagine a policeman in any other Central American country so careless of his image. My mind filled with memories of the dark glasses and puffed-out chests, swagger and self-importance I had come across so often in this part of the world. They did not mix with the toads and watervoles that were captivating this constable. But when the sergeant came up the stairs to the porch to see who we were, he snorted in disgust at the impression his subordinate was giving of Belizean law enforcement.

"Fockin Bogs Bonny," he sneered as he glanced at the book's childproof cardboard cover and outsized, easy-to-

read print. *"If you're goin to read, you might as well read sumtin worthwhile."*

Turning to us, he announced that while we waited for the customs and quarantine officials to arrive from Belize City, fifteen minutes away by light aircraft, we were not allowed to wander further than a restaurant up the street. To ensure that we did not slip anchor surreptitiously, he took our passports from us.

It was an unnecessary precaution. I had been dreaming of a Belizean breakfast since we'd left Cozumel, and the "Jade Gardens" lived up to my expectations. Run by two retired British squaddies who had served a tour of duty in Belize and decided to stay, the restaurant offered the classic British workingman's breakfast—bacon and eggs and toast and tea—redolent of the grease and sullenness found only in English cafés.

The constable came to fetch us as we wiped the last of the bacon fat from our plates, and we ferried the health inspector back to our boat in the inflatable. His examination was hardly rigorous, comprising one question—had anybody died on board since we left Cozumel?—and ten seconds' reflection as to whether he should order us to destroy our eight mangoes. He decided that this was not necessary, and I was free to go. Alan would deal with the customs official when he arrived.

I was anxious to get away: I was planning to meet my wife, Edith, that afternoon on the next island down the string of small cays lying along the reef. But none of the skiffs tied up at the low jetty were going to Cay Caulker. I would have to fly into Belize City and take a boat from there.

On this quiet Good Friday the sun was high as I walked

down the village street, a beaten sand path just wide enough for one of the monstrous, low-slung Chevrolet sedans so popular in Belize as status symbols or souvenirs of a couple of years' wetbacking in the United States. The street was lined by low wooden houses set on pilings, neatly painted in pastel shades, roofed with rusting zinc. Their shady verandahs were decorated with plants sprouting from old powdered milk or marmalade tins.

The municipal airstrip, paved but potholed, lay at the end of the village. A twin-engined Cessna was waiting for more passengers, and my arrival made it worth the pilot's while to leave. Fifteen minutes later we were dropping down into Belize over a confusion of rusted roofs, rotting timber frames and foul grey canals feeding into a muddy bay.

The settlement was founded nearly 400 years ago by English adventurers who drifted south when the Spanish drove them from the Mexican coast, and found they could make a living in the thick forests and murky swamps by cutting logwood. These thorny, twisted little trees were valued for the dye extracted from their timber, and the loggers would spend weeks at a time out in the bush felling them. Dragging the tree trunks to the nearest river they would then float them downstream to a boom set from bank to bank, such as once must have existed at Burrell Boom, to await collection by trading vessels.

These loggers were "a rude and drunken crew," according to one English merchant who visited them in 1726. "Rum punch is their general drink which they'll sometimes sit several days at." They made no effort to set up any local government, felt no need to build a church for 150 years, and devoted themselves to "Murders, Fraud and Confusion" in the words of a British admiral. By the time "the

Baymen," as they called themselves, did build a church
they were using the money that mahogany, not logwood,
had earned them. Chemical dyes had outmoded natural
extracts, but the great English cabinetmakers of the eighteenth century had promoted a taste for exotic hardwoods
and Belize, or British Honduras as it became known, was
well placed to meet that demand too. By this time, however, most of the jungle work was being done not by the
white settlers but by black slaves bought in from Jamaica
or elsewhere on the coast.

Belize's status always remained ambiguous and precarious. Throughout the seventeenth and eighteenth centuries, Spanish men o' war launched repeated assaults on the
settlement, burning down the shacks and forcing their inhabitants to flee. As soon as the Spanish had withdrawn,
the settlers would return from the cays, rebuilding their
wood and thatched huts within a few days.

In various treaties ending one or other of the wars that
England fought with Spain, Madrid granted increasingly
large concessions to English logcutters in the Bay of Honduras but never ceded sovereignty over the area, nor did
London seek dominion. Belize became effectively British
territory, however, as a result of a bizarre military en-
gagement in 1796.

As the Spanish fleet gathered for an attack on Belize,
the English naval captain sent from Jamaica to assist in the
settlement's defence found the Baymen drunken, unruly
and reluctant to take orders. Against thirty-two ships of
the line carrying 2,000 Spanish troops, the Baymen could
rally only 240 armed men and six vessels, four of them
merchantmen with the unwarriorlike names of Tickler,
Towzer, Teazer and Swinger.

Whether the Spanish admiral feared that this handful of

ragged drunks were just bait to tempt him into an ambush is not known. In any event he withdrew after a week of inconclusive maritime sparring and the Spanish never threatened Belize again. The Battle of St. George's Cay, as the incident became known, is now embalmed in local legend, celebrated annually as an illustration of the brave Baymen's indomitable spirit and refusal to bow to the Spanish yoke.

Few visitors to Belize City have been polite about the place, and it is easy to see why. Though the town smells less powerfully than it did before the Canadian government paid for a new sewage system, the open drains that border many of its narrow streets still take some getting used to. Many times in its history hurricanes have knocked the town back into the swamp it is built on, and the result is a strange air of impermanence: The rickety wooden homes, badly in need of shoring up, their paint faded and peeling under the violent sun, radiate a sense of impending doom.

An old colonial presence too is palpable, appearing through dilapidated cracks in the ramshackle town: ancient English pillar boxes, bright red, with the royal insignia stamped above the slot where you dropped your letters; the Edwardian phrasing of notices over the entrance to shops "licensed to sell fermented and spirituous liquor, not to be consumed on the Premises."

Beneath Belize City's general air of lassitude lies a deeper uncertainty about just what it is there for. It doesn't produce anything, its port is so shallow that cargo boats have to offload onto lighters and it isn't even the capital of the country anymore since a new town was carved out of the jungle fifty miles inland. Yet everybody wants to live there. It is home. All the government's efforts to lure people elsewhere have failed miserably. There are only

160,000 people in the whole country, and well over a third of them are crammed into Belize City, immune to the rats, insects and periodic invasions of landcrabs that plague the town. Moreover, they are proud of their home. The taxi driver waiting at the airport was excited by my plan to write a book about Central America's Caribbean coast.

"Dat a big mission, mon," he said. *"Dat shine a light on Belize we haven't seen yet. Cos dis a virgin country yet, you know. An I tell you one ting, mon: he nebber set one foot in Belize, but Christopher Columbus, he bury here."*

I expressed surprise. I knew that cathedrals in Seville and in Santo Domingo, the capital of the Dominican Republic, both boasted that they housed the great explorer's bones, but I had never heard that Belize, too, had staked a claim. The driver paused. *"Ah, yes, you mebbe right dere, mon. It's not Christopher Columbus, it's de Baron Bliss."*

Baron Bliss? Who the hell was he, to rank equally in a Belizean taxi driver's mind with the discoverer of the New World?

Henry Edward Ernest Victor, the fourth Baron Bliss of the former Kingdom of Portugal, is probably remembered nowhere in the world except Belize. There, however, he is a national hero, his name emblazoned on monuments and public buildings all over the country.

Born in Marlowe, Buckinghamshire, in 1869, Bliss amassed a fortune before being struck by paralysis at the age of forty-two. He then sold everything, built himself a luxurious cruising yacht and headed for the Bahamas to spend the rest of his life sport-fishing. He died of food poisoning fifteen years later while fishing off the cays, but not before he had made out a new will leaving just about everything but his pocket watch to Belize. The trust fund he created contained over a million dollars. He gave no reasons for doing this. As the taxi driver had told me, Bliss never set foot on Belizean soil. But he ensured that somewhere in the world his memory would be honoured, for he specified that any project built with trust-fund money worth over £500 should bear his name.

Belize is thus littered with nursing schools, arts centres, cricket pitches and town halls named after Baron Bliss. The first object a traveller spots as he arrives in Belize harbour is the Bliss lighthouse, beneath which the Baron is buried. The first building you see when you land at the airport is the Bliss transit lounge. The Baron barred the use of any of his money, however, for the construction of educational establishments (except agricultural or vocational schools), dancehalls or churches. Again, he gave no reason for this eclectic list of prohibitions. It is a curious little story, which strikes me as peculiarly Belizean: inconsequential, but charming and unexpected, like the country.

Down the road from the Bliss lighthouse, the taxi dropped me at a bridge over the river mouth, where skiffs from Cay Caulker were tied up. Finding one whose captain said he was leaving *"right now, mon,"* I dropped my rucksack in and jumped after it. Twenty minutes later, still tied up to the dock, I began to adjust to Belizean Standard Time and realised I had plenty of time to go and find a cold drink. All the other passengers were sitting in the shade of a nearby petrol station. I joined them for the hour we had to wait before the boat eventually left.

The forty-minute trip out to the island took us across a wide lagoon sheltered by long belts of mangrove trees growing on submerged cays. None showed any sign of life, save the odd fisherman's shack, nor any trace of their old role as an English loggers' haven from Spanish attack.

My fellow passengers on the speedboat looked nothing

at all like the blacks who had filled the streets of Belize City. Bronze-skinned with slightly indian features, they were island dwellers, descended from refugees who fled the Mexican Caste Wars, an indian-peasant rebellion at the end of the last century. Their Mexican heritage showed only in their faces and their facility for Spanish. But even that language they spoke with an English accent, and when they danced, it was not to the strains of salsa, but calypso.

The boat dropped me at the end of a long wooden jetty, and I surveyed the scene. It was a familiar one, for I had visited Cay Caulker several times over the previous few years, and fallen helplessly under its spell. Apart from anything else, it was here that Edith and I had decided to get married.

Cay Caulker has all the ingredients of a Caribbean paradise: with a stretch of coral sand two miles long and a few hundred yards wide and coconut groves down to the limpid waterfront, the island is home to only a few hundred people. Their village consists of two sandy tracks running parallel to the beach, Front Street and Back Street, bordered by simple clapboard houses, natural lawns of short, tufty grass and casually planted gardens of blood-red hibiscus, lemon trees and ornamental bushes.

The hotel that Edith and I were to stay in stands twenty-five yards back from the shore. I could see it from the jetty, through a clump of shade trees beneath which hammocks swung in the wind. "Vega's Far Inn," as its name suggests, dates from the time when Belize was on the Latin American hippy trail, and tends now to cater to those same hippies fifteen years later, spending shorter holidays and more money now than they used to. A solid, two-storey wooden building painted white, with two flights of stairs running up either side of its façade to a balcony, the hotel looks like a warehouse with pretensions to being an antebellum mansion in Louisiana.

I walked up the pier towards the hotel, expecting my wife to appear at any moment. But as I dropped my rucksack at the foot of the stairs the proprietress emerged to tell me that Edith was not there. She had rung from our home in Managua to say she could not find a seat because all the planes were full over the Easter weekend. I went to drown my sorrows at Martinez's bar down the beach.

The television was on behind the bar, perched above shelves of rum, and what should be on but the Chicago Cubs in spring training. Dennis Martinez was watching it avidly. What had happened to cricket, I wondered, in this bastion of empire?

What had happened to cricket was satellite television. Belize happens to lie under the "shadow" of the satellite that carries Channel 7 from Chicago, and the local television station, rather than spend money making local programmes, simply pirates the signal. Chicago television is thus Belizean television. Chicago news is Belizean news, and Chicago's baseball team is Belize's team too. Everybody with a television, I found, was a Cubs fan, and cricket pitches all over the country have been transformed into baseball diamonds. On one visit to Belize in 1985, I found the city empty save for the route of a procession, and thought perhaps the queen was making a state visit. In fact, everyone had turned out to see Gary Matthews, a star Cubs player, making a lightning tour of this unexpected nest of fans.

And he had plenty of fans on Cay Caulker, for there are plenty of televisions. Their aerials, sprouting from tin roofs, are the only sign that this modest little community is the wealthiest village in Central America. Though the competition is not stiff, of course, some Cay Caulker fishermen are well off even by US standards, making upwards of $50,000 a year. They owe these staggering incomes to the spiny lobster that live and feed on the nearby coral reef, and to the cooperative they formed nearly thirty years ago that broke an American businessman's monopoly on the lobster trade. The only outward signs of their wealth, however, apart from the television aerials, are the ferociously powerful outboard engines fitted to the island's speedboats. Nor do the islanders seem unduly affected by the steady stream of tourists who have discovered Cay Caulker over the past fifteen years. One householder has erected a white picket fence around his yard, along with a notice that reads TRESPASSERS WILL BE VIOLATED, but everybody else was relaxed about the presence of foreigners.

Indeed, the tourists were pampered, in small and discreet ways. Several women offered bacon-and-egg breakfasts in their cramped front rooms or squeezed fresh orange juice for sale, and when cinnamon buns or lemon meringue pies came out of the oven, chalkboard advertisements would appear at kitchen windows.

When Edith arrived the following day, we melted into a few days of self-indulgence, stumbling sleepy-eyed down the deck in the early morning to wake ourselves with a swim, sifting sand through our toes as we lay on the beach, drifting underwater alongside eagle rays and parrotfish when we went diving, mixing coconut water with our rum as dusk fell, choosing between fish and chips and lobster and chips at supper.

This was all very well, but it wasn't getting me any further down the coast. It was time to get moving.

To go south, I first had to go north. The transport manager for Belize Sugar Industries—the national sugar company—had arranged for me to ride on one of his molasses barges from the northern port of La Libertad, near the Mexican border, down to Belize City. All he had asked was that I sign a release form, to the effect that should I fall overboard, drown in molasses or otherwise come to harm it was my own fault. This whole adventure was my own fault. I signed.

The bus to La Libertad took me through the heart of Belizean sugar country, where the cane reached thick and green to every horizon. It also took me into indian country: though the bus itself was full of creoles bouncing on unstable seats to the reggae blaring from the driver's radio, the workers in the fields were of Mayan descent. When we stopped in Orange Walk for a ten-minute break the smell of steamed corncobs, rubbed with chili powder and lime juice, recalled similar bus journeys in Mexico.

Spanish is the dominant tongue in this part of the country. The Mexicans who introduced the language as they escaped from the nineteenth-century Caste Wars have since been joined by refugees from more recent violence: the farmhands and cane cutters in northern Belize were once peasants in El Salvador and Guatemala who could no longer stand the brutality of their governments' armies.

Another band of refugees have made their home around Orange Walk, fleeing not the tumult of war, but the disorders of the modern world. Returning to my seat on the bus as I chewed on a corncob, I spotted a family of them through the window. They were sitting pink-skinned and sober-faced in an open buggy, pulled by a weary-looking horse. The father, dressed in dark blue pinafore dungarees and a curl-brimmed straw hat, twitched at the reins. Beside him sat the mother, looking rigidly ahead, her eyes shaded by a broad-brimmed straw hat, her neck stiff above a long mauve dress that hung heavily down to her black ankle socks. In the back seat sat two little blonde girls, smaller versions of their mother.

The Mennonites look as out of place in Belize as would a Victorian sepia family portrait in a gallery of brash primitivists. They stay close to their farms, shun motor vehicles and most other twentieth-century inventions and provide the country with almost all its chickens, eggs, cheese, beef and milk. Some of the younger Mennonites, however, while retaining their decorous appearance of rectitude, have adopted a more modern approach. Diversifying their production away from Northern European staples, they have turned to Belize's most profitable export cash crop —marijuana. Orange Walk was scandalised, when I passed through, by the news that three Mennonites had just been arrested for drug smuggling. Until then, the government had been content to blame the whole drug problem on "aliens," by which they meant *ladino* refugees.

The *ladinos* undoubtedly make up most of the workforce in the dope industry, hacking out remote clearings in the forest, tending to the marijuana plants and guarding them until harvest from rival growers. But they are paid little more than any other agricultural day labourer, and they run the biggest risk of getting caught.

None of the really big operators have been caught yet, and they act as though they believe they never will be. On Christmas Eve a few years ago, one particularly daring smuggler landed his DC-3 on an invitingly straight stretch of the main road out of Belize City. The police arrived just in time to watch him take off. The highway is now lined by fifteen-foot-high poles, designed to take the wings off a plane flown by anyone who tries to follow that example. But the government cannot erect such defences along every farm track in Belize, and even though antidrug teams spend a lot of time blowing up clandestine landing strips, it would be regarded as rank ingratitude if they were to blow up the roads so kindly built with British and American development aid.

Furnished with a choice of ready-made landing areas, and scarcely deterred by the Belizean Police Force, which is made up mainly of unarmed constables on bicycles, drug smugglers have had a field day in Belize. And though a US programme to spray all the grass plantations with herbicide has discouraged marijuana growers, the smugglers have simply turned to carrying packets of cocaine in the small planes that once transported bales of grass. Out of the frying pan, and into the fire. If the drug trade was flourishing, sugar was in the doldrums.

The old sugar mill where I was due to pick up my molasses barge had been closed, and the bus no longer made the two-mile detour into La Libertad village. Getting off at the junction, I walked down an empty road as the sun sank behind sweet-smelling clouds of smoke. They were burning the sugar fields in preparation for the harvest, to strip the cane stalks of their razor-edged leaves.

The guard at the main gate of the deserted sugar mill could not offer any suggestions when I asked where I might find something to eat. La Libertad, I had discovered walking down its one street, was a ghost town, silent as the surrounding acres of cane that would now be processed at the country's sole remaining refinery, nearby Orange Walk.

Ignoring my hunger, I decided I would do a little work. The boss of Belize Sugar Industries lived nearby; I would ring to see if he had time for an interview on the state of his company, and maybe I could work it up into a piece for one of my newspapers. I had been working in Central America for the previous three years as a reporter for the *The Christian Science Monitor* and the *Financial Times* and thought I might perhaps earn some travelling money by filing some stories as I journeyed down the coast. It was to prove an idle hope. I hardly came across a postbox, let alone a telex or a fax or a telephone, until I returned home.

Mr. Browne sounded overjoyed to hear a new voice. Ten minutes after I called, his driver had arrived to take me out to the fenced-in compound where senior company officials lived.

Micky Browne led me into his spacious, ranch-style house, built by Tate & Lyle in the days when that English multinational had run the sugar industry in Belize. Mr. Browne's predecessor had been an Englishman; he himself was from Jamaica, but apart from that not a great deal seemed to have changed. On a table beside my armchair I noticed a pile of newspapers, on top of which was *The Times* of London. It had been years since I'd seen a copy of *The Times*, and I flicked through one casually.

"The post here is simply dreadful," Mr. Browne said in polished tones as he handed me a glass of beer. "I'm afraid the papers are frightfully old, but they do help to keep one in touch." In fact, the most recent edition had been published only four days earlier, which didn't seem bad considering where we were.

"My office hours are an awful bore as well," my host went on. "I don't get home in time to hear the cricket report on the BBC, I'm afraid, so I can scarcely follow the games. You don't happen to know how the Test went today, do you?"

I coughed out some excuse about the batteries in my

radio being too low for decent reception. In the presence of such an Anglophile, a confession that I wasn't interested in the fate of the English cricket team would have been tantamount to renouncing my nationality. I turned the conversation to a carved wooden bird perched on a branch of dry twigs on the coffee table between us.

"Ah yes, well you don't find that sort of pigeon here in Belize, of course," he explained. "That's a Jamaican pigeon. But I get some fairly decent shootin' in here anyway, when I have the time. The local birds give me a little sport."

I felt time warped into a Somerset Maugham short story and had to pinch myself to remember that this was no longer British Honduras: since 1981 Belize had been an independent nation. The evening continued in the same vein, as we sat down to supper. We ate Jamaican patties, spicy meat wrapped in a pastry envelope, sent especially from home. And when we had finished, I was offered a choice of four malt whiskies and a giant box of cigars, each with Micky Browne's name printed in gold on its crimson wrapper.

Replete with luxuries, I was returned to a very different reality back at the sugar mill, where the floodlit riverside dock had come alive in my absence. Picking my way through hulks of abandoned machinery and coils of rusted cable, I found the *Donald,* a 180-foot-long storage barge lying low in the oily water, full of molasses. The sweet stench of the sugary refuse was overpowering as I explored the maze of tubes and hatches on the *Donald*'s deck, their silver paint sticky with spilt molasses. A stevedore, readying a thick canvas pipeline through which the molasses would be unloaded onto another barge that night, noticed my curiosity.

"You wanna taste dis stoff, mon?" he asked, pulling an old rubber hose from the river and opening a hatch. I peered down into the hold as he dropped an end of the hose in and hauled it back up. I wiped off a thick smear and licked my finger. It was delicious, rich and sweet and cloying. I had been allowed the occasional spoonful of molasses as a boy, when my mother was cooking a Christmas pudding. Now I was standing on top of 450 tons of the stuff. Enough to make me really sick. As my nose became accustomed to the syrupy pungence of the molasses, the smell faded, and the stink of sump oil rose from the river, slick with grease. A heavy harvest moon rose over the mangrove swamp on the opposite bank, and I heard the rumble of a powerful engine straining up the river. My ride to Belize was coming in.

The tugboat *Terry* came round a bend, towing an empty barge. Through the night, the molasses on board the *Donald* would be pumped into the *Gretel,* and at dawn, we would set off downriver for the sea, then turn south to Belize City.

I lay down to sleep on a makeshift mattress of sliced up tyres, woven together like a crude hammock, that I found at the stern of the *Donald.* The shouts of the stevedores and the thunder of the pumps as they worked through the night did not disturb me. I dreamt that I was driving at reckless speed down a motorway. A sudden bang startled me awake—a tyre had blown out. A second loud clang, and I realised that day had broken, the loading had finished, and that the dock hands were slamming the hatches shut.

"Weyik op, cook is hailin you for caarfee." An old man was peering down into my face, shaking my shoulder. I stumbled to my feet and climbed on board the *Terry.* A plateful

of fried sausages, fried eggs, bread and an enamel mugful of tea awaited me in the galley. I was not going to starve on this trip.

I had barely finished my breakfast when the *Terry*'s engine roared into life, shaking the whole boat. Captain Anderson stood at the wheel, with the top two buttons of his shirt done up and a spreading paunch pushing out beneath. A squashed nose in the middle of a wide, bulldog face gave him the air of an ageing prize fighter, accentuated by his lack of any top teeth. The three front teeth on the bottom were intact, splaying out of his jaw like a fossilised fleur de lys and fitting neatly into the naked gum above. His demeanour, though, belied this fearsome aspect. Captain Anderson moved gently and ponderously, handling his tug with delicacy and precision. He backed the *Terry* up until she was dead ahead of the *Gretel,* and then softly put the engine into forward gear. As we inched forward, the rope hitched to the barge rose gradually to the surface of the river, skittered for a moment and then came taut with a crack.

As the *Terry*'s engine revved wildly, we stood stock still in the water, and then, minutely, the barge began to move. Seven hundred and fifty tons of barge, and four hundred fifty tons of molasses in its hold.

"*Laat o' weyit for a likkle tog.*" Captain Anderson smiled. After eighteen years as a tugboat captain, he was still proud of what the diminutive boats could do.

We ploughed down the inky river, the barge swinging slowly from bank to bank as we rounded the meandering bends. A hawk eyed us suspiciously from a treetop, and a pair of grey-bodied herons, stretching their russet necks forward, lifted from their perch on a mangrove root to flap carelessly across our bows. But the forest wildlife seemed accustomed to the passage of these monstrous barges along the narrow river: Two ducks swam sedately ahead of us at our prow, diving in unison only when Captain Anderson forced the engine to a higher pitch to pull the *Gretel* off a bank.

The barge hit the banks at almost every bend, no matter how carefully the captain nudged the wheel. Gouging through the soft mud in the shallows, and tearing off branches above that got snagged on the hatches and valves, the *Gretel* was festooned with foliage after an hour or so.

As we neared the sea, the river cleared to a rich green in a reflection of the overhanging vegetation. Shafts of sunlight refracted through the rippled surface shot below the water like pillars of jade, and electric-blue butterflies floated around the boat as if mocking our clumsy struggle. On either side of us, mangrove trees dropped their roots straight down into the water from branches twenty feet up, creepers trailed from tree to tree, and bulbous pock-marked termite nests clung to treetrunks like obscene tumours. The smell of damp plant life and foetid mud was heavy on the air, and I was relieved when we rounded the last bend in the river and came out into a clean wide bay, fresh with a salt breeze. All afternoon we chugged our way across the mirror-flat sea, the sandy bottom a steady ten feet below us, devoid of any kind of life.

The wind dropped, and the sun baked the air into shimmers. The horizon melted into an indistinguishable pale blue blur of sea and sky. The engine throbbed monotonously and our course did not change; we laboured across the endless expanse of water like a crippled waterbeetle.

The *Terry* was a waterborne donkey, devoid of any sense of seafaring romance. Forty-three feet long, painted a workmanlike battleship grey, the tug had no pretensions beyond housing a 220 horsepower engine, and floating. She was the bare minimum of a boat, functional and stripped of any fripperies. Only Captain Anderson dignified the vessel with the feminine pronoun: The other three crewmembers referred to the boat as "it," as if she were no more than a machine.

It was hard to hold much of a conversation on board the *Terry*. The wheelhouse was as far as one could get from the engine while staying out of the sun, and even there I could only make myself heard by shouting above the din. Captain Anderson was a man of few words, and he seemed uncertain about what I was doing on board his tug.

"Yes, yes, yes, yes, yes," he would say in response to my questions, or give me a long, laughing "Noooo" if I had misunderstood something. He thought the idea of travelling from Belize to Panama was peculiar enough—the whole of Central America was simply violent confusion as far as he was concerned, and any sensible man stayed out of it. *"Dat a mess, mon,"* he told me. *"Dose people go to work shootin each other an at de end dey got to reach a decision of some sort. An aall dose men lost, dere lives gaan."* And if I had to make the journey, why on earth was I spending twenty-seven hours on a noisy tugboat when there was a perfectly good road to Belize City? But he was happy to give me a ride if that was what I wanted.

Andy, the engineer, said little throughout the trip, and the cook spent much of his time in the galley, frying up eggs, sausages and beans for breakfast, preparing chicken stew with onions and okra and fried banana for lunch, or baking johnny cakes from a basic dough of water, flour, salt and baking soda, which we ate for tea with hunks of cheese.

Only Hansell, a wiry little grandfather with dimming

eyes and a wolfish grin, was very talkative, though he didn't get the joke I made about Hansell pulling the barge *Gretel*. As night fell and he took the wheel while the others slept, he took to reminiscing about his days at sea.

"My daddy was a farmer, bot he couldn't keep me on de farm. I waark in sea waark since I eighteen years of age, traalin shrimp off Nicaragua, haalin sugar from Cuba. You goin to Caarn Island, mon, down Bluefields side?"

I said I hoped to go there.

"Dass de place I seen de biggest women, mon. I got a boy by one of dem women, but I got trobble, too. I come home from Nicaragua one day, 1952 or so, an my wife say 'no more back, Hansell, no more sea. You gaan too laang.'" He cackled as he remembered, bending over the wheel. *"De whole ting dat smash it op, she go in my suitcase and she see the photo of de girl. She say 'she prettier dan me, no more back, Hansell.'"*

So he never went back to Nicaragua, but took a job instead on a cargo boat carrying Cuban sugar to Miami. *"Den when Castro tek over, everyting smash op,"* and he came back home to work on coastal steamers. *"I a coptin, bot my papers went down in a boat I was runnin right here in Belize, she spring a leak out in de blue. Now dey use me as a sailor. I sixty-five, bot dey caant get rid of me."*

When Hansell got onto the subject of his four women and his twenty-one children, I decided it was time for bed. He was liable to go on all night, and now we were out of the bay the wind was growing cold. I checked the compass before climbing into my bunk. Due south. Just where I wanted to go.

Late the next morning we sighted the World War II oil tanker, moored in the lee of a small island, where we were to leave the barge. The tanker crew would pump the molasses aboard later, and then, when they had a full load with the contents of other barges, await the arrival of a US ship that would take it all away to make cattle feed in America.

Five hundred yards away, Captain Anderson stopped the engines, but the barge was still making headway as we came abeam of the tanker, its concrete, mineproof hull stained an industrial brown with age. Two hundred yards wide of our goal, the captain was twisting the wheel this way and that. *"Gotta kill dat headway, mon, odderwise we caant do nuttn. We bruk up de boat, cos dat a cement ship, and she caant tek no lick."*

It took us over half an hour to manouevre those last 200 yards, and after all that he brought the barge in six inches too close, buckling a few steps of an iron ladder down the tanker's side. A lengthy argument between the tugboat crew, who maintained that the steps had been damaged before, and the tanker crew, who insisted that everything had been in perfect order before we arrived, did not resolve anything. Captain Anderson grunted, and went to record his version of events in his logbook. Doubtless the tanker crew boss did the same. Nowhere in Central America but Belize, I reflected, would anyone give a damn about a few bent steps. Here, however, reports would be filed, competing accounts of the affair would be compared, and after judicious consideration by a bureaucrat from Belize Sugar Industries, somebody's pay would be docked.

That prospect did not dim the mood, though, as the *Terry,* freed at last from her burden of molasses, steamed eagerly back into Belize City. The job was done, the crew was going home, and I was anxious to find a slightly faster means of transport for the next stage of my journey.

———

I was out of luck. Hansell had told me that seeing as how it was Friday, one of the British Navy motor patrol boats would probably be heading south. Fisheries protection was apparently best done over the weekends in the south, which I presumed had something to do with the fact that the beaches there are better. But the boat had already left by the time I arrived at the dock.

So I took the bus. My intention, planning this journey, had been to cover as much as possible of the distance from Belize to Panama by boat or on foot. Railways were acceptable, I reckoned, for no particularly justifiable reason other than that I am fond of trains, and a light aeroplane or two might be unavoidable in some of the darker reaches of Honduras. But I hoped to resort to standard forms of public transport only when absolutely necessary.

Avoiding them was not going to be terribly difficult. Standard forms of public transport are unheard of along most of the coast, so I would not often be tempted to choose speed and convenience over improvisation. The real problem in most places was going to be finding any sort of transport at all, and I was by no means sure that the trip I had dreamt about for so long, and was now beginning, was actually feasible. Certainly I knew of no one who had done it.

The whole journey was an act of faith—faith and a little bit of logic. If people lived along the Caribbean coast of Central America—and in most parts they did—then presumably they sometimes visited friends, or went to a nearby town to trade their goods. And if there were no roads, then they must go by sea, and some of them must have room for the occasional passenger. But here in Belize City, it was a question of either taking the bus, since there was one, or waiting indefinitely for some sort of boat. Since none of the dockworkers I consulted thought it at all likely that anything would be leaving until next week's Royal Navy outing, I opted for the bus.

The Southern Highway is rather a grand name for the red dirt road that runs through tropical forest at the foot of the Maya Mountains. When it is not being used as a landing strip by drug barons, it carries little traffic except for the ancient American school buses, offloaded as part of some US aid programme, that ply from village to village.

I was heading for a valley in the mountains that has been turned into the world's first jaguar reserve, though I had been warned by everybody who knew anything about it that I stood no chance whatsoever of seeing any jaguars there. The Duke of Edinburgh, president of the World Wildlife Fund, had once visited the park, and a government official planning his trip had been so worried about the jaguars' elusiveness he had tried to persuade the Belize zoo to drug one of the cats there and plant it in the jungle. In the end, all the duke saw was a footprint, and apparently he was happy enough with that. He had more luck than I did. The most unusual species I came across in the forest was a pair of English art students, commissioned by the makers of Jaguar motor cars to draw a poster for the World Wildlife Fund's campaign to protect the jaguar. They too had been forced to resort to the zoo to get a look at a real jaguar, and had come to Cockscombe Basin to study the natural habitat that they would paint in as background.

Park wardens had cut narrow trails through the forest, tunnels winding through the thick, green subaqueous gloom of the jungle floor. Hushed, but for the occasional squawk of an unseen bird, the luxuriant riot of vegetation was overpowering. Ropes of lianas hung from the branches above, clusters of orchids draped themselves around tree trunks, buttress roots as tall as a man supported the "chicle" trees that ooze chewing gum from cuts in their bark. In the treacly heat, the exuberance of the jungle's rapid growth was cloaked by the silence of decay.

Somewhere in the tangle of undergrowth, about forty jaguars were prowling. Or sleeping, since they hunt mostly at night. Wildlife experts say that Belize harbours the densest jaguar population in the Americas, numbering in the hundreds. For an animal that once ranged from Oklahoma to Argentina, the Belize jaguar retains a last tenuous grip on existence.

Jaguars once roamed these forests as undisputed kings. The Maya indians, whose civilisation flourished 1,000 years ago in Belize and neighbouring Mexico and Guatemala, held the animal in such awe that their most sacred hieroglyph, the most powerful symbol in their alphabet, was a fanged jaguar head. "Balaam," a symbol used apparently interchangeably for a jaguar or a senior priest—in a society ruled by priests—recurs over and over again in Mayan carvings and paintings. In Mayan mythology, the jaguar guarded the underworld by night, and the Sun God took on jaguar characteristics in the underworld, controlling everything to do with death. It is not difficult to see why the Mayas venerated the jaguar so deeply. As the biggest, most fearsome animal in their daily world, it became the most powerful and awesome god in their religious pantheon. Killing its prey unlike any other cat—crushing the skull with one snap of its jaws—the jaguar is unique.

And until the advent of the rifle, it was virtually untouchable. Modern-day Maya indians, who live and farm in southern Belize, are not so much in awe of jaguars as terrified by them, and shoot them at every opportunity. A creation story they still tell seems designed to justify this attitude.

The jaguar already existed when the Creator decided to make men, and was watching as He took some mud and began to fashion human limbs. Not wanting the jaguar to see how man was made, the Creator sent him to the river to fetch some water, giving him a calabash with holes in it. The jaguar tried and tried to fill the calabash, but succeeded only when a frog suggested that he cake it with clay to block up the holes. And by the time he had managed to do that, and brought back the water, the Creator had already made thirteen men and twelve guns. As the jaguar returned, he saw the Creator was making a dog too out of mud.

"That animal will be for me to eat," he said.

"No," said the Creator, "this animal will serve man, and his guns will teach you to respect him."

"I'm not afraid of guns," the jaguar replied. "I'll catch the bullets."

"We'll see about that," the Creator said. "Go and stand by that tree over there."

One of the newly created men fired a shot at the jaguar, wounding him in the paw. As he bandaged him up, the jaguar insisted again that he wanted the dog. But the man said, "No," and sent the dog after the jaguar, driving him up into a tree, and again shot him in the paw. "You have learned your lesson," said the man. "You can eat anything except man and dog. Now go away and live in the bush."

A handy sort of legend to have around, that, crediting the Creator with making guns at the same time as man. It certainly hasn't helped the conservationists reawaken the old respect for the jaguar that the Mayas' ancestors showed.

As I left the reserve I reflected that the jaguar would make an ideal national animal for Belize: proud, sleek, invulnerable, instilling fear in allcomers. But Belize had rejected such a macho image. Instead, the country had chosen as its national symbol the tapir, known here as the mountain cow, which mooches through life rooting for leaves and fallen fruit. It was hard not to feel sympathy for a nation that had adopted such a homely, peaceable and ungainly creature as its emblem.

TWO

KINGFISH, QUEENFISH, CALIPAVER, ALVACORE,
SAILFISH, BLACK, MUTTON, REEF SNAPPER, CABILLO,
DOLPHIN, POMPANO, TUNA AND HOGFISH.
$1.50 PER POUND

Never had I read such a musical price list as the fading
noticeboard outside the concrete blockhouse that served
as the Dangriga fish market. The neatly painted blue letters
continued:

JUNEFISH, GROUPER, AMBERJACK, TARPON,
YELLOWTAIL, SILKSNAPPER, DOGTEETH, MACKEREL,
SNOOK, BARRACUDA, MULLET AND CREVALLE.
$1.35 PER POUND

The poetry of the reef, the changing rythms of the sea,
embodied in a straightforward presentation of the price
of fish.

PETER FORD

STONEBASSS, DRUMMER, PORGY, GRUNT, BAY SNOOK, SILVERFISH, SHARK AND OTHER TYPES NOT ENUMERATED.
$1.05 PER POUND

Well naturally. How could a fish called a porgy compare in quality with an alvacore? How could the flesh of a grunt be half as sweet as a pompano?

On a slimy wooden table outside the market, a group of fishermen were gutting their morning's catch, hacking at the gleaming fish with blunt knives and broken machetes and throwing the entrails into the river. They sank cloudily onto a bed of old coconut husks and fish heads on the muddy bottom.

I was about to make my first attempt at a scenario I had run through so many times in my imagination, and placed so much faith in to make my journey possible: asking local fishermen where I might find a boat to take me down the coast. And it worked! One of the fishermen looked up from his butchery, wiped his hands on his trousers and pointed up the riverbank to a family stepping out of a small dory. They had just arrived from a village further south, he said, and would doubtless be returning home that day.

Sure enough, talking to the father as he made fast, I found he had come to Dangriga to do some shopping, and would be leaving back for the village of Hopkins in a couple of hours. And certainly there was room for me, he said, introducing himself as Ben. I felt the excitement, physically, of my first success. And for the first time I knew that the journey I had planned was going to be feasible.

A hundred yards upriver from the sandy bar that marked the rivermouth, Ben had hitched his dory's painter to a paddle stuck upside down in the mud. A fifteen-foot narrow dugout, powered by an eight-horsepower outboard motor, the *Mamy Joan* offered a foretaste of all the other canoes that awaited me further down the coast. She leaked slightly and needed constant bailing with an old plastic cup kept at the back for that purpose. Loaded with two bags of cement for the house Ben was building, four crates of rum and Sprite and a block of ice for the village pub, we were low in the water as we poled our way across the bar and into the open sea.

It was not long before the waves roughed up. Sitting in the prow, wearing just a pair of shorts, I felt the spray on my feet, then my knees, then my chest, then over my whole body in a glorious salty wash I had to suck from my moustache, never quite dried by the sun between splashes. The water was doing the bags of cement no good at all, but it felt great to me. I leaned back on my rucksack to ask Ben about places to stay in Hopkins. Could I sling my hammock on the beach, did he think?

"Mon, no one sleep on de beach in Haapkins. De sandflies dere, dey liff you out yaar hammock an corry you away. Bot a cozzin of mine, she gaat a room you can stay."

The village was barely visible as we approached it forty minutes later, just a few scattered houses poking through the coconut palms. Closer in, however, I saw that it stretched a mile or so along the beach, a string of 200 or so simple shacks raised on pilings, devoid of paint and bleached a sharkskin silver-grey by the sun. Beside each house stood a separate kitchen building, thatched rooves blackened by smoky cooking fires. Above the tideline, dories lay tilted on their sides in various stages of disrepair. Stray dogs roamed the beach, nosing families of chickens away from interesting piles of refuse. In the heat, nothing else moved.

I found Ben's cousin, Gloria, sitting on a bench in the shade of her tiny grocery store. I was welcome to stay in her house next door, which she was repairing, so long as the American who had rented the place for a month did not mind. I climbed the stairs, peered through the open front door and found a tall fair-haired man in swimming trunks lounging in a hammock stretched across a room bare of any furniture. He was eating bread and oranges. Bread and oranges, it turned out, were all he ever ate, except for the occasional fingerful of peanut butter.

Kevin had landed in Hopkins by chance, having heard of Belize for the first time a few months earlier from a CBS television programme. He had decided to stay and to write a novel. Broke, he wasn't going to spend unnecessary money on food. Frustrated by the villagers' constant demands for favours, he wasn't going to go out more than he had to. He simply lay in his hammock and wrote unceasingly, a bold longhand scrawl, onto a yellow legal pad. He had been in Hopkins for six weeks and said he was setting his novel there. This I found rather daring, since Hopkins is inhabited by Garifunas, a bizarre and little-known ethnic group whose culture, Kevin was the first to admit, he found inscrutable.

So did I. Arriving in Hopkins, I found myself for the first time in years outside the European-rooted cultures with which I was familiar: Here, among a people who looked like Africans but spoke an Amerindian language, I was way out of my cultural depth. I simply did not know how to tell what was acceptable behaviour and what was not. How, for example, did I take a piss?

Since none of the houses in the village had running water or lavatories, I assumed that men simply peed against a convenient coconut tree, as discreetly as possible. But when I went in search of such a tree on my first afternoon in the village, I found they were all slap bang in front of somebody's house. After a couple of hundred yards, I came to a short jetty sticking out into the water, at the end of which was perched an outhouse. This was clearly where the women went, and it would serve my purpose perfectly, I thought.

But when I stepped into the rickety shack, I found it was a two seater. And the other seat was occupied. The old man sitting on the hole over the sea was quite undisturbed by my arrival, but something told me that wherever men pissed, they did not bother to visit the outhouse. I could hear the village gossip already, about the strange new white man who went all the way to the outhouse just to take a leak. There was nothing for it but to dissemble. I pulled down my trousers, sat on the privy and pretended to shit. I felt extremely foolish, and extremely foreign.

The Garifunas are a unique people with a remarkable history blended from two continents into a new culture.

Some time before Columbus arrived in the New World, Carib indians from the Orinoco Basin in what is now Venezuela began to migrate northwards. Carried by the currents and the prevailing winds, they landed on the island of St. Vincent, in the eastern Caribbean. They stayed there, after conquering the Arawak indians who lived on the island already, and settled down to a life of fishing and basic agriculture, calling themselves "Carífuna," or "Carínago," which in their language meant "the brave people." Columbus, in his journal, corrupted these names into the Spanish "caribales," from which the English word "cannibal" is derived.

In 1635, or 1645, or 1675, depending on which historian

you believe, a ship carrying blacks from the West African coast to the Spanish Caribbean colonies ran aground off St. Vincent. The survivors found their way ashore, attached themselves to indian women, learned their language, Africanised the tribe's name to Garifuna, and a new people was born—the Black Caribs. Then, as now, the Garifuna looked like West Africans, talked with West African intonation, danced to West African music. But the language they spoke was Amerindian, the songs they sang came from the Orinoco and they cooked the food they ate according to Carib tradition.

As England, Spain and France vied for control of the Caribbean, the Garifuna on St. Vincent allied themselves with French settlers. But the guns they secured from their patrons did them little good. When the Garifuna rose up in 1795 against a British edict confining them to reservations, they were doomed. British soldiers and local militiamen hunted them down, burning their crops, their houses and their canoes, and only a few hundred escaped the onslaught. Close to 5,000 were rounded up and held captive, nearly half of them died of "malignant fever," and the rest were tossed below decks aboard British men o' war and carried away, as their African ancestors had been 150 years earlier.

The British dumped them on Roatan, a deserted island many hundred miles away off the north coast of Honduras, and left them to their fate. Here there were no friendly indians to welcome them, nor ground cleared for planting, but the Spanish garrison at Trujillo on the Honduran mainland opposite Roatan invited the Garifunas to settle and work with them. This they did, prospering in a quiet sort of way, and earning a reputation as hard workers resilient in the face of the tropical diseases on the coast that ravaged

Europeans and indigenous indians from the interior. But just as they had allied themselves with the French against the victorious English, the Garifunas chose the wrong side again when war disrupted their lives once more.

By the end of the 1820s, Central America had won its independence from Spain, and Francisco Morazan ruled the region as president of a federated state. But Spanish royalists had not given up their dreams, and when they sought to regain their lost territories, they recruited the Garifunas as footsoldiers. They lost, and when Morazan accused all rebel troops of treason, they feared retribution. From Trujillo, they fled east, into the remote territory of the Miskito indians, and north, into Guatemala and Belize. That last upheaval fixed the current boundaries of their existence.

Those who live in Belize speak English as their second language; those in Guatemala and Honduras speak Spanish. But they all speak Garifuna, they have all chosen spots within 100 yards of the beach to build their villages and they all share a heritage of which they are extraordinarily proud. It is a heritage of enormous suffering, of constant setbacks, convulsions and dispersal, that makes their survival itself remarkable and has forged a sense of kinship across three national frontiers. And the Garifuna are flourishing: The 3,000 ancestors marooned on Roatan nearly 200 years ago have grown into some 70,000 today, still anxious to set themselves apart.

From their days on St. Vincent, when the Black Caribs pressed newborn babies' heads between two wooden boards to flatten their skulls for life, the Garifunas have been proud to differentiate themselves from other blacks who have been slaves, or whose ancestors were once enslaved. For the survivors of the seventeenth-century slave-ship, Garifunas all along the length of the coast were quick to tell me, had never been sold into slavery. They had been captured in Africa, but they had never worked for a white master.

The cultural similarities between Garifuna villages all along the coast are offset, however, by some peculiarities. In Hopkins, for example, no one ever says thank you. Kevin, trying to write his novel about the Garifuna, found this especially unsettling and had tied himself into a cultural knot in his relations with the villagers. Because, he had found, it is not that people in Hopkins are particularly rude. Just that if you do someone a favour, you expect a favour in return, not just a "thank you."

Saying thank you, it appeared, implied that an exchange was complete, and for the villagers of Hopkins, give and take had to be constantly reinforced by practice. Since stinginess, to the Garifunas, is a cardinal sin, Kevin was trying hard to be understanding about this, even though the only way he could return favours was by paying for them, which was playing hell with his efforts to live on one US dollar a day. But it seemed to me there was a good deal of hypocrisy involved in this business. Although the Garifuna regard themselves as a generous people—and I found them almost always extremely generous with me— they resort to all kinds of trickery to avoid giving things away to each other, at least in Belize.

In Hopkins, for example, women went to the village shop to buy miniscule portions of what they needed, pinches of salt, single oranges and so on, and it wasn't that they were so poor they could not afford more. If they could use what they had right away, they would not have anything left over to give if they were asked. But if they did have it, and a neighbour asked for it, they would feel morally obliged to hand it over, of course.

One invitation I was given for free. Walking gingerly down a scorchingly hot sand path one morning, I nodded hello to a wide-hipped woman in a bright orange headscarf standing in her kitchen doorway. She waved me over, and I went to see what she had to show me. I ducked into her large kitchen hut, its walls made of slim treetrunks lashed together, slivers of sunlight cutting through the gaps and through the smoke that filled the dim interior. A hen pecked at the beaten sand floor, among the feet of a group of raucous women all sitting on low stools, laughing and joking as they bent over two long wooden troughs. One was full of brownish cream roots, resembling outsized parsnips, which some of the women were washing. Two other women were grating the cleaned vegetables into the second container, using wooden boards studded with tiny sharp-edged pieces of gravel.

The atmosphere in the hut, full of women working together at well-practiced tasks, was heavy with ritual. And the manufacture of the Garifunas' traditional bread, from the root of the cassava, or manioc, plant, is indeed a major ritual, an anchor embedded deeply in Garifuna culture. Martha, whose kitchen I was in, and whose sisters and cousins were helping her with her chores, was anxious that I learn how cassava bread is made. It was a relatively simple process, but it involved no implement I had ever before seen used to bake bread.

Once the cassava had been grated into a damp mush, Martha brought out a serpentine tube woven in basketwork from a local creeper. She slung a loop at one end of it over a rafter, and it hung down sinuously like the trunk

of an elephant, nine feet long, its closely meshed fibres
stained ebony black. Then she stuffed in the cassava mush
until the *ruguma* was full, and pushed a stick through an
eyelet at the bottom. As she and a sister sat on the stick,
stretching the *ruguma* downwards, the basketwork con-
stricted, squeezing its contents. The sides ran with juice.
This was the key to making anything from bitter cassava—
ridding it of the toxins that the vegetable contains, and
which make it inedible unless it is grated and squeezed.

Pressed dry into a tubular cake, the cassava flour would
sit overnight and then be sifted through a loosely woven
sieve made from "basket tie-tie," the same vine used to
weave the *ruguma*. Martha would make a fire on the floor
in a corner of her kitchen, set a wheel-sized griddle over
it and sprinkle on the flour. That is all there is to it. Miraculously, the dry flour congeals on the griddle, forming
a thin cake the consistency of a prawn cracker, only slightly
chewier. It is said to last for months, and to have sustained
the Garifuna refugees on their journey to Roatan.

Martha delved into a plastic bag to give me a piece of
the finished product, and I munched appreciatively, not
daring to tell her that the bread of which she was so proud,
a cornerstone of her culture, tasted to me like lightly
toasted stale cardboard. The Garifunas, however, prize
their cassava bread highly and are deeply worried about
its future. For the number of men who know how to make
a *ruguma* is dwindling rapidly.

Down the beach from Martha's kitchen, I found Octavio
Magdaleno squatting on a treestump in deep mango shade,
weaving a sieve for sifting the flour. In a threadbare checkered cotton shirt and dusty trousers, he had a kindly, puzzled face beneath a mop of white hair.

"*De yong men dese days, mon, dem no care for dis business,*" he said looking up, his thick fingers finding their way alone to each alternate strip of fibre as he wove a new piece in. *"My daddy laarned me how to mek rugumas when ah joss a boy. Bot ah got sixty-nine year now, and who gonna do dis when ah gaan?"*

The situation turned out not to be quite as critical as all that. Octavio had taught his nephew, now fifty-six, to do the basketwork. But they were the only two men in Belize who could make *rugumas,* and they sold them all over the country. In Honduras, he told me, things weren't much better. Lying on the ground by his side was a square basket lashed onto four frame poles, broken and frayed and clearly useless.

"Dat a gadauri, *you know, like dem rocksacks you see. Used to use em for carryin tings,"* he explained. *"One man bring dat from Honduras laas year, say dem people dat side forgotten how to mek it, aask if ah know how. Bot my daddy never laarned me dat. It too caamplicated, aall mash op like dat."*

I remembered having read somewhere that the national anthropology museum in Honduras had looked in vain for a *gadauri* a few years earlier. This one in Octavio Magdaleno's yard was possibly the last in existence. And no one could be found to copy it.

In only other place in the world do people weave *rugumas*—in the Orinoco Basin, where the Garifunas' Carib forebears came from. And incredibly, the link has not been broken. Or rather, it has been reforged in the last thirty years. The Garifunas have spread, working on merchant ships, to the United States. But living in houses or apartments where the process of making cassava bread would be impractical, to say the least, they would normally have had to do without it. Except that Garifuna seamen, travelling to ports in Venezuela and neighbouring Surinam,

45

discovered there the same bread they had eaten at home in Central America. It was being made by Carib indians in the same way they had always made it. Today, reaching back 600 years into their past to satisfy a yearning that has not died, the sailors buy cassava bread in Maracaibo, and sell it in Queens.

In Hopkins, I began to get the measure of the coast, and to fall in step with its slow, steady pulse. Time ran in a circular motion, not straight ahead to any goals, but round and round through the daily, weekly, monthly chores that made up the unchanging village life.

A little rain or thunder marked a highlight in the pattern. An especially vicious assault by sandflies one night would be remembered for weeks. Changes in the wind direction and the moon's effect on the snapper at the reef paced out the steady cycle. For the men, weeklong fishing trips to the cays revolved around bouts of drunken lassitude, induced by a homemade brew called "bitters," a sugarcane liquor in which a sour root lay soaking. The women's lives turned around the steady routine of cooking, washing and feeding the children. And every minute of the day, the awesome bloody endlessness of the waves falling gently on the beach: splash, hiss, suck, wave after wave since the beginning of time, round and round with the moon.

For three years I had been living with a driven purposefulness, the lunatic schedule of a foreign correspondent, a new direction every day. In Hopkins, I sloughed off that attitude gratefully, lost my speed and slowed my mental metabolism to a crawl. One old woman I talked to told me someone had once taken her photograph, but that she hadn't recognised herself when she saw it. *"Even I to myself, my lookin was deceivin to me."* I knew how she felt.

There was no way out of Hopkins by boat, I discovered, so I was obliged to hike five miles inland, down the dusty track that led to the Southern Highway. The road was deserted, and the sun bore down into my skull like a drill as I trudged along. A red-and-black banded coral snake, one of the deadliest in the tropics, writhed into my path a few feet ahead of me. I froze. He hesitated, sniffed the air and considered whether I was worth the venom. Apparently not. He wriggled back the way he had come into the long coarse grass.

At the junction with the highway, waiting vainly for a bus, I hitched a ride south for the three hour drive to Punta Gorda. Stanley Usher, who picked me up, turned out to be the chauffeur of Minister of Natural Resources. It didn't take him long to ask me Belizeans' favourite question of foreigners at that time, especially foreigners they took to be American. What did I think of Jesse Jackson?

In the middle of the 1988 primary campaign, Stanley was ecstatic about Jackson's performance. Paying scant attention to the road ahead, he acted out the speech Jackson had made the night before, broadcast on the Chicago television station, WGBN, that serves as Belizean national television. Pulling his West Indian vowels into an approximation of Jesse's urgent preaching, thumping the steering wheel as Jackson had thumped his podium, reaching out to embrace his daughter in the passenger seat the way Jackson had embraced a weeping white woman, Stanley exulted in the black preacher's success, revelled in the discomfiture that he was causing the white Democratic party hierarchy and howled with delight at even the remote possibility Jackson might become vice president.

"*I see dat mon op dere an I see* myself. *I proud of dat mon,*" he shouted gleefully. Then, catching himself, fearful he may have offended me with his fervency, he stopped short and looked back over his shoulder at me. "*Not that I've nottin against white people, mon,*" he assured me. "*I used to work wid Englanders once.*" A broad grin slowly split his face. "*Bot you know, dere's nottin like one of your own.*"

Tunelessly, but with enthusiasm, he launched into Peter Tosh's reggae anthem of black pride.

> *No matter where you come from,*
> *So long as you're a black man,*
> *You're an African.*

It occurred to me that Belizeans' ardour for Jesse Jackson—even the conservative Prime Minister Manuel Esquivel, who was white, had phoned him with congratulations when he won the Michigan primary—derived from more than just black peoples' pride in a black American doing well in a white man's world. WGBN, as a Chicago station, was probably giving more coverage to Jackson, a Chicago politician, than was any other station in the United States. Did the owners of WGBN realise that they were helping to foster international black solidarity? I wondered. At the same time, Stanley Usher's dependence on US news emphasised the ties that bind Belizeans to the United States. The old royal coat of arms over the courthouse in Belize City might reflect a colonial heritage, but London is a rapidly fading pole of influence. Today, America is the magnet, and almost as many Belizeans live in the United States as in Belize, according to some estimates.

Just short of Punta Gorda, though, we drove past one of the last vestiges of the British presence—a British army camp. Neat rows of Nissen huts, like elongated igloo entrances roofed with corrugated iron, sat squat in a verdant pasture. The British troops were there to fend off any threat of invasion by neighbouring Guatemala, which claimed Belize as its own territory, but such a prospect seemed remote as a squad of Gurkha soldiers formed up on parade in the evening sun. No barbed wire, trenches or gun emplacements guarded the base. Just a flowering hedge of hibiscus, a flagrant scarlet, long stamens drooping provocatively from the broadly opened petals, like the mouths of listless whores waiting for the squaddies to get off duty.

Arriving in Punta Gorda, I found myself a room in a cheap bugfree hotel and went to find some supper. PeeGee, as residents call the town, offers little in the way of diversion for the traveller, or indeed for the 2,000 people who live there. The bus line that delivers Guatemala-bound voyagers the day before the ferry boat leaves must be in league with the local chamber of commerce, I decided, obliging us to while away our time at the two restaurants and one bar on offer.

I chose Mahung's, the Chinese restaurant, and was encouraged to find that the menu promised pigeon and duck, as well as the standard fried rice dishes. But the local shots had clearly failed Mr. Mahung that day. Pigeon and duck were off. I asked the waitress if there was any seafood.

"Yes," she said. "Swims."

"Swims?"

"Little tiny things," she explained, holding her thumb and forefinger close together.

I thought I understood. What we were talking about here were whitebait or sardines, I decided, the local variety of which were called—in charmingly direct creole English—"swims" because that is what they do. After all, in Hopkins they had equally blunt ways of naming their dishes. Turtle was called "seameat," game was "bushmeat," and tubers such as yams or manioc were known as "groundfood."

I ordered a plate of fried swims, and asked for a slice of lime to squeeze over the heap of crispy brown little fish I was imagining. Half an hour later, as the dish was set before me, I realised that the waitress suffered from a slight speech defect. I was confronted by seven fried shrimps, sitting on a bed of wilted lettuce. Perhaps I would do better tomorrow, in Guatemala, where they spoke Spanish.

I had fallen in with a Rasta on the ferry to Livingston, a tall, proud-looking Creole with luxuriant dreadlocks tumbling halfway down his back, wearing a T-shirt emblazoned with Bob Marley's portrait. To my innocent enquiry as to what he did for a living, he bent close to my ear and told me in a dark whisper that he worked for the United Nations, but he was not at liberty to tell me exactly what he did. Secretively, he slipped me what he said was his business card, bent and grubby, identifying him as Raymond Craig, attaché at the Belizean mission to the UN in New York.

This was preposterous. I gave him what I hoped was a hard "I got you sussed, mate" stare, to which the unlikely diplomat seemed impervious, and dropped the subject. So did he, offering no objection when the friends he had come to visit called him John as we ate a standard fried-fish supper together in a shack at the edge of town.

Later, we went down to the beach, where a cluster of bamboo lean-tos at the edge of the surf each played Peter Tosh and Bob Marley and Gregory Isaacs tapes at top competing volume. They were all empty save one cavernous barrack at the far end which was offering tonight's star attraction—live music.

The Bambu Bay, a spare, cement-floored, characterless structure with a few tables and benches arranged around the walls, was dimly lit by one naked bulb over the bar and a greenish-purplish glow from an art deco flower-petal glass lampshade that hung from a ceiling fan turning lazily. The band—a nameless collection of Garifuna youths—set up their gear in a dark corner: an electric organ, a bass guitar, a battery of drums, a brace of bongos and a collection of river-turtle shells strung together that one boy strapped onto his chest like a washboard. Percussion was clearly where this music was at.

The musicians appeared to be seriously stoned, as was most of the audience, and had yet to fully master their instruments. The rhythm was halting and unsure at first, but soon picked up the insistent beat of the *punta,* a traditional Garifuna dance driven by the jungle drums of West African music. The bongos thumped out a framework bottom line, while the drums and the turtle shells laid down more complicated runs along the top. The rhythms echoed and reechoed in ricochets from the walls, boring their way through the steamy air. The singer, pulling at a bottle of rum and sucking hard on a joint whenever his voice gave out, grew steadily more crazed. Brandishing the microphone like the head of a venomous snake, he twisted and squirmed in a frenzy of passion.

On the floor, pairs of dancers in a sweaty pack kept their upper bodies stiff as they shook their bottoms, shuffling their feet flat while they flexed their knees. It was a free-for-all. The singer took a break to rearrange his woollen dreadlock cap, which had fallen over his eyes, and held the microphone to the drunkenly slavering lips of a one-legged man on crutches who crooned guttural moans.

But the dancers had tuned out this unessential surface music, their heads and hips and shuffling feet locked into the drums. Gradually the musicians tired and fell away from the beat, and the dancers sagged back to their beers. The waves outside the door took up their own relentless rhythm. No fury, no exhaustion, just that endless splash and hiss of Hopkins that will drive you loco unless you take refuge in *punta rock,* impose your own noise on the noise of the sea.

In amongst the wriggling mass of dancers I had noticed a European woman, out of place not only for the colour of her skin, but for the flowing hair, flat sandals and indian-print frock, drab against the flash and slick of the young Garifuna couples. I learned that she was Italian and had lived here for two years with a local fisherman. Her sister had done the same. Here was a topic for one of the aspiring anthropologists who have descended on the Garifunas over the past few years, tilling a virgin culture into Ph.D.s: the socio-sexual-cultural impact on a Garifuna community of two nubile Italian girls.

Not that they were the only outside influence on this town. Livingston's exotic inhabitants and spectacular location on a bluff overlooking a forested gorge as it opens onto the sea have attracted large numbers of Guatemalan tourists, and increasing numbers of foreigners. The signs were everywhere, from the bars on the beach to a new luxury hotel that a Swiss entrepreneur had built in tiers dropping down the hillside. And though no road connects Livingston with the rest of Guatemala, the country's indigenous indian majority was clearly in evidence. Kekchi indians from upriver had settled in the town to run shops and small restaurants, their flower-embroidered blouses and woven wraparound skirts the only reminder that this was indeed Guatemala, in Central America, not a Caribbean island or an African village.

The town's two paved streets were lined with clapboard houses and shops, their tatty mildewed paintwork and faded Coca-Cola signs testimony to the humidity and neglect they had suffered. On the concrete steps that raised the buildings above street level to save them from flooding in the rainy season, shopkeepers had set tables under bedsheet awnings and piled them with plantains and bananas, oranges and corncobs, avocadoes, onions, melons, tomatoes, coconuts and cassava. Bundles of chopped firewood stood outside doorways that led into dim interiors crammed with bins of beans and rice, drums of cooking oil and stacked piles of plastic buckets. On the walls, shelf upon shelf held soap, matches, mosquito coils, kerosene lamps and tins of sardines, bolts of cloth, needles and thread, plastic sandals and plastic jewelry, the junk and driftwood of international trade, washed up on this forgotten shore.

I staggered up the steep rutted path that led from the Bambu Bay back into town, and down the main street, deserted at two in the morning save for a couple of teenagers sitting together in the shadows cast by a solitary streetlamp.

Back in my hotel, as I lay down to sleep, I heard behind

the shrill of the cicadas a distant throb of drums. I remembered an account of the Caribs written nearly 400 years ago by a German ship's doctor:

> Since they are a barbarian, idolatrous and heathen people, they are very given over to sorcery and magical, devilish works in that they talk and dance with devils, which come to them in person . . .

Tomorrow, I decided, I would try to find out more about those drums.

To find out anything amongst the Garifunas, you need to talk to the women. Anthropologists call Garifuna society "matrifocal": what that means in practice is that women, and especially older women, take care not only of the cassava—the central, almost sacred staple food—but of the whole culture. They nurture group memories, keep alive folk customs, breathe meaning into the events of daily life.

A Garifuna man follows his bride to live in her family compound. He owes his mother-in-law and sisters-in-law unquestioning respect. He is, after all, a secondary being, of relative unimportance beside the womenfolk. His responsibilities—to clear the bush for planting, to catch the fish in the sea—are light in comparison with the women's. They are the ones who bear the burden of keeping Garifuna culture alive.

So I went looking for Antonina Alvarez, an elderly woman I had heard of who liked to talk about the old ways. Asking my way from door to door, through a maze of wood-and-thatch huts, tripping over chickens and piglets rooting along the dusty paths, I found Antonina's house, and heard her arranging pots and pans in her kitchen.

"*Buiti binaffi,*" I called, my only two words of Garifuna. "Good morning."

She emerged from her hut, her coppery face creased like an old paper bag with laughter to find a white man speaking her language. She uttered a stream of unintelligible greetings as she pulled out a low stool for me to sit on outside her kitchen door, and I had to resort to Spanish to tell her that actually, I did not speak much Garifuna. She was crestfallen, but not surprised, and my initial effort had been sufficient. She was glad to hear a *merigué* saying anything in her language, she said. I explained that I was not American, but British, but the difference was clearly too slight in her eyes to warrant further investigation. I was not a Garifuna and I was not a "Spaniard"; that was all she needed to know.

Antonina launched into a long lament about how useless all the young people were nowadays. "See these clothes I'm wearing?" she asked, pointing to her red-and-white checkered skirt and matching headscarf. "These are traditional Garifuna clothes, what my grandmother wore, what all the women wore. But girls don't want to put these clothes on now. They wear any kind of blouses, they wear any coloured skirts, they even wear trousers." It was a standard grandmother's complaint. "When I was a girl, I got up in the morning and I had to go into the bush with my mother to cut cassava. Or we planted bananas, or sowed plantains. But my grandchildren don't want to go into the bush anymore. They don't want to plant, so we have to buy all our food now. It didn't used to be like that. We didn't used to buy any of our food."

She obviously had enough money, though, to buy her food. She had enough money to pay for a new house, built of breezeblocks instead of wooden planks, that was under construction across her yard. If nobody farmed anymore, where did this money come from?

"Oh, my son sends me money every month," Antonina explained. "He went to *merigué* fifteen years ago and he's a good boy. He hasn't forgotten me. But life is hard now. When my mother was alive, life was easy, we grew our cassava, we grew our plantains. But now life is difficult."

"What is most difficult?" I wondered.

"All the men now, they're being thrown out of *merigué*. I heard it on the radio. And one boy from right here, in Livingston, he came back last week and he told me. Men can't go to *merigué* anymore."

So that was it. Life had been good in the old days because the townspeople had planted plenty of cassava and grew what they needed to eat. Life was hard today because of Simpson-Rodino. US immigration policy, not the rains or the fertility of the soil, determined the town's standard of living.

Slowly, I brought the conversation round to the drums I had heard the night before as I lay awake. I had thought that the Garifunas' religious beliefs and practices might be a delicate topic, to be broached gently by a foreigner. Not a bit of it. Antonina was delighted to tell me all about them.

Last night's drums, she explained, had come from a "nine night," a celebration to mark the ninth night after a death. As at an Irish wake, the family and friends of the dead person expressed their sorrow with a party, playing cards, telling stories, drinking hard and dancing *punta* to the beat of the bongos. The "nine night" is a Catholic ceremony Garifunised into a social occasion and an excuse to have some fun, but it is essentially the same ritual as Catholics throughout Central America observe. Much more interesting, Antonina said, her eyes brightening, was a *dugu*. And a family was giving a *dugu* tomorrow, to placate an angry spirit. I must go and see it. She would tell a nephew to take me.

Unlike most people on the coast, evangelised by English, German and American missionaries into Protestant faiths, the Garifunas are Catholics. But finding no contradiction between their *dugus* and the teachings of the church, they also rely on the spirits of their dead ancestors to cure their ills.

The Garifunas attach enormous importance to their dreams, especially when a family is suffering some misfortune. If your son is constantly misbehaving, or you have been plagued by a run of bad luck, or—most commonly— you are ill, your dreams, properly interpreted, can reveal the source of the problem. Garifunas take their dreams to a spirit medium, a *buyai*, to unlock their secrets. Marked since childhood by special signs and powers the *buyais*, who are generally older women, can distinguish between natural illnesses and those caused by the anger of a dead ancestor. And should an ancestor be at the root of the trouble, they can divine which ancestor it is, and what should be done to placate his spirit.

In case of serious problems, the *buyai* decides that a full *dugu* is called for, a nonstop ceremony lasting several days that can take up to a year to prepare. In this case, in Livingston, a woman living in New York was seeking to heal her daughter who was suffering from a lingering illness that American doctors were unable to cure. The woman had returned home to Livingston, consulted a *buyai* and been told that a twenty-four-hour ceremony was needed, a shortened form of the *dugu* known as a *chugu*.

Antonina's nephew, himself in his sixties, led me along

a track that took us out of town, towards the bush. *"Dis woman, her grandaddy died laang years ago, an she givin dis feast for him,"* he explained. *"If she no give him dis* chugu, *one of her daarters is gaan."* It was only eight-thirty in the morning, but we stopped for a drink anyway: Emeterio felt more comfortable with an eighth of a bottle of rum in his belly and another in his back pocket. I followed suit. It seemed best to blend in.

After we had been walking for fifteen minutes, the huts on either side of the path petered out, and the forest thickened. Around a bend, I saw a long, low building, its walls made of bamboo poles lashed together with twine, its roof a thick thatch of interleaved palm fronds. This was the *dabuyabe,* the cult house where the ceremony was to be performed. By the entrance, in the shadow of a thatched canopy, a group of bulky middle-aged women lounged in hammocks, eyeing me curiously as I approached.

I let Emeterio explain what I was doing there, that I was anxious to watch this *chugu* if they would let me, that I would stay out of the way. He passed his bottle of rum around to smooth our arrival, and again I did the same. One of the women folded her yellow-and-white checkered skirt protectively around her treetrunk thighs, leant over to a neighbour and consulted with her in a low murmur. The other women busied themselves conspicuously—rearranging their blouses, picking invisible bits of grit from between their toes, glancing at me from the corners of their eyes as they awaited a decision.

The first woman looked up at me and nodded gravely, her multiple chins wobbling. *"Tenki reyabon,"* I said. The Guatemalan Garifunas, I had discovered, did have a word for "thank you"—they had corrupted it from the English.

The woman smiled broadly. Everyone else laughed. I could stay.

Enjoying the cool shade inside the *dabuyabe*, other women sat around quietly, waiting for the ceremony to start. They were all dressed alike, in checkered frocks and blouses whose colours—yellows and greens and greys—the spirit medium had specified. Round each head of bushy hair was tied a matching headscarf: the knots of chatting, joking women blended into a soothing uniformity in the dimness.

Three drummers arrived midmorning, all men, wearing identical tartan shirts, one bearing a snare drum, another a bass drum and the third a bongo. They arranged themselves on a bench at the far end of the cult house, and nonchalantly began to beat out a soft rhythm. It was a signal. One by one, the women lifted themselves from their hammocks, which they slung over the rafters, and filed up in loose formation, three or four ranks of them, hip to hip, across the *dabuyabe,* facing the drummers. In the dust of the beaten earth floor, they began to shuffle their feet and sway in slow, dreamlike unison. No orders had been given, not a word of organisation had been spoken, but in the space of a minute disparate knots of women had fused, group by group or singly, into a solid phalanx, rooted in the drumbeat, the ritual, their sisterhood.

For five minutes they danced in silence, moving their feet slightly in a waddling stomp to the steady *one* two three, *one* two three thump of the drums. And then an older woman at the front sang a line of melody, a clear, simple tune, and the dancers responded with a verse of tonal, moaning plainsong. On and on they danced, as the sun outside rose to its zenith. On and on went the chant, rising and falling, woven delicately into the rhythm of the drums. I did not know what they were singing; I could not make out the words, let alone understand them. But I did not need to, for their purpose was clear. They were calling to the *gubida,* the ancestor spirit, the soul of the dead grandfather.

In a clearing behind the cult house, a handful of men were preparing the food that would be offered to the spirit. Banking up enormous wood fires, they plucked and gutted two dozen chickens, hacked up the carcass of a pig and peeled mountains of thick green plantains. The grass was carpeted with feathers, banana peels and bloody meaty bones. Two mangy dogs gnawed their way through the refuse as huge tureens, balanced on the fires, bubbled and frothed. Inside the cult house the chanting died away, and the dancing slowed. Mopping their brows and breathing deeply, the women drifted back to their hammocks. The floor was cleared for a line of trestle tables stretching for twenty feet and loaded with dishes of food.

Tin plate was piled upon tin plate, each heaped with rice and beans and cassava bread, chicken and pork, fried bananas and mashed yams. Set amongst this precarious pyramid of provender were several bottles of Coke and Fanta orange juice, and a bottle of rum. The Garifunas are thoughtful when it comes to the offerings, and always lay out the spirit's favourite food and drink. Grandfather clearly had a fondness for the bottle and was being indulged.

Two candles were lit, one at each end of the table, and a group of prayer women bent their heads to say an extended grace. Everybody filed out, the doors were closed, and the spirit was left in peace to eat his fill.

I left the women to rest through the afternoon, and went to ask the local priest what he thought of all this. The grace the women had recited had been a Catholic prayer, addressed to the Lord. And as I peered behind a partition at the far end of the *dabuyabe,* in a cramped sanctuary where only the spirit medium entered, I had seen an altarlike table on which candles were burning before portraits of various saints.

The priest turned out to be an Irishman, Father Jerry, who had lived in these parts for over twenty years. He had never been invited to a *dugu* and didn't ever expect to be, but he was quite prepared to respect the Garifunas' belief in the powers of their ancestors' spirits.

"They come to mass, and then they'll go on to a *dugu,*" he said in his soft Irish brogue. "They act as though it's an extension of the liturgy."

Father Jerry had come to accept his flock's varied extracurricular religious traditions. He was particularly fond of the Kekchi indian faithful, whom he found very Irish. "They get married, one man, one woman, they have kids, they come to mass, they could be from Tipperary. Sometimes they tell me they're going off to a cave somewhere for a ceremony, and I suspect there may be a little idolatry involved, but what the hell."

He was a little less patient with the Garifunas, whose habit of always demanding a favour for a favour he found exasperating. "They wouldn't even carry the cross for Jesus Christ unless you gave 'em a tip." And he wondered just how deep their Catholicism went.

"They don't go much on marriage," he acknowledged. "Some of 'em might settle down when they're fifty or so, but not all of 'em. I had an old man in here the other day, ninety years old, wanted to get married. I had to tell him, marriage is not the last rites."

When I got back to the cult house, I found the tables had been cleared. All the food, Emeterio told me, had been carted down to the beach and thrown into the sea. What the spirit had not eaten, man could not touch. But there was plenty of other food. Sitting on the ground before the ceremony resumed, I was urged to eat a proffered plate of chicken and coconut bread, and when I had finished that, another of the growing crowd of women who were gathering in the dusk pressed an enamel mug of cocoa and a bowl of beans and salty, crumbling cheese on me. I dared not say I was no longer hungry, but took advantage of the quickly falling darkness to scrape half the plateful into a nearby bush when no one was looking.

And then the drums took up their call again. The room was full now, dense with women swaying and heaving in the faint golden glow cast by two weak lightbulbs hanging from the rafters, the air thick with the smoke of incense wood burning in a brazier. Ranged side by side in close ranks, undulating en masse to the hollow beat of the drums and overlaid rattle of a pair of maracas, their breasts swinging pendulously beneath their full blouses, the women pulled greedily on bottles of rum and passed them from hand to hand, gyrating ever more fluidly, chanting louder and louder, first in rough, growling voices, then in a higher-pitched whine.

I stood in a doorway, the only man around except the drummers, Emeterio and the *buyai* who was managing the proceedings. But even he stayed on the edges, prowling around this mass of matronhood, looking mysterious in aviator shades, tight white shirt against his jet black chest, a tasselled baton in one hand, like a Congolese secret policeman.

As much as an invitation to the spirits, this was a massive celebration of womanhood, a sacred female gathering that excluded men entirely. In between songs, the women told jokes in loud voices and laughed bawdily and richly. They swigged at rum bottles like sailors in a drinking contest, shaking their shoulders and rotating their elbows like drunken rugby heavies. Suddenly, piercing the repetitive chant in an instant, a woman in the middle of the pack shrieked inhumanly, and slumped into the arms of the woman behind her. Her head lolled senselessly on her chest, and without missing a beat, the crowd around her opened up.

"Hear dat noise?" Emeterio whispered into my ear. *"Dat de spirit."*

The possessed woman, her arms draped limply around the necks of two sisters, rolled her eyes until only the whites were visible, a ghastly supernatural mask wailing and squealing like a child. Her helpers heaved her to a stool, and set her down, an elephantine rag doll. Like a deaf-mute asking for food, the woman signed to her mouth with a handful of fingers, stamping her foot petulantly. Someone brought her a bottle of "Old Friend" whisky, and she drank deeply. Only her helpers and I were paying her any attention. The rest of the room shuffled and rocked incessantly, each woman bound up in the net of rhythm that the drums cast over the room.

After a few minutes, the entranced woman staggered to her feet, brandishing the whisky bottle, and half danced, half stumbled through the dancers, shouting and crying above the din of their voices. When the song ended, her assistants led her around the room for talks with individual women. She was telling them some home truths, Emeterio told me, and answering questions put to the spirit that had taken possession of her body. Her comments drew a lot of laughter, and no one showed a trace of fear.

This was a family affair, I realised. Many of the women in the room had known the grandfather when he was alive, and they were just as comfortable with him when he visited in spirit form. The atmosphere was that of a particularly raucous gathering of sisters and aunts and mothers and cousins, deepened by a sense of supernatural mystery that joined the participants more tightly together.

An hour later, two more women had gone into trances, possessed by other spirits, helped around the room by other women as they grunted and wailed, splashing the earthen floor with rum and offering around both the bottle and small moulded balls of processed cheese. I never found out the significance of the cheese. But when one of the spirit-women rolled across the room to where I stood, stared blindly into my eyes and thrust a piece into my hand, along with some rum to wash it down, I ate it readily. Swallowing the oily little pellet, astounded that I had been included in this magic, I felt entranced myself.

Sometime after midnight, I left, as unsettled as I had been fascinated. For although I had been superficially included by the Garifunas' kindness and openness, I was, in the end, wholly excluded by my ignorance. These people had found ways into the past of their ancestors that I could not conceive of, which gave their present existence a meaning I could never grasp.

THREE

No one travels south by boat from Guatemala to Honduras. There is simply no cargo, nor enough passenger traffic to make it worth a boatman's while. There is no road connecting the two countries either, unless you want to follow a roundabout route far inland, which I did not. My rules for this journey stipulated that I should stay as close to the coast as I could. That left only one option, to walk. But I was not sure this was wise.

Three years earlier, starting out in Central America as a low-budget freelance journalist, I had sought the cheapest way of reaching Belize from Honduras, and had hitched to the port of Cortes, where I had hoped to find a steamer. I discovered, however, that only a large passenger dugout made the trip, and only once a week at that. Seeking to avoid the five-day wait that lay ahead, I had asked around about a land route, but wherever I enquired, I heard the same response. Honduras and Guatemala had agreed, twenty years earlier, to build a sixty-mile connecting road from the Honduran port of Cortes to Guatemala's Puerto Barrios, around the bay. Honduras had duly gone ahead, but the Guatemalans had reneged on the deal. Cortes is a much larger, busier and more convenient harbour than Puerto Barrios, and the Guatemalan government had realised that if its exporters could carry their goods along a paved road to and from Cortes, they would do so, leaving Puerto Barrios jobless.

People in Cortes had told me that unless I spent eighteen hours on buses, following the road deep inland, there was no way to Guatemala by land. There were paths through the forest, of course, but it was unthinkable that I should make my way on foot. I would lose myself, and anyway, the area was full of bandits. Even local travellers had been hacked to death with machetes merely for their horses and saddles, I was warned. A foreigner carrying dollars would be certain prey.

I knew that in Central America, as anywhere else, those who do not care to travel invariably exaggerate the dangers that lie outside their range of experience. But eventually I had been convinced by story after story of brigands, trackless jungle and the absence of any immigration posts. I waited for the dugout to leave, spent a miserable, soaking, seasick fifteen hours on it and regretted ever after my lack of courage.

This time, I was determined to brave the alleged dangers, and in Livingston I found Jimmy, an old man who had once worked on a banana plantation close to the border, and who said he knew the route. He himself had not taken it for close to a quarter of a century, he pointed out, but he did remember the names of the villages through which I had to pass. Armed with this skeletal itinerary, I decided to take my chances.

The ferry to Puerto Barrios left Livingston at five A.M., early enough to take the teenage children who had to be in school by seven-thirty. Beside me in the half light on the deck, a girl frantically cribbed her homework from a friend's exercise book, pausing only to decide where she should make a few deliberate mistakes to conceal her duplicity. In return, in true Garifuna style, she braided her friend's hair into beaded plaits as the sun came up.

In Puerto Barrios I walked quickly away from the wharves of banana boats and container ships to find the bus station. On an oily forecourt in front of what might have been a disused aircraft hangar, ranks of ancient buses revved their engines furiously, filling the air with diesel fumes. Small boys scampered through the milling crowd of passengers, screaming out destinations at the tops of their voices, and grabbing the luggage of anyone who showed interest before he had a chance to find a competing bus.

I was going only ten kilometres up the road towards the capital, to a junction that had a name, but which was certainly not a final destination for any of these buses. So I reversed roles, standing on the edge of the crowd and shouting "Entrerios, Entrerios." It took only thirty seconds before a barefoot boy had pushed his way through to me and tugged at my sleeve. I followed him to the bus he represented, and climbed on.

The bus was going all the way to Guatemala City, its smoked-glass windows and well-upholstered seats proclaiming its exalted intercity status. But so many other buses plied the same route, they were all obliged to take any passenger they could find, however derisory the fare. During the twenty-minute journey to Entrerios we stopped eleven times to pick up or drop off somebody, and several passengers stayed aboard barely long enough for the conductor to give them their twenty-five-*centavos* tickets.

I got off at a collection of Coca-Cola stands, which the driver assured me was Entrerios, and looked around for the railway that Jimmy had told me about. There was nothing but a dirt track leading down the hill. At the end of it, a woman standing by the side of the road promised me, was a railway station. I set off down the path, which ran between patches of maize carved from the scrub on the hillside, and nodded good mornings to groups of peasant farmers as they headed for their fields. The farmers here were not from the coast themselves. They were indian and mestizo peasants who had despaired of their dirt-poor future in the highlands and migrated here in search of land. They looked like caricatures of Central American peasants in their cartoon straw hats, grubby shirts and patched trousers, carrying machetes over their shoulders.

I fell into conversation with one of these *campesinos* a man in his mid-thirties who told me his name was Angel, and that the train to Cinchado would not leave for another two hours. At Cinchado, Jimmy had told me, I would have to get off the train and cross the river to find the Guatemalan customs post, before beginning my walk.

"If you don't want to wait for the train, I can take you on my *pooshcar,* Angel suggested, the English word unintelligible at first on his Spanish-speaking tongue.

I had heard of the *pooshcars* that ran along the banana railroad, and had imagined them as pioneer Wild West contraptions, worked by two men facing each other pushing down on a lever between them. Angel had only one arm, but I reckoned we could do it together.

With a price agreed upon, we reached the railhead, a dilapidated cluster of shacks at the end of a narrow gauge line. *Pooshcars,* it dawned on me as I saw a row of them

chained together, were exactly what their name said they
were—cars you pushed. I dumped my rucksack on the
four-wheeled wooden platform and prepared to help push
it, wondering whether this was really worth the fare I was
paying. I might just as well have walked along the rails, I
thought.

"Jump on," Angel urged me, so I did, while he started
pushing.

Once he had worked up some speed, however, Angel
too leapt aboard, took up the long wooden stick he had
brought with him, and began poling us up the track as if
we were in a gondola. I felt like a tropical Doge, planted
regally atop my backpack, surveying the surrounding countryside, as Angel worked up a furious sweat, the stump of
his amputated right arm swinging uselessly in time with
his poling. Now I was wondering whether I was paying a
high enough fare.

I assuaged my guilt by insisting on taking over from him
for a while. It took some time to find the rhythm, digging
the end of the stave into the ground just in front of a
sleeper, pushing off hard, bringing the pole back up
through my hands and ahead, choosing the next spot to
push off from. I had to be careful to keep the stick well
out to one side: If it had caught on the front end of the
cart, I would have been catapulted head over heels into
the ditch, like a pole vaulter. After ten minutes of this I
was exhausted and had to concede that even with only one
arm, Angel could propel us a good deal faster than I could.
He took up the job again, and we steamed along through
wide expanses of cattle pasture, dotted with stumpy cahoun
palms that bore giant clusters of chocolate-brown nuts the
size of chickens' eggs high on their trunks. The early morn-

ing mist rose in swathes from the rough, cropped grass, and snowy cattle egrets flapped away languidly at our approach.

Every so often we would come across another pushcar coming in the opposite direction up the single track, and I found that a strict protocol had to be followed. One of the cars had to be heaved off the tracks, obviously. But this was a laborious business, so a set of rules decided who enjoyed the right of way. On the flat, a man carrying a group of children took precedence over a man giving a woman a ride. A man carrying a woman took precedence over a man carrying another man. A man on his own took precedence over a man and a woman. And Angel on his own, with his one arm, was always given precedence by other single men, he told me. On a gradient, it was simpler. The pushcar going downhill always gave way to the pushcar going uphill. And where the track ran over rivers and creeks, the cart that reached the bridge first took precedence.

What happened when two men on their own, each with two arms, met on the flat, I did not find out. It probably came down to a banana railway version of "chicken." But my presence as a fully fit male passenger, and the fact that we were generally going slightly downhill, meant that Angel and I had to bodily lift our pushcar off the rails every few minutes.

After an hour or so of this constantly interrupted journey, the cattle fields gave way to banana plantations, massed ranks of pulpy stems sprouting broad green leaves and unexpected blue plastic bags tied round the fruit itself, to protect it from the birds. In the middle of nowhere, Angel stopped poling, and we glided to a halt. This, he announced, was Cinchado. I looked around. Nothing but row upon row of banana trees, swaying in the wind, and not a soul in sight. This was where I got off?

"Yes," Angel insisted. "You see that track there, through the plantation? Follow it until you reach the river, then shout for someone to come and fetch you."

It seemed highly improbable, but there was nothing to be done about it. I paid Angel his fare, shouldered my rucksack and set off down the path. The stillness was oppressive, and I could not see more than a few yards through the banana trees. I began to wonder whether I should not have taken the bus. But sure enough, ten minutes further on, I came to the river, broad and sluggish, a brilliant silver band cutting through the vegetation. On the far side, 200 yards away, I could see a woman bent over a boulder, doing her laundry. At least this place was inhabited.

"Halloo," I shouted, through cupped hands. The woman looked up briefly from her washing, surveyed the tree-lined bank I was standing on, didn't see me, and went back to her work.

I tried again. "*Oyé, Señora;* how do I get across the river?" I could see no boat anywhere.

This time, shielding her eyes with the palm of her hand, she spotted me, and gestured that I should follow the river-bank downstream. I found a vaguely defined path through the undergrowth and pushed my way down it. A hundred yards on, the path ended in a slithery, muddy slide down to the water. Below me, sitting wordless in the stern of a long, narrow dugout canoe, sat an ancient, bony man, a paddle across his knees.

"Can you take me to the other side?" I asked. He raised his head, and I found myself face to face with Rasputin, an unkempt grey beard reaching to his chest, crazy deep-sunken eyes and a manic grin. He nodded his assent mutely.

My doubts about this whole enterprise deepened. I could see nothing on the far side of the river to indicate that this was really where I needed to get to, just a line of unbroken forest. Around me, nothing moved but a dragonfly, its darting hum amplifying the silence. The sun reflected off the water in a blinding glare. Rasputin stared up at me unblinkingly. If I wanted to get to the other side, I went with him. I clambered unsteadily into the rocking canoe and we pushed off, Rasputin paddling steadily, his lunatic smile fixed on his face as I squatted in the prow, scanning the riverbank for a sign of life.

The dugout crunched against the gravelly shallows, and I stepped out into ankle-deep water. "Fifty *centavos*," the ferryman demanded. He wasn't dumb after all. I asked him if he knew anyone who could guide me into Honduras, but he simply waved in the general direction of the woods.

Following these somewhat unhelpful directions, I came across a hut. It was closed up and deserted, but under the circumstances I took its very existence as an encouraging sign. And indeed, there was a village further on. Scrutinising my approach from the steps of his house as he fiddled with a stick was a slim youth, the ubiquitous straw hat tilted over his eyes.

My plan was to hire a guide to show me the way across the border, and a donkey to carry my rucksack, since I had no intention of carting it up and down mountainsides if I could avoid it. No sooner had I explained to the diminutive Don Justo what I was looking for, however, than he had whipped my pack onto his back and set off at a trot down the path. I had not even had a chance to discuss a price, but given Don Justo's enthusiasm, and his willingness to act as a beast of burden, I did not have the heart to bargain. Customs and immigration, he told me, were at the far end of the village by the football field. We had to go there first.

The village, which turned out to be Cinchado, was not actually on the border, but as the nearest settlement to the demarcation line, it housed the army post responsible for customs formalities. The three young National Guardsmen doing their military service, however, were not at all sure what to do with me and sent Don Justo off to find the *jefe*.

He showed up fifteen minutes later, dressed in T-shirt and shorts, with a hook and line wrapped round a wooden block tucked into his waistband. Roy, as he introduced himself, had been fishing at the river. He was clearly not a busy man and was thrilled to find a real foreigner passing through his hands. He turned the rigmarole of crossing a border into a ritual dance, donning a pair of long trousers to lend the occasion an air of formality. Step by carefully completed step, he led me through the procedure with grave and exaggerated courtesy. I could not start filling in Form B until he had checked and countersigned Form A. He declined to accept my exit tax money until I had entered my name, age, profession, destination and purpose of journey in a Dickensian ledger. And once the paperwork was completed, he directed one of his green-uniformed minions to empty my rucksack and shoulder bag, item by item. Not that he suspected for a moment that anything was out of order. When a soldier found a phial in my toilet bag that he suggested smugglers sometimes used to carry *cocalina*, Roy dismissed the implied suspicion with a contemptuous sniff. I was, after all, an Englishman, he told his subordinate severely, and thus undoubtedly legitimate.

But the rules required, he informed me apologetically, that all travellers be searched alike. Roy was clearly terminally bored in this boondocks outpost, the fishing was lousy that morning, and he was going to spin this little bit of theatre out to savour every moment. It would probably be another year before he got the chance to do it again.

It took rather more than an hour before Roy acknowledged, regretfully, that we had exhausted this game and that I was free to go. I asked him about the risks of being held up by bandits between here and Honduras, and he looked deeply pained.

"Bandits? Who told you there were any bandits here?" he asked.

"Well, just about everybody I've talked to said this was a dangerous area to walk through," I said.

"Nonsense. There were guerrillas here once, before I was posted here, but that was years ago. And since I've been in charge, there hasn't been any trouble. I've got patrols out all the time, and everything is well under control, I can assure you."

I had obviously hurt his feelings by casting doubt on his mastery of the bandit situation. But I was glad to hear him sound so categorical anyway.

Don Justo led the way out of the village into pasture land. Growing hot in the midmorning sun, the fields had lost the gauzy haze that had shrouded them earlier, and they offered no shade. I was relieved when the path led into the forest, though under the canopy of leaves the air was heavy and close. Every now and again we would emerge into wide spreads of empty pasture, and I could see a low range of grey-blue hills in the distance. Though we were heading in their general direction, the fields were crisscrossed by so many narrow trails, no clearer than rabbit

tracks, that I was grateful for my guide. I could not explain
to his satisfaction just why I was following this route, and
he kept reminding me how much more comfortable I
would have been on the bus. But he was happy to be
earning the equivalent of three days' paltry wages, the price
we had negotiated as we walked, and I was happy to be
sticking more or less to the coast.

Suddenly, at midday, we emerged from a wood of
twenty-foot-high bamboos into open country. Verdant cattle fields lay to our left, a patch of burnt-off land to our
right, and by the path a squat plastered pyramid, mossy
with age. On my side it read "Guatemala." On the other
side was carved "Honduras." Along a third edge, "Laudo
1930" recalled the year in which the two countries had
agreed where their territories met. The stone marker was
the only suggestion that anything had changed. The countryside ahead looked much like the countryside we had
been walking through for the past two and a half hours,
only more mountainous. But it did indicate that we had
made some progress, and that we were not hopelessly lost.
Don Justo and I, pleased with ourselves, celebrated with
a sip each from my water bottle.

We needed the rest. The sun was at its hottest as we
began to climb a slope so steep we had to pull ourselves
up by the roots and branches of trees that encroached on
the little-used track. Pausing for breath every five minutes,
we toiled our way up to a narrow ridge, as the sweat
dripped from my forehead into my stinging eyes, and my
heart pumped alarmingly.

I had hoped for a view from the ridge, but found myself
surrounded by dense grass taller than I was. Every now
and again the reeds thinned sufficiently to allow a glimpse
of higher mountains to our right, draped with clouds, and

a wide plain of cattle pasture to our left, sweeping monotonously to the sea beyond the horizon. My nose was
caught by the sharp tang of cat urine, but whoever had left
that signal was no domestic tabby. This was jaguar, ocelot
and margay country, the savage scent a reminder that we
were trespassers up here.

From now on it was all downhill to the village of San
Carlos, where I planned to pick up the road, but I had
given up asking Don Justo how much longer we had to
walk. Never having owned a watch, his sense of time was
vague, and patterned on different measurements. Setting
off from Cinchado, Don Justo had told me our hike would
take about two and a half hours. We had already been
walking for three and a half hours, and our destination was
nowhere in sight. The march would eventually last for five
hours, and the final thirty minutes were the most trying.
The land was flat and the paths easy across the ranchland,
but the fields were divided from one another by barbed-
wire fences with gaps marked by posts set too close together to allow Justo through with the rucksack. Exhausted
as we both were, we were obliged to keep stopping, taking
the rucksack off, passing it over the wire and putting it
back on again. Don Justo told me, with longing in his voice,
that the shop in San Carlos had a fridge and sold litre
bottles of soft drinks. We set our minds on the prospect
of ice-cold sodas as we plodded through the fields. Never
before had Coca-Cola been the key element in my defi-
nition of civilisation.

Around half past two, we staggered into San Carlos, a
dusty group of huts shaded by mango trees, lifeless in the
heat of the early afternoon except for the occasional
chicken picking listlessly at the dry earth. Draining a bottle
of Coca-Cola, I recovered my strength as the sugar buzzed

through my veins, and began to explain to the curious shopgirl how I was glad to have done this journey, however knackered I felt, after three years of thinking about my fear of bandits.

"It's a good thing there aren't robbers around anymore," I said, "or I wouldn't have done it."

"What do you mean there aren't any robbers?" Don Justo piped up. "What do you think I carry this machete for? Just a couple of days ago the *bandidos* held up some men from Cinchado. There were three of them, one had a carbine, and the other two had machetes. They stole a cow, two horses, a tape recorder and a corn grinder. Who knows where they are now."

FOUR

San Carlos was too far off the beaten track for the Hondurans to have bothered putting an immigration post there, so I had to hitch a ride thirty miles to Omoa. No more than a village itself, Omoa had nonetheless been an outpost of central government authority ever since the Spanish first built a fortress there in the eighteenth century, in an unsuccessful effort to keep the English away.

Just as the fort had signalled an authority the Spanish had been unable to impose, the immigration office was but a façade. The man behind the plywood desk took no interest in my explanation of why I was there, and paid no attention to my request to enter the country. Instead, he simply demanded my passport and inspected it closely, upside down.

As politely as I could, I pointed out his mistake, and he proceeded to examine all the stamps he found, reading them out aloud as he leafed through the pages. When he came across some Nicaraguan entry and exit stamps he looked disturbed, put my passport down beside his antique typewriter and told me the office was closed.

"But your door was open, you are here, and it's only four o'clock," I pleaded. "Can't you do me the favour of letting me in now? Otherwise I'll have to come back tomorrow. It'll only take a minute."

He took his glasses off and pondered this, evidently deciding that it wasn't worth continuing to pretend that he was shut. "I'd willingly do you the favour," he said, "except that you need a visa to enter Honduras, and you should have got it in Guatemala. I can't let you come in."

This was rubbish. I had been in and out of Honduras countless times and knew perfectly well that British passport holders did not need a visa. I offered to show him all my previous Honduran entry stamps, unaccompanied by any special permit. The official sighed, realising he was beaten.

"You can't enter the country here because I haven't got any entry forms," he acknowledged. "You'll have to go to the office in Cortes. But don't tell them you stopped here and that I didn't have any papers left, okay? Just say you went straight there."

That was fine by me. As long as he wasn't telling me that I had to walk all the way back to Cinchado, anything he said was fine. I would happily get my papers fixed in Cortes. But first I wanted to have a look at the fortress.

I found it at the end of a straggle of modest houses set in quiet gardens blooming with sprays of purple and orange bougainvillea. It was hard to imagine this haven of lower-middle-class domesticity as the malarial swamp that the Spanish found when they began building their *castillo* 250 years ago.

The fortress itself was a heavy, uninspired triangular

structure of red stone and brick, pointing towards the sea. Built around a grassy courtyard that presumably once served as a parade ground, it comprised merely a flat-roofed, three-sided parade of cavernous, vaulted cata-combs, indistinguishable each from the other save for two kitchens, identifiable by massive fireplaces in the gloomy shadows at the rear. Along the rooftop lay rows of cannon, which would have been all very well, except that they were pointing out to sea. Overlooking the fortress from the rear was a hilltop, which the designers of the redoubt apparently ignored. This oversight was to have grave consequences.

The Spanish began clearing land for the fort in 1752, but sickness oozed from the rotting marshland right from the beginning, and hundreds of indians died trying to get the project under way. It took fourteen years just to drain the swamp and lay the foundations, and scarcely had the building been finished in 1779 than the English cap-tured it.

King Charles III of Spain had declared war on England in the hope of winning control of the Central American coast, and his first move had been to seize Belize. Two British officers, Captains Luttrell and Dalrymple, who had arrived too late to save the settlement there, decided to retaliate by attacking Omoa and spent a couple of weeks sailing up and down the coast gathering recruits from amongst the Baymen who had escaped from Belize and England's Miskito indian allies. Dalrymple led his 500 men through the mangrove swamps on a march "unlike any ever made by European troops" and seized the hilltop to the south of the fortress. Luttrell landed cannon, pushed them to the top of the hill and subjected Omoa to crossfire from the hill and from frigates in the bay. At the whispered order "Britons strike home" the raiders swarmed over the ramparts and captured the fort. A little over a month later, however, the Spanish counterattacked and the British slipped away without even offering a fight.

Having fallen within days to each of its first two assaults, the fort's subsequent history was no less ignominious. In 1832, Spanish royalists followed the English example, taking the southern hilltop before seizing the fortress from Francisco Morazan's revolutionary troops, but a few weeks later they too discovered how little protection this sorry pile of brick offered when Morazan's men took it back.

Omoa suffered one last defeat in 1853, falling to 400 Guatemalan soldiers, before the Honduran government decided that the building was probably harder to get out of than into, and made it a prison.

Puerto Cortes is the foullest blot on Central America's coastline. Honduras's largest port is resolutely grimy and degrading, from the dead cockroaches on my hotel bedroom floor to the raw concrete blockhouses outside my window, garishly lit by meretricious violet lampbulbs, empty but for a few tawdry whores sitting in the windows.

Built this century, long after military defence was important, it has none of the furtive charm of other Spanish harbours along the coast. Nor does it display any of the redeeming gaudiness and eagerness to please that can make even the grubbiest port appealing. The town is stifling and it stinks: sump oil coagulates the air at the wharves, each litter-strewn doorway reeks of piss, rubbish barrels sicken the atmosphere with putrefying fruit. At every street corner your nose puckers at the stench of rancid fat boiling in snackbar kiosks, for the port caters to both of man's basest urges—fried chicken as well as fucking.

By day, flatbed trucks transport industrial poisons by the

sackful. By night, the air is so heavy I could sleep only if I did not move. And I was woken at half past two in the morning when the brothel next door suddenly started playing a mournful Country and Western song, then a snatch of a faked Euro-reggae number, then a wailing, macho-mestizo love song.

Brazen, cheap, vulgar and selfish too. In the lavatory at my hotel, the management had scrawled a warning to patrons: "Don't piss on the seat, you'll have to sit on it yourself later."

I visited immigration, got myself legal and left town as fast as I could.

Armed security guards at the port entrance had not even allowed me onto the dock to seek a passage down the coast, and anyway it seemed unlikely I would find any small boats hopping from village to village amongst the towering tankers bound for Hamburg and Buenos Aires, so I took a local bus for twenty minutes to escape the metropolis.

It dropped me in another world, the reassuringly familiar surroundings of a Garifuna village with its palm trunk-walled huts topped by high-pitched thatch roofs and spread out down a wide beach. Travesia was as far as the bus went, I was trying to get to the next village, Bajamar, where I had been told the existence of a fishing co-op improved my chances of finding a boat.

Behind the beach a sandy track ran towards Bajamar, but at midday I could not face the six-mile walk. This was the moment, I decided, to try out my mouth organ for the first time.

I am not remotely musical. I played the triangle at nursery school, progressed to the recorder when I was ten, and that was it. But planning this trip, I had expected to be alone, with time to pass, quite often, and a mouth organ had struck me as sufficiently simple, and sufficiently portable, to be worth taking along. When I bought it in New York I had imagined myself at the end of some deserted jetty at dusk, stranded until the next canoe showed up, playing wailing homesick travelling blues over the darkening water. What I had bought turned out to be more suitable for playing military marches.

It glinted impressively in the sunlight as I put it to my mouth and tentatively blew a few experimental notes. After a quarter of an hour and a lot of repetitions I was playing a rudimentary but recognisable beginning of Mendelssohn's Wedding March and the first few bars of the theme song to the Lone Ranger, which I had found to include many of the same notes, played in a slightly different order and at a different rhythm. But my feeble efforts were clearly unworthy of my instrument. Its maker, Herr Matth. Hohner, of Trossingen, Germany, left me in no doubt that if I couldn't play this mouth organ it wasn't any fault of his. Carefully engraved on its bright silver casing were replicas of the various medals Herr Hohner had won at international trade fairs for his finely crafted harmonicas. Gold at Ulm in 1871, gold again at Vienna in 1873, a disappointing bronze at Philadelphia three years later, but a triumphant, vindicating gold again at Stuttgart in 1881. And there the laurels ended. At any event I had got no further than the third bar of the Lone Ranger by the time a jeep bumped down the track towards me. Relieved, I stuffed the mouth organ back in its case and jumped in.

The driver was almost as frustrated as I was. A travelling salesman for a tobacco company, he was at the far reaches of his beat, which ended where the road petered out in

Bajamar. He was not having much success amongst the Garifunas, he told me, with the new brand of mentholated cigarettes he was trying to introduce. But he kept at it, and the short drive to Bajamar dragged out endlessly because he would pull up to hand out free sample packs at every tiny kiosk that sold anything at all. By the time we reached our destination, he was distributing free packs to anyone we saw along the road with a cigarette in his mouth. Menthol, he assured me, was an acquired taste. With time, perhaps, he could get the Garifunas hooked on it, too.

Bajamar was asleep when I arrived, its inhabitants resting in the shade of their huts from the fierce sun. But lying on the beach, shimmering in the heat, was just what I had been hoping for: a dugout with its outboard motor still attached, suggesting that it might be going somewhere soon.

At the village shop I found a gargantuan woman perched precariously on a low stool outside her doorway, puffing uncertainly on a mentholated cigarette. The boat, she told me, had come in this morning and would probably be leaving for Rio Tinto later in the afternoon. Rio Tinto was not as far as I had hoped to go, but at least it was in the right direction. I found Antonio, the dugout's owner, lounging on the patio of his aunt's house, a yachting skipper's cap tilted over his tightly curled hair, dunking cassava bread into a bowl of fish stew. He was not leaving until the next day, he said, but in the morning he would be happy to take me. For four dollars, he would carry me beyond his village, which was surrounded by mangrove swamp, to a point from where I could walk to my next destination, the banana port of Tela.

It turned out that Antonio had brought his elder brother to Bajamar so that he could catch a bus to the city of San

Pedro Sula, sixty miles inland, where he would then take a plane to join his cousins in New York. But how true to his origins could Antonio's brother hope to be in America? I wondered.

Driven by forces beyond their control, travel and displacement are more than a way of life for the Garifunas, they are almost a cultural imperative. For 200 years their numbers have multiplied and their culture has flourished, seeming to feed on hardships. Deported from St. Vincent by the British, dumped on Roatan, drawn by the Spanish to Trujillo, scattered along the Caribbean coast, periodically uprooted by hurricanes, Garifunas are now being tempted to go to the United States.

In the past the Garifunas have always settled along the coast. Of the fifty or so Garifuna villages, only one is not on the beach. I wondered whether the lost corners of American cities will allow them to recreate, in their minds at least, the breezy shores of the Caribbean? Or will the din of freeway traffic drown out the thump of *dugu* drums and the shuffle of the Garifunas' flatfooted dance? However the Garifuna emigrants to New York fare, they are a long, long way from Bajamar. The village's lassitude soon overcame me, and I spent the afternoon asleep in my hammock. I awoke to find two small boys marvelling at my rucksack, wondering at its size and weight as they tried unsuccessfully to lift it off the sand, each trying to impress the other with his strength. One of them poked at a sidepocket, bulging with cassette tapes, a tin of corned beef and a pair of socks, and took a couple of guesses at the contents. A loaf of bread? No. A pistol? Certainly not. Was this what I should be carrying? I asked myself.

The boys' father approached after a few minutes to tell

his sons to stop bothering me, and to introduce himself as Eugenio Tomás, the owner of the hut in front of which I had slung my hammock. I would stay the night with him, he announced, but first he wanted to show me around.

Eugenio's tour of Bajamar involved two stops—his house and the village bar. It was clear as soon as we stepped through the door of his hut that wherever Eugenio planned to put me up, it was not there. He, his young wife and three children lived in two rooms. The windowless bedroom was dark and cool, clothes draped over rafters cut from tree branches, a double bed covered with a thin blanket beneath which Eugenio slept with his wife and baby, and jammed into a corner, a simple platform of planks lashed to four legs, on which his two boys slept. The other room, its beaten earth floor swept immaculately clean with the bunch of twigs that stood in a corner, looked out towards the sea. Furnished spartanly with a cheap table and two stools, the room nonetheless was brassy and colourful, for its walls were papered from floor to ceiling with pages torn from magazines brought back by seafaring friends.

A lissome blonde in a tight, sky-blue Lycra swimsuit demonstrated aerobics exercises from the pages of *Oggi*. Princess Caroline of Monaco, her smile bent by the corner around which her portrait had been plastered, grinned from a four-year-old edition of *Paris Match*. Beside her, bright and glossy, shone an advertisement for chloresterol-free margarine that *People* magazine once ran.

"Pretty, huh?" Eugenio said proudly as I inspected his walls.

"Unusual," I acknowledged.

At the bar–cum–grocery store down the beach we leant

on the short counter drinking shot after shot of cane liquor, thankfully a good deal more palatable than the "bitters" I had tried in Hopkins, and Eugenio introduced me to everyone who came in as a Peace Corps volunteer. I was not sure how to take this, since the Peace Corps had been instrumental in setting up the village fishing co-op that later folded ignominiously, but nobody seemed to harbour any grudges, and I soon gave up trying to explain that I was English. The small group of men who had gathered round me were not so interested in where I was from as in where I was going. None of them had ever visited the furthest-flung Garifuna settlements, and they were excited to find an outsider interested in them.

Depressingly, though, few of them knew more than the sketchiest outlines of Garifuna history, and I found myself in the peculiar position of giving them an account of their own past. They were fascinated, pestering me for details they hadn't heard about and filling in gaps in my knowledge with items they remembered from their grandmothers' stories, until a barrel-chested young man walked into the bar, pushed his way to my side, told me he was a teacher and pompously took over the proceedings. The epitome of the boring pedagogue, he pontificated superficially and often incorrectly about early Garifuna history and insisted on tearing a page from my notebook in order to list all the Garifuna settlements from here to the Mosquitia, "at least those that have municipal status." I kept trying to turn the conversation back to the fishermen's tales I had been enjoying earlier, but the young teacher had been a semi-professional soccer player before injuring his knee, and had travelled as far as neighbouring El Salvador, so all the others deferred to him.

I went back to Eugenio's, hung my hammock in the hut

next door to his, left empty by a brother now living in Chicago, and soon lost sight of the stars hanging over the endlessly pounding surf.

I was barely awake at dawn the next morning when Antonio was at the door, urging me to get ready quickly. I just had time for a hurried gulp of tepid herb tea before I was down at the surf, helping to heave the cumbersome dugout into the water. Antonio, two friends and I were unable to move the thirty-foot boat, carved from a single mahogany trunk, but a couple of youths walking down the beach came to give us a hand. Launching a canoe appeared to be the one communal action the Garifunas willingly joined in, without expecting reciprocal favours.

Once the boat was in the water, a boy at the prow poled fiercely while Antonio, controlling the outboard at the stern, used a short paddle to keep the canoe's nose pointing into the rolling breakers. At one point, careless in his yelping eagerness to get under way, the boy with the pole nearly turned us over when a crashing wave caught us broadsides. I sat in the middle of the canoe, gripping the edges tightly and not daring to let go even long enough to wipe away the seawater that was pouring down my face. We hung in the shallows until Antonio saw a break in the wave sequence, gunned the engine to a scream and shot us over the breaking crests, the prow smashing down into troughs with such force that the boy up front was thrown high into the air. He landed with a crack painful enough to persuade him to join me amidships.

For forty-five minutes we stayed half a mile offshore, following the beach, and not once did I relax my hold on the gunwhales. The canoe heaved and rolled with every incoming wave, but more alarmingly it would heel over

sharply at my slightest movement. Trying to be a sphinx
in a pitching canoe is not an easy trick, and I was deeply
relieved when we passed Rio Tinto and entered the rocky
mouth of a sheltered lagoon. There the jade-green water,
darkened in patches by turtlegrass waving on the bottom
five feet below, washed in gentle ripples against the prow.
Beyond Rio Tinto, no more than a clump of houses nestling
by the beach, lay a long headland, indented by two bays.
Antonio pulled the canoe up to a muddy mangrove bank
at the far side of the first bay and told me this was where
I started walking.

Plunging into the mangrove swamp alone, I was nervous
about finding my way. But after five minutes of fighting
off clouds of mosquitos I came out of the forest to see a
tropical paradise before me. A bay of silver sand, backed
by gently leaning coconut palms and lapped by barely per-
ceptible wavelets, curved away from me in a horsehoe. It
was half past eight in the morning: the sun was well up
but not fierce, and I set off at an enthusiastic pace along
the firm sand, following the water's edge and the crab
tracks—the only other sign of life.

Half an hour later, after I rounded the bay and followed
an indistinct track through more mangrove and wild banana, I emerged on the other side of the promontory, at
the head of an endless, sweeping beach that stretched in
an arc of blinding sand towards the grey-blue haze of the
horizon. Somewhere down there was Miami, the next village along the coast, and ninety minutes' walk away, according to Antonio.

"More like two hours, and that if you're quick," said a
fat old grandmother who came out of her thatched hut,
dabbing cinnamon oil onto a painful tooth, to see who was
passing by.

"Okay, two hours," I told myself. "That sounds manageable."

Tucking my flip-flops into my pack and walking barefoot, I headed directly into the sun. I soon found that I could not walk in the dry sand high up on the beach. It was too hot, and the weight of my forty-five-pound rucksack drove me up to my ankles into the uncertain surface. I discovered that the only way to walk along these shores was to follow the line of the most recently broken surf, as it crashed and receded, leaving the sand firm enough to take my weight.

As the sun rose higher, and the pack cut more deeply into my shoulders, I set my eyes downwards, fixing them on the surfline. But the damned line kept changing. Though the tide was coming in, forcing me slowly up the beach, its reach varied with the incline of the shore, and I found myself zigzagging like a crab, concentrating only on the next few steps.

When I raised my eyes, the distance was clouded by a fine haze flying from the pounding spume. It was not an encouraging view, and to make it worse, whenever I held my head upright sweat dripped from the corner of my eyebrows into my eyes. I abandoned my sunglasses, which merely dribbled the sweat across my vision, and squinted at the foaming surf at my feet. I gave up following the breaking waves, finding that the sand underwater was firm enough. So I waded, sometimes dragging myself through freak waves that broke as high as my waist, and wondered to myself why the hell I was doing this.

Today, I remembered, was my thirty-fourth birthday. I should be having a party, lying on the beach, not trudging along it on my own.

With my mouth tasting like the inside of a gum bottle,

my legs weary and my shoulders burning, I set myself thirty-minute stretches between breaks. As the appointed minute for a rest approached, I had to steel myself against the temptation to look at my watch. I savoured each moment of my rest stops. First, a few scribbled notes while I was still, theoretically, dry, although the sweat on my hand and forearm made half of each page unreadable. Then I would stagger down to the sea and throw myself into the cool waves, just to float mindlessly in the sandy breakers. Then back to the shade for a light sip of water to rinse my mouth of salt and prepare it for the full flavour of the highlight of my fifteen-minute reprieve, a cigarette. I lovingly smoked it to the filter, took another, heftier swig of water from my flask and spent a few minutes contemplating my foolishness.

Why *was* I doing this? Partly because the road to Tela, along which buses ran, went a long way inland. Partly because in Bajamar I had not found a canoe that would take me all the way to Tela by sea. Partly because I had not appreciated quite how gruelling this walk would be. But I was mainly doing it because I had read that beachwalking was a venerable Garifuna tradition, *the* way to travel when visiting relatives. And I had not seen one sodding Garifuna all morning on this godforsaken beach. Any of them with any sense, I realised, would be taking the bus.

This was particularly distressing because for a long while, whenever I looked up and back, my starting point had receded, but my destination, a gap in the palm grove, had not grown any closer. Without the encouragement of an approaching goal, my insteps aching, my ankles nagging, my shoulders screaming and my groin smarting with friction and salt water, I gave myself up to the power of inexorability.

Eventually Miami did come into view—a collection of thatched hovels on the far side of a sandbar. Another thirty-minutes' walk and I was there, only to discover that I had missed the tide, and the bar was no longer crossable on foot because white crested waves were breaking through the channel in a riptide. I didn't even have the energy to stamp my foot. But just then I spotted a miniscule dory in the sheltered lagoon inside the bar, and hailed the two boys fishing from it. They paddled over and I heaved my pack and myself on board. I held my breath as they steered the canoe, only seven feet long and eighteen inches wide, to the far bank.

I scuffed my way through the knifegrass at the village edge, into the cluster of filthy little huts that I discovered were mostly occupied by *ladinos* who had taken them over from their original Garifuna inhabitants, who had gone abroad. In one of them, I found a man with a little ice and a Coca-Cola in his cold chest. A wizened grandfather came and sat by me as I slumped, shattered, over my Coke, and tried out the broken English that he had learned forty years ago in Belize. What was I doing, he wondered. I explained. Was I being paid for this, was it some kind of a job? No, I said, I was doing it for fun.

"*I see, mon, you juss tekkin a waalk.*"

Yes, man, just *tekkin a waalk*.

The prospect of continuing this walk as far as Tela was too horrible to contemplate, but I was in luck. The daily lorry running from Miami to the neighbouring village of San Juan was leaving soon, and I had time for a quick swim before finding just enough space to stand in the back. The truck bumped its way down a rutted, sandy path that led along a classic Caribbean beachscape. The view was a good deal more pleasing from the back of a moving vehicle than from underneath a backpack, I decided.

San Juan is almost on the beaten track. Only a few kilometres outside the town of Tela, its beach is popular with day-tripping Hondurans, and I had no trouble catching a ride around the bay into the port. Well, into the former port. Tela was once the Central American headquarters of the formidable United Fruit Company, whose writ was law throughout the region in the early years of this century, and which made or unmade governments depending on their insistence on a banana export tax. The company's last victim, Guatemalan President Jacobo Arbenz, fell in a 1954 coup d'état cooked up in a conspiracy between United Fruit and the CIA. But *El Yunai*, as the company is known locally, moved away years ago, and Tela slumbers now as a genteel resort for the richer Honduran on holiday. The old United Fruit residential compound, in fact, has been converted into a hotel—rows of tidy stilted bungalows that increase in size with their proximity to the beach-front and the importance of their former occupants. I had arranged to meet a couple of friends from the capital, Tegucigalpa, at this hotel, to celebrate my birthday and a month of travelling. I relaxed into a day of unaccustomed comfort.

On my Texaco map of Honduras, the only one I had, a dotted line indicating a steamer service joined Tela to La Ceiba, the next port, 100 kilometres down the coast. Since the map's main purpose was to indicate the existence of Texaco petrol stations around the country, shipping routes were not a priority, and I had assumed that any that were marked must be regularly plied. I had assumed wrong. When I asked at the dock about boats to Ceiba, an old man looked up from his fishing line just long enough to cackle scornfully and tell me he hadn't seen a coastal boat leave Tela since sometime in the 1950s.

I got the same reaction from a tramp sitting in the shade of the railway station as he methodically combed his chest-length beard with overgrown fingernails. The tracks to Ceiba, laid by United Fruit, had fallen into disrepair a quarter of a century ago and had been so shoddily rebuilt the year before that the first rains had washed all the bridges away, he told me. The road, which had put the tramp steamers and the railway out of business, ran along the foot of increasingly impressive mountains whose higher reaches were covered in virgin forest and shrouded by the misty blue smoke of fires that peasant farmers had started on the lower slopes to clear bushland for their plots of corn. To my left, rich, lurid green cattle pasture ran away towards the sea.

In Ceiba, I went looking for a hotel, but the first one I tried was well beyond my budget. As I turned away from the desk, a young man who had overheard my enquiries jumped up from a sofa in the lobby.

"*You lookin for a cheap place tonight, mon?*" he asked. "*I show you won place got good rates. Ten lempiras a night. Fifteen seventy-five if you carry op a woman.*" Cheap at either price, I reckoned, and I took a room there.

Ceiba was just the sort of shabby, goodnatured town that a port well past its heyday ought to be—seedy but still somehow dignified. All the action centred on the wharf, for La Ceiba was still the heart of operations for *El Yunai's* historic rival, Standard Fruit. The *Rio Areboyo* out of Guayaquil in Ecuador was tied up, her huge bulk throwing the long wooden jetty into shade as she loaded bananas ceaselessly through five gaping hatchways in her hull. Up the narrow gauge tracks laid on the pier, an oily yellow locomotive pushed strings of battered goods-wagons, and from inside the wagons, the unseen hands of stevedores threw box after box after box of bananas onto tracks of rollers and conveyor belts that ran, mazelike, into the ship's hold. All that afternoon, all that evening, all that night, all the next day the boxes trundled, back to back in an endless stream. "Dole Fruit Company Dole Fruit Company Dole Fruit Company."

The *Rio Areboyo* was bound for Hamburg according to the loading schedule chalked on a blackboard hung over her side. The Germans, I gathered from a Standard Fruit official, are the most enthusiastic banana eaters in the world, each man, woman and child peeling his or her way through more than twenty-five pounds of the fruit each year. This load would keep them going for a few days.

Above the din of the rattling banana wagons, a siren sounded the end of a shift. Fruit handlers streamed out of the *Rio Areboyo*'s frozen hold, pulling off leather gauntlets and slinging empty lunchsacks over their shoulders. "*Qué calor, hombre,*" one of them muttered as he emerged into the sunlight. "*Fock.*" The stevedores were Spanish speakers from the interior, but the coast's English language heritage had left its mark.

Their day's work over, the dockers headed up the quay to Ceiba's central street, split down its middle by the railway track leading onto the wharf, and lined by bars. Over the years, respectable businesses have moved a block or two away from San Isidro Street, and their place has been taken by oversized rabbit hutches with swing doors that cater to sailors. At a distance, it was hard to distinguish one bar's blaring jukebox from the next, they all blended into a cacophony of cheap goodtime noise, and fair-haired, blue-eyed boys from the nearby Bay Islands, on the prowl in groups of three or four, lapped it up, roughhousing but careful not to dirty their shore pants.

I was heading for the Bay Islands, intrigued by stories I had heard of an improbable independence movement among residents who wanted to break away from Honduras and declare their tiny archipelago an English colony. That night, in one of the grubby little bars decorated with posters of various breeds of anthropomorphised dogs playing billiards, I joined a table of Bay Islanders. They were delighted to find I was English, and took my presence as a new excuse to badmouth Spanish-speaking Hondurans. In Ceiba, they explained, they walked around in groups of at least three not so much for the company, as to give themselves protection against being beaten up by "Spaniards," and they never ventured more than three blocks into town. *"I fock on San Isidro, no further,"* a stubble-chinned old man with calloused hands told me firmly. *"If you beat a Spainyard op now on the meenland, dey put you in jail, mon. You doan waant to mess wid dem Spainyards."*

On the islands, however, it seemed, you could beat a *"Spainyard"* up without any risk of jail at all. My drinking companions turned out to be the crew of a cargo boat sailing to the island of Utila the next day, and the boat took passengers, they told me. I had a ride.

FIVE

The *Tona C.* was due to leave Ceiba at nine o'clock,
but she didn't get away until nearly noon because
Captain Lejourn Cooper kept hoping for a little
extra cargo.

The hold was already full of beer, soft drinks, flour,
sugar, meat, ice cream, cigarettes, lumber and butane gas
cylinders, and the crew had stacked piles of timber along
the gangways on either side of the bridge, but there was
still a little space on deck, behind the parlour set of sofa
and chairs, two beds, a stove, bundles of plastic piping and
sheets of corrugated iron, and Captain Cooper was loath
to leave it empty. Eventually two men panted up the pier
pulling cartloads of oranges, cabbages, bananas and plantains, and once they were on board the Captain decided
he had loaded as much as he could take. Captain Cooper's
business, he told me proudly, was *"keepin the oisland in
food"* and doubtless he did it well. But his mundane cargo
of daily twentieth-century necessities would scarcely have
tempted the buccaneers who once prowled these waters.
The likes of Henry Morgan, whose brother is said to be

buried on Utila, made the Bay Islands a den of piracy in search of fatter Spanish prey.

The original corsairs, both French and English, descended on the western Caribbean in the latter half of the sixteenth century, less than a hundred years after Columbus had first explored the region. They found the three Bay Islands, thirty miles off the coast of Honduras, an ideal refuge to careen their boats and divide up the spoils of their raids. For a while the pirates concentrated their attacks on the Honduran coast, robbing warehouses full of gold ingots and animal hides in Trujillo, for example, but they soon exhausted that town's possibilities and the buccaneer fleets operating from the islands of Utila, Roatan and Guanaja turned their attention to juicier targets.

In the seventeenth century, when the Spaniards' pillage of South American gold and silver was at its height, the galleons loaded with this wealth passed through the Bay of Honduras on their way from Portobello in Panama to Havana, and thence to Cadiz. Dutch pirates alone, professionally organised and acting under the auspices of the Dutch West India Company, captured 547 Spanish ships—at the rate of almost one a week—and 118 million Guilders' worth of goods in just 15 years between 1621 and 1636.

And that was before the buccaneers really came into their own, in the second half of the seventeenth century, when they virtually ruled the Caribbean. Their numbers swelled as sugar, which was grown with black slave labour, replaced tobacco that had been cultivated by white indentured field hands, as the West Indies' primary export crop. Poor whites were kicked off the land all over the Caribbean, and rather than return home to England, Holland or France, many of them joined pirate fleets that could muster as many as 1,000 men at a time. Others did not go to sea

at once, but retreated to wild and uncultivated bays, building rude shelters of animal skins and leaves, to hunt boar
and feral cattle. They cured the meat in a style first learned
from the local Carib indians, smoking it on a barbecue of
green wood over a fire fed by the fat, bones and offal of
the animals they had killed. The cured meat was known
as *boucan* jerky, and the men who made it *boucaniers*. It is
from that French word that the English "buccaneer" de-
rives, for as the herds of wild animals diminished, most of
the *boucaniers* gave up trading with passing pirate ships and
signed on as crew members themselves.

One such man was François Lolonois, a Frenchman who
arrived in the Caribbean in the mid-seventeenth century
as an indentured servant, and whose exploits suggest the
nature of life as a pirate in those days.

Lolonois joined the *boucaniers* in the woods of Hispaniola when he had served his time, and then went aboard a
pirate ship as a common mariner. His bravery attracted
the notice of the French governor of Tortuga, known today
as Grand Cayman, who offered him a ship and made him
Captain. Lolonois then began to walk the ill-defined line
between outlaw pirate and officially commissioned pirate,
or privateer, plundering the Spanish not only for his own
glory but for that of his government too.

Alexandre Esquemeling, writing his pirating memoirs in
1684 under the title *Bucaniers of America*, recalled that
Lolonois's "cruelties against the Spaniards were such, as
that the very fame of them made him known through the
whole Indies," and he did well for a while, seizing considerable amounts of Spanish booty, before a great storm blew
up off the coast of Campeche, in Mexico, and he lost his
ship. Though he and his crew reached dry land in a longboat, the local Spanish garrison pursued and killed or cap-

tured most of them; Lolonois himself was wounded, but mixed sand with the blood from his gashes, smeared it on his body and crawled under a pile of his comrades' corpses to hide until the Spanish had left the field.

Later he bound up his wounds, disguised himself as a Spaniard and made his way into the town of Campeche, where he persuaded two slaves to steal a canoe one night, and in return for their freedom come away with him. Thus he escaped, "and came safe to Tortuga, the common place of refuge for all sorts of Wickedness, and the Seminary, as it were, of all manner of Pyrats and Thieves." Having found himself another ship, Lolonois raided a town in Cuba, where he executed all his prisoners before making off with tobacco, sugar and hides, surprised a galleon off the north coast of Colombia to steal its cargo of plate, and then launched his biggest project yet—an assault on the wealthy port of Maracaibo in Venezuela.

Gathering over 650 men in eight vessels, and pausing on the way only to knock off a Spanish cargo ship laden with cacao, Lolonois arrived in the Gulf of Venezuela and proceeded to storm the port. Meeting little opposition, his men took over the best houses in town, since their oc-cupants had fled into the forest, and found them

> well provided with all sorts of Victuals, such as Flour, Bread, Pork, Brandy, Wines and a good store of Poul-try. With these things the Pirats fell to banqueting and making good Cheer: for in four weeks before they had no opportunity of filling their stomachs with such plenty.

The pirates left a month or so later, richer by 50,000 pieces of eight that they had stolen or extorted as protection

money not to burn the town down. They retired to an
island off Hispaniola inhabited by *boucaniers* to divide up
their spoils according to seniority, first recompensing the
wounded for any loss of limb and all swearing an oath that
none had concealed any plate, jewelry or other valuables.
They returned to Tortuga rich men, the meanest cabin boy
rattling over 100 pieces of eight in his purse, but

> as to the common Pirats, in three weeks they had
> scarce any money left them, having spent it all in things
> of little value, or at play either at cards or dice.

Lolonois met his end on an ill-fated expedition to pillage
Nicaragua. Desperately short of food, he was putting into
shore so that his men could hunt monkeys and other wild
animals, when he ran aground on a sandbank in the middle
of the Miskito Cays. He made camp on one of the cays,
broke up his vessel and made a longboat from its timbers,
and then set off in search of canoes in which to transport
his stranded shipmates.

> But God Almighty, the time of his divine justice being
> now already come, had appointed the Indians of Dar-
> ien to be the Instruments and Executioners thereof.

As Esquemeling put it,

> The Indians within a few days of his arrival took him
> Prisoner, and tore him in pieces alive, throwing his
> body limb by limb into the fire, and his ashes into the

Air; to the intent no trace or memory might remain of such an infamous, inhumane Creature.

At one time or another Lolonois surely put in to Utila to mend his rigging and catch turtle. As the *Tona C.* slowed her engines and edged around a sandbar at the mouth of the harbour, the bay before us appeared an ideal pirates' lair. A rocky, coral-strewn headland to our right protected the village, a string of white painted clapboard houses running around the foot of a low hill down to the water's edge, many of them standing on stilts in the crystal shallows of the lagoon. Where the village petered out, mangrove bushes grew thickly, a tangle of yellowing green lining the sweep of the bay into the hazy distance. Behind the mangroves, thickets of coconut palms rose into the air—a reminder that at the turn of the century this island was exporting three million nuts a year—and beyond the village lay a low flat-topped hill like an upturned pudding basin, partly covered in scrub and partly cleared for small farming plots.

Though some buccaneer blood may still run in Bay Islanders' veins, it is not pirate genes that make almost half of the population English speakers. Once the Spaniards had cleared all the indigenous indians off the islands in the mid-seventeenth century, in an attempt to deprive freebooters of provisions, no one except a group of Garifunas settled permanently until the second quarter of the nineteenth century, when a wave of Cayman Islanders arrived to seek their fortunes after the abolition of slavery in the Caymans in 1830. They were followed by many of their former slaves, who had won their freedom but who often could not find work.

The former slaveowners were English, and in 1852 London officially claimed the Bay Islands as a Crown colony, a step it had never formally taken during the previous century of disputed ownership with Spain. But by this time the English foreign secretary and Prime Minister Lord Palmerston was in his prime, assuring settlers around the world that "a British subject, in whatever land he may be, shall feel confident that the watchful eye and strong arm of England will protect him against injustice and wrong." For the colonists in those days "injustice and wrong" were synonymous with *"Spainyards,"* and although England relinquished its claim to the Bay Islands in 1859, that sentiment prevails today. The attempt to redeclare the islands a British colony, I learned, had been squelched by the Honduran authorities, but fond memories of Palmerston's days live on.

Those memories, it turned out, had been rekindled only recently, sparking brief hopes that maybe England had not after all abandoned the islands. While I was sitting one afternoon in a coconut grove where I had gone for a picnic of stewed fish and a half gallon of rum with Lejourn and some friends of his, the conversation turned to the Falklands conflict. I have always had my doubts about the manner in which Margaret Thatcher fought that war, but this was clearly no place to air them. Lejourn's voice rose as he jumped to his feet in the sand. The west country vowels of his ancestors surfaced in an explosion of English pride, his bleary eyes fixed on mine.

"Oi tell you, mon, the British when dey tell dose modderfockers one ting, dey mean dat ting. Margaret Taatcher, she waalk troo dose Spainyards loik she waalkin troo a field o roice."

I heard the same story, expressed in a more cautious and refined manner, when I went to visit an old man in his nineties who, I had been told, would give me "an earful of history" if that was what I was looking for. He talked to me on the condition that I not mention his name, but *"use a little diplomacy—call me 'a gentleman born of British parents.' They are very fonny people here."* He perched, bird-like, on a swinging chair on his porch, surrounded by carefully tended flowering bushes, his pale papery hands shaking, his thin white hair combed neatly over a skull blotchy with age as he launched into a lament over the moral decadence into which Utila had fallen since the proper days of his youth. Every now and again he paused to check that I was still paying attention and to peer through dim and watery eyes at the manifesto that he had once written but thought better of distributing.

"You lissen and face the facts, then you decide and past your own opinion whether we've degraded and degenerated or not," he said, fixing me with a warning stare, as if I was about to suggest that maybe life on the island today was not all that depraved.

"We had six flower gardens well kepp along our road fenced in. We had six groups of young men and young ladies gatherin on Sunday mornins singin, and we only had one liquor shop. No vulgar expressions on the streets, especially by young ladies supposed to be. We had some dirty characters, oh yes, but they were precautious in their deeds owin to the law. Lots of rummers too, but only six or seven public drunkards. The girls were taught music lessons, and we had one of the best bands of music around. Our young ladies, white or black, were at home at six P.M. We had any kind and class of food to buy but we didn't buy anything from the coast, oh no. All foreign goods, USA, France, England, Germany. I think you can put two and two together and decide for yourself. We had carts hauled by oxen or horses to haul our provisions from the farms, and we also had a buggy hauled by a horse to ride through the town.

"*My father come from Southampton, far down in history. He come with his father, a shiprigger and a sail maker. I haven't taken a drop of liquor in my life, you know, but I've had three strokes. The last time, the doctors looked at me, they didn't find a trace of VD. I said not unless they put it in my food.*

"*I wanted to get to London but I only made Liverpool. That was in 1919. They was hard days, eighty-two days from Newport News to Belfast, thirty dollars a month for the sailors and only on Sunday they give us a little ice cream. In them days we had wooden ships and iron men. I've stood on the spot where Lord Nelson was shot, you know. In Tampa, Florida. Oh yes, they brought his ship over that side then in 1920 they towed her across to British Honduras. Come in here, I'll show you something.*"

He trembled to his feet, leaning on a mahogany cane, and I followed him indoors. In the parlour, plaster ducks flew up the walls and an ancient leafed table was stacked high with dusty books and papers. The gentleman born of British parents paused to let me admire a commemorative mug from a Methodist conference one of his nephews had attended, and beckoned me into his bedroom. Stooping over a battered sea chest in the corner, he pulled out an immaculately folded flag and laid it gently on the bed. It was a white ensign, the colours of the Royal Navy, the red cross of St. George on a white background with the Union Jack in the top left-hand corner.

Don't tell me he's got the Victory's standard stashed away here as well, I thought to myself. But no, it was a more recent flag, given to his school by HMS *Renown* and presented to him in 1922 for coming top of his engineering class.

"*I cherish that,*" he said, gazing lovingly at this old emblem of English might. *"But don't say who showed it to you, will you. Just say 'the informer' cos I livin in a treacherous place, and they prejudice here. You English, you know well enough, ever since England took world power away from Spain, any Spainyard from whatever part of the world, he be enemy of you."*

For this old man, Sir Francis Drake's defeat of the Spanish Armada in 1588 was not merely a historical event he had learned about as a boy. It was an element of his daily life, full of vibrant meaning. And he wasn't even English. He had been, until his twenty-first birthday, but he had decided that to avoid unnecessary problems with the local authorities he would become Honduran. *"I British at heart,"* he confided, *"England's the mother country of the world. But you've got to adjust matters to suit yourself."* He rummaged again in his seachest and looked back at me over his shoulder. *"What year Churchill die?"* he asked me sharply.

For a moment I thought he was simply curious to know, but then I understood. I was being quizzed.

"1965?" I ventured.

"Correck, young man. See here."

He proffered a tattered and yellowing magazine. Churchill's face glowered from the front cover of the edition of *Life* that had marked the statesman's death. *"You see the old bulldog, you see the old bulldog."* He pointed to the portrait with a shaking finger and sighed.

In the face of such resolute determination to feel British, I wondered how the municipal officials, Spanish speakers imported from the mainland, managed to impose their Honduran authority. An announcement chalked in a looping Victorian copperplate on the village noticeboard hanging outside a small grocery store gave me a clue.

TEKKIN A WAALK

TO ALL CITIZENS OF UTILA

*I would like you all to cooperate by clearing up your graves
that are fenced in. I am clearing the graveyard now and
I would appreciate your cooperation.*

> *Thanking you*
> RONALD RAMON
> CHIEF OF POLICE

The Honduran police are not known for their politeness
or delicacy. Ronald Ramon, it was clear, had learned to be
diplomatic.

On my way to find a boat that could take me to Utila's
neighbouring island, Roatan, I spotted a large man loping
down the sandy path towards me. Although he was black
he was much too stocky for a Bay Islander, and anyway,
no one on Utila wears a sarong. I could not resist the
temptation, trying not to be too blunt, to ask him where
he came from and what he was doing here.

Vilimaina Vono came from Fiji, and he was Utila's Methodist minister. He had been on the island for two months,
he told me, and he already felt right at home: the people
ate the same food and John Wesley had had an equally
strong influence—Methodism having arrived in Utila in
1852, seventeen years after its introduction to Fiji.

When England handed the Bay Islands back to Honduras
in 1859, a clause in the treaty allowed the inhabitants to
continue worshipping as they pleased. The Catholic church
excommunicated Honduran President Santiago Guardiola
for his weakness on this point, but he was, after all, only

facing up to the same reality that police chief Ramon had to deal with. Nonconformism is the Bay Islands' style.

Scarcely had the *Utila Tom* left harbour than the wind sprang up. She was a high-powered fibreglass craft, built along the lines of a speedboat but large enough to carry several thousand pounds of fish in her hold and two great ice chests buckled down astern. She belonged to the islands' fishing co-op, collecting the catch from outlying branches and bringing it in to be processed in Coxen Hole on Roatan before it was flown to the States. The fishermen on Utila had complained that life was growing harder for them and that they had to cast their nets further and further afield to find the shoals that had once been plentiful onshore. But fishermen, like farmers, are born to moan. At the height of the previous year's season, the captain of the *Utila Tom* told me, the 30 dories fishing out of Utila had shipped 52,000 pounds of red snapper to America in just three weeks.

Captain Henry was in a hurry to get home and he didn't give a damn about the weather. Sitting in a highly sprung armchair at the wheel, munching on pieces of fried chicken fed to him by his assistant, he forced the boat through the towering swell at a relentless speed. Sitting on a built-in couch along one side of the wheelhouse, I soon tired of being tossed around and cracking my head against the ceiling every time we crashed into a trough, so I went outside. There I found a spare rope lying on the deck and tied one end around my waist and the other to a chrome handgrip bolted to the gunwhale. Crouched against the wind and holding tight to the handrail, I watched the sun set behind us, gilding our foaming wash and colouring the gathering waves ever deeper shades of purple and violet until night fell heavy and black with storm clouds.

After a couple of hours, though, we were running in the lee of Roatan, sheltered by its long, crooked finger of land, and by late evening we had tied up under the arc lamps of the co-op's concrete wharf. Stiff and aching from the strain of constantly steadying myself against the lurching of the boat, I paid for a room in the nearest boarding house, tried to ignore the stench drifting down the corridor from the sole lavatory, which was blocked, argued just long enough with the proprietor to obtain a pair of clean sheets to replace the stained rags that I had found covering the lumpy mattress, and fell asleep.

The inhabitants of Coxen Hole like to tell visitors that their town is named after a seventeenth-century pirate named John Coxen who used to live there. It is hard to reconcile this piece of folklore, however, with the fact that the name does not appear on any map of the island until 1843. Regardless of the town's origins it is an ugly, dusty, unkempt straggle of a place today, the Bay Islands' administrative centre and the only settlement of any size on Roatan, but with nothing to detain the tourists who pass through on their way to resort hotels overlooking secluded bays elsewhere on the island.

It had been some time since I had been in touch with friends of mine in the capital, Tegucigalpa, who were keeping tabs on my progress and relaying reports to my wife in Managua, so that morning I decided to give them a call. I was encouraged to find a bright new telephone office in Coxen Hole, all gleaming plate glass, bright orange plastic bucket seats and polished floors, but having climbed a set of steps up the hillside to its entrance I discovered it was

closed. A soldier on guard outside, lounging on the butt
of his M-16 assault rifle in the shade, told me that the
exchange had been shut so as to be inaugurated.

Marvelling at this example of Honduran logic, I was
about to go back down into town when I saw a press of
paunchy, well-groomed dignitaries mounting the steps towards me, trailed by a television crew and a gaggle of
reporters. This was the inaugurating party. I slipped in
amongst the journalists and pushed my way past the guard.
The inauguration of the island's first telephone link with
the mainland was a solemn affair, timed to coincide with
Honduras's annual National Day of Dignity. That celebration marked the day in 1861 when England finally relinquished control over the Bay Islands and handed them
over to Honduran sovereignty. But Honduran national
dignity had taken a severe beating since then.

The archetypal "banana republic" in American eyes,
Honduras in the late nineteenth and early twentieth centuries was only as important to Washington as the fruit-
growing lobby could make it. But when the Sandinista
revolution shook neighbouring Nicaragua in 1979, US pol-
icymakers took a new interest in the second-poorest country in the Western Hemisphere, better off only than Haiti.
Rendered pliable by its traditional dependence on the US
market for its fruit exports, and wooed with hundreds of
millions of dollars to relieve its misery, Honduras rapidly
became a bastion of US policy in Central America. The
contras set up their bases in Honduras, USAID officials
poured in by the score, US soldiers flew in by the thousands for endless joint exercises, and it was no secret who
was really running the country. Although the Honduran
flag flew over the pink stucco presidential palace, the Stars

and Stripes flew higher over the American embassy, where the ambassador was generally known as the proconsul.

As this year's National Day of Dignity dawned, US Drug Enforcement Agency officials had decided a few days earlier that they would like to talk to a well-connected Honduran whom they suspected of smuggling cocaine into the United States, and rather than trouble themselves with the normal Honduran judicial channels, they had swooped into Tegucigalpa and kidnapped the man, flying him to Miami without so much as a by your leave.

The panjandrums gathered at the Coxen Hole telephone office, though, had come to forget about all this. They were here to tie another knot in the rather tenuous links between the mainland and these very un-Honduran islands, to reaffirm the country's sovereignty and then to get drunk on a Caribbean beach before being flown home by the army. The minister of communications was here to preside over the ceremonies, the colonel in charge of the national telephone company was here to remind everyone that communications are a national security concern, the entire local government of Roatan was here to bask in the reflected glory of these bigwigs, and the local priest was here too, to sprinkle holy water over the newly completed project.

Crowded into the exchange, we all stood at attention while the national anthem was played over a tinny tape recorder. We then bowed our heads as the priest intoned a prayer over a maroon telephone placed with exaggerated precision in the centre of a silver platter that sat on a royal-blue velvet mat decorated with golden tassels. A vase of plastic flowers on a lace doily to one side emphasised the importance of the occasion. As the colonel cut a ribbon strung across the room, marking what he called "this transcendental moment in the institutional life of Hondutel," we clapped politely.

And then, the highlight of the morning, the first official phone call. The minister gravely picked up the receiver and a flunky dialled the number of the presidential palace in Tegucigalpa. The audience held its breath and the German technicians who had installed the exchange kept their fingers crossed. Over the loudspeakers rigged up to broadcast the other end of the conversation we heard the phone ringing in the capital. The technicians uncrossed their fingers. A girl at the switchboard answered.

"*Palácio presidenciál,* can I help you?"

"The president's office, please."

"One moment, I'll put you through."

A certain amount of clicking, a prolonged silence amplified by the hiss of the loudspeakers, and the president's secretary came on the line.

"I'd like to speak to the president of the Republic, *Ingeniero* Jose Azcona, please."

"I'm sorry, sir, he cannot be disturbed at the moment," we heard faintly.

"This is the minister of communications, calling from Roatan," the minister replied icily. "I would like to speak to the president."

"I'm very sorry, *Señor Ministro,* but the president told me he could take no calls at the moment. He is in an extremely important meeting."

"This is the inaugural telephone call from Roatan to Tegucigalpa using the new exchange," the minister insisted. "The president is expecting my call. Please put me through."

The secretary's response was testy, and, he clearly intended, final. "The president was quite clear that no one was to disturb him," he said. "He is meeting with the American ambassador."

The minister went pale, the dignitaries grouped around him shifted nervously and the journalists with their tape recorders held close to the loudspeaker did their best to conceal their sniggers. "This telephone call is being broadcast live on national radio," the minister spluttered, reduced in his shame to a blackmailing lie.

There was silence from Tegucigalpa, and then a simple "Oh." The minister wiped beads of sweat from his brow, and then at last the president's voice crackled over the sound system.

"Señor Presidente," boomed the minister, drawing himself up to his full height as if he were in Azcona's office. "I have the honour of addressing you by telephone from the Hondutel office in Roatan to mark the inauguration of the new exchange here. We are celebrating another magnificent achievement of your administration.

"Thank you," said the president. "Congratulations to Hondutel. Salutations to everyone up there. Glad to talk to you. Carry on." He hung up, intent on more important business.

Three cheers for Honduran dignity and sovereignty.

I was trudging down Coxen Hole's scrubby little main street in search of a bus to somewhere more scenic when Captain Henry skidded to a halt beside me on his bicycle. Tipping his mariner's cap back on his head, he told me he was just leaving to pick up some more fish from French Harbour, down the coast aways, and asked if I wanted to go with him. Half an hour later we were pulling into the well-sheltered little port that French buccaneers had once made their own, but which was now full of tidy blue-and-white lobster boats lashed one against the other around the basin in mass homage to their captains' sisters, wives and sweethearts. *Miss Janet, Miss Selina, Miss Lorraine, Miss Heather, Miss Lani,* the *Sandie J.,* they all bore girls' names as charms against the perils of the sea.

French Harbour turned out to be little more than a ramshackle collection of vegetable stalls piled with green bananas, tuberous cassava and young coconuts, but buses stopped there on their way to Oak Ridge, ten miles further east, where the road came to an end. I would have done better to have walked to Oak Ridge. Public transport consisted of Japanese minibuses packed with seats too small for a midget to sit comfortably and totally inadequate for the crush of bulky fishwives who were crowded into the bus, the multicoloured rollers in their hair scraping the ceiling. I threw my rucksack onto the roof and twisted my way into a seat already half occupied by a matronly thigh, to sit there suffocating while the driver revved his engine mercilessly and his assistant hung out of the sliding door shouting at the top of his voice to attract still more passengers. Only when he had bullied all the children under the age of ten into sitting on their mothers' laps and squeezed a couple of late arrivals onto the transmission tunnel, legs astride the gearstick, did the driver consent to leave. He then drove so recklessly along the rutted, dusty track that wound up and down the island's mountain spine that I could concentrate on nothing but my grip on the seat in front of me. I caught an occasional glimpse of the sea, glittering at the foot of wooded hillsides, and once in a while the fiery parasol of tangerine flowers crowning a flame tree flashed by the window. But I was in no position to enjoy the view.

After half an hour of this misery we made a jarring and precipitous descent and pitched to a halt at the edge of a secluded lagoon, protected from the sea by a low sandbar. The village of Oak Ridge—a string of small painted wooden cottages on stilts—was built on the bar. The water lapped underneath their verandahs and each one had a long slim skiff tied up outside. These offered the village's only form of transport. A number of these boats were rocking at the jetty where the bus had deposited me, but none of their owners was around. An old black man was sitting at the end of the jetty. I asked him, in Spanish, how I might cross the lagoon to a boarding house I had heard of.

"When de man come, de man come," he told me laconically. I sat down beside him to wait.

Benito Caballero, it turned out, was from the only Garifuna village on Roatan, an hour's walk away on the north side of the island. He had strolled over to see some friends, he told me, and was waiting for a water taxi. I wondered how Benito came to speak English. The descendants of the white settlers in the islands and their former slaves spoke English, but didn't the Garifuna in Honduras speak Spanish? I asked him.

He explained that his mother had taken him to Belize as a boy, and left him there with a friend. *"She tek me when ah five years old, to laarn to spik English way, dat what she tek me over dat side for.*

"Well you see, dere's Garifuna over dere. My mudder she say it is better laarn it in Belize not here in Honduras because aal dese people here dey only knows to spik Spanish. A person dat don't spik English by de times dat is comin, he is nowhere. If ah carry you to Belize an you could laarn to spik English den

*you be sumtin big dere for de days dat comin. Quit dis place,
let us go to Belize. Dat is de way my mudder tek me to Belize."*

It had been over seventy years since Benito had returned
to Honduras as a teenager, he told me, and since he didn't
leave his village very often he had little cause to speak
English anymore. I told him how impressed I was by how
well he spoke it after so long a time.

*"Well, see, some of doze fellers from Belize, de niggers daan
dere, dem taalks it diffrent, fonny. But ah stay wid a nice
young lady dere name of Alice Price, dat is de lady dat put me
to spik dis way."*

A typical Garifuna, with his pride in being different, I
thought. And he was also typically Garifuna in his enthusiasm to teach me a little of his people's culture. He would
sing me a song, he told me. *"One of dem oold-time saangs."*

He sucked in his breath and began a wavering chant in
Garifuna, his voice cracking on the upper notes and growling at the lower ones. As he ended he broke into a cackle
of laughter. I asked him what the song had been about.

*"It say dat him was sick, and him was to caal de doctor of
his nature to see what happen to him. An de doctor toles him
dat it is true, sumtin was haarmin him. He says sumtin was
haarmin him in waater, sumtin like dis, er, you know, sumtin
dat aal de time stay in waater, dis we caal it a merrymaid. A
merrymaid goes to worry him."*

What, I asked him, was a merrymaid?

"A merrymaid? Dat stay in de sea."

Of course. A mermaid.

*"Well we says merrymaid. It is true, de doctor say, it is dat
haarmin you, humbuggin you. So him cure him."*

I looked up to find that we were no longer alone. A
boatman was standing over us asking where we wanted to
go. Benito and I jumped into his skiff, and we chugged

across the still water. As I hopped out at the jetty behind the hotel I planned to stay in, Benito called to me.

"You got time, you go down Port Royal side. Dat where we Garifuna come from."

The only way to Port Royal, a few miles further down the island near its tip, was to take one of the skiffs powered by inboard motors that sputtered regularly around the lagoon. The next morning I hailed one, negotiated a fare with its teenage skipper, Tennyson, and set off along the coast, the wind lifting curtains of spray from the bow and blowing it into my face.

Port Royal is almost deserted today, although the crystalline turquoise waters of its bay, ringed by white coral sand and steeply wooded slopes, will doubtless reflect the frontage of a tourist hotel as soon as the government builds a road there. Three hundred years ago, however, it was one of the busiest spots on the Central American coast; its huge natural harbour, protected by a headland and a string of coral cays, was large enough to hold a fleet of buccaneer brigs, sloops and schooners. In the lee of the largest of the cays, Fort George, a wide expanse of gently shelving sand offered an ideal spot to haul up a ship in need of careening. For the captive Garifuna, rowing ashore from their prison boats, though, the sawtoothed mountains hemming in the beach and the unbroken forest and scrub that covered them must have presented a poor prospect. For it was here that the Garifunas were unloaded on 12 April 1797, after their long voyage from St. Vincent.

Port Royal had not been long uninhabited by the time the Garifunas were dropped there. Only fifteen years earlier Englishmen had been living around the bay in considerable numbers. At the edge of Fort George Cay I found the remnants of the British defences. But first I had to ask permission to look them over because the island, Tennyson told me, was now private property.

I had wondered who owned the twin-engined light plane sitting on a trim grass runway stretching past a tall stilted house, and I found Al Hundemere, an ancient, pale American, sitting on his mosquito-netted porch reading *Playboy* magazine and enjoying the sea breeze. He was happy to let me explore the ruins, but said he knew no more about them than that they were English and that the Spanish had destroyed them in some battle once. He had not found the name that the English had given the island, Fort George Cay, romantic enough for his taste, and as owner of the property he had decided to restyle it Fort Morgan Key, after the pirate Captain Henry Morgan.

I refrained from asking him what right he thought he had to rename historical sites and keep Hondurans off a piece of their national heritage, and instead walked down to the shore where Mr. Hundemere's man Friday was forking piles of seaweed into a trailer hitched to a wide-wheeled red beach buggy. He nodded to me sheepishly, as if acknowledging that this was a pretty pointless pastime but what the hell, he was well paid for it. (Later I found him on the other side of the island, up to his waist in the sea, digging up seagrass from the sandy bottom. Mr. Hundemere's young wife, he explained with wonder in his voice, did not like the way it looked.)

Where the sandy beach gave way to mangroves, I found what I was looking for. There was not much left of it. A few tumbled ramparts a couple of feet high stood at the lapping water's edge, constructed of slabs of ochre granite and grey lumps of gritty coral, bound together roughly with a yellow, sandy mortar. Iguanas baked in the sun, rustling the dead leaves gathered in the gun emplacements set into the earthworks. They have been deserted since Spanish soldiers broke up the fortifications in March 1782 after subjecting the English garrison to a sixty-gun cannonade for two days and forcing them to surrender.

That was only one of scores of battles fought between English soldiers and settlers and Spanish militia over more than 150 years of their struggle for the coast. It was that rivalry that spawned all the region's oddities and quirks today.

English settlers on islands in the Caribbean had visited the coast as early as 1633, sowing the seeds of an alliance with the Miskito indians they found there. This was to guarantee an English advantage for the next two centuries, and that advantage was sealed when Oliver Cromwell's troops seized the pivotal stronghold of Jamaica in 1655, furnishing English strategists and colonists with a springboard from which to launch their incursions. It was then that London really began to threaten Spain's position on Central America's eastern seaboard.

In the early years, the English pirates ventured to Central America only in search of loot. The logwood cutters were satisfied with limited riches. But by the middle of the eighteenth century, settlers from Belize to the southern reaches of Nicaragua were interested in the longer term, more solid benefits that could be gained by trade with the Spanish-inhabited interior, and so was the mercantilist-minded government in London. There were no more than a few hundred of these traders and their slaves, but in Madrid's eyes they were all illegal smugglers posing a threat to Spain's sovereignty and trading monopoly. They had to be rooted out.

In 1732, a logwood cutter from Belize named William Pitt, fed up with constant Spanish attacks on the settlement there, founded a new village at Black River, about sixty miles east of the Bay Islands on the Honduran mainland, and established a profitable business smuggling British goods inland to Spanish colonists whom Spanish traders could not service. When the War of Jenkins's Ear broke out between England and Spain in 1740, the military authorities in Jamaica envisioned Black River as the nucleus of an official British presence on the shore that could dominate any route connecting the Caribbean with the Pacific, and thus facilitate more extensive contraband.

The governor of Jamaica, Edward Trelawney, sent a detachment of soldiers to Black River under the command of Captain Robert Hodgson. He reaffirmed England's alliance with the Miskito indians, and then sailed to Port Royal, where he oversaw the construction of a seventeen-gun rampart in what is now Al Hundemere's back garden. William Pitt was put in charge of the new settlement, which was soon home to some 1,000 people scattered around Port Royal Bay.

The 1748 treaty ending the war decreed a return to the territorial "status quo ante," but the settlers at Black River resisted. They had established the rudiments of civil administration, the contraband trade was profitable, and London argued that since the Central American shore had never been Spanish territory, the English were under no obligation to hand it over. Black River stayed.

The same problem arose in 1763, at the end of the Seven Years War, when England pledged in the Treaty of Paris to dismantle its fortifications in Belize and in other parts of "the territory of Spain." That vague wording, however, allowed the English settlers in Honduras and Nicaragua, who had become known as "Shoremen," to recycle their old argument that the shore had never been Spanish and that the fortifications could therefore remain. They did.

After seeking to evict the English from the Central American shore by winning over the Miskito indians, and failing, King Charles III of Spain sided with England's rebellious North American colonies and launched a major offensive on the coast in 1779. Spanish troops attacked Belize, lost and then retook Omoa, fended off an English siege of a major fortress in southern Nicaragua (during which young Captain Horatio Nelson nearly died of fever), seized Black River and recovered Roatan. When the Treaty of Versailles was signed to end the war in 1783, English diplomats decided that the game on the coast was no longer worth the candle. England agreed to evacuate the Central American shore in return for possession of Gibraltar.

In 1787 over 2,500 British subjects abandoned some dozen settlements stretching from Black River to Nicaragua's southern frontier with Costa Rica, and moved to Belize, Jamaica and the Cayman Islands. The Miskitos, however, remained loyal to their retreating English allies, and Spain's attempts to colonise the area that the British had left behind never prospered. Soon British smugglers were again operating in Honduras from their base in Belize, and it was not long before Spain was to lose Central America altogether to *independistas*. New governments would have to cope with the Miskitos and their stubborn refusal to accept Spanish-speaking rule.

I returned from Port Royal that evening and walked through Oak Ridge at dusk searching for the village's only restaurant, which turned out to serve nothing but pizza. Waiting for mine to bake, I sat drinking a beer on the verandah over a lagoon marked on old maps as "Pitt's

Lagoon," perhaps because William Pitt had farmed here while he was superintendent of the Port Royal settlement in the 1740s. A young man munching away at the table next to mine looked up at me and smiled. I asked him how the lagoon had gotten its name.

"Dis lagoon here, mon? Dis lagoon get its name short time back. Before times, we juss caals it 'de lagoon.' Bot den dis restaurant opens, an now we caals it 'pizza lagoon.'"

SIX

At this stage I was obliged to abandon the coast, temporarily lifting my self-imposed ban on travelling far inland. Two hundred miles down the coast lay the frontier between Honduras and Nicaragua, and that frontier had been closed since 1982, when Miskito indians, armed by the CIA, had declared war on the Sandinista government in Managua. The Honduran authorities, beholden to Washington for economic and military aid and no friends to the revolutionary government in Nicaragua, had sealed off the border area by posting army checkpoints on all roads and allowed the Nicaraguan rebels to establish training camps, logistical bases and other rearguard facilities on Honduran territory. Officials in Tegucigalpa, the capital, repeatedly tried to conceal this violation of international law by denying all Managua's accusations about the aid they were affording the contras. Their efforts, though, were less than convincing in the light of a stream of press reports by journalists who had visited the camps and knew perfectly well where they were.

Further away from the border, and by no means clandestinely, tens of thousands of Nicaraguans were sitting out the contra war in United Nations refugee camps. Afraid either of the fighting that had made normal peasant life impossible in large areas of their homeland, or of being called up to do compulsory military service in the Sandinista army, they had fled their homes. A string of UN camps in the jungle of eastern Honduras housed several thousand Miskito indians, some of whom had been living there under the watchful eye of the Honduran army for six years. By the end of 1987 most of them were growing increasingly restless in their exile and were anxious to return home, so the United Nations had agreed upon a plan with the Honduran and Nicaraguan governments to repatriate as many of the refugees as wanted to leave.

An old frontier post on the Coco River had been reopened, a ferry service across the river was organised, and once a week, a convoy of lorries flying the pale blue flag of the United Nations High Commission for Refugees would transport between 200 and 300 Miskitos at a time the 35 miles from their camps to the river. My only chance of crossing into Nicaragua near the coast was to accompany the refugees, but the frontier post had been opened exclusively for the indians. Before leaving on my journey I had secured the Sandinistas' permission to cross the river, but I still needed special authorisation from the UNHCR and from the Honduran government. That meant going to Tegucigalpa.

So I took a plane from Roatan and waited two days for an interview with the UNHCR chief. He was happy to sign a letter of authorisation allowing me into the refugee camps and to give me permission to cross into Nicaragua with the *repatriados,* but, he regretted, his permission was worthless. He told me I needed to convince the Honduran government's own refugee agency.

For three days I patrolled the agency's offices, awaiting a summons from the retired army colonel who ran the place. When eventually he received me in his bare little office he too was all smiles and very understanding. But the lack of paperwork on his desk and the empty shelves behind the easy chair in which he was reading the morning papers suggested that he was not a man at the heart of the decision-making process.

He confirmed that impression as soon as I had explained why I needed his help. He envied me the adventure, he said. It was high time that a journalist took a first-hand look at how successfully the refugees were being repatriated, he said. But he was not the man I needed to talk to about crossing the border. Only the *Oficina de Migración* was empowered to make a decision on that. The colonel rang a friend of his who happened to be the deputy director general of *Migración*, and I set off through the twisting narrow streets of Tegucigalpa, which were choked with traffic and thick with exhaust fumes.

Only at the central plaza did I find a little comic relief. A bronze equestrian statue of a military-looking man in ceremonial regalia dominated the square, erected to the glory of Francisco Morazan, hero of Central America's independence, some years after his death. But the victorious general on his horse is not Morazan at all. The group of Honduran dignitaries dispatched to Paris by the Congress to commission a statue were too easily seduced by the delights of the French capital and spent the money with which they had been entrusted on satisfying their fleshly appetites. But returning home empty handed was clearly out of the question. As they hunted round in search of a cut-rate sculptor, though, they were blessed by a stroke of luck. There, in the dusty corner of one of the ateliers they visited stood a forgotten and unwanted monumental figure on horseback. *"Le Brave des Braves"* read an inscription on the plinth. No matter, said the Hondurans, a new inscription could easily be carved. Who in Tegucigalpa would recognise the supercilious sneer of Marechal Ney, one of Napoleon Bonaparte's top generals before he quarrelled with the emperor and fell out of favour?

The deputy director of *Migración,* whom I found taking shelter in his soundproof office from the hordes of petitioners waiting patiently in the corridor for the grace of his signature, looked like the sort of man who would have been picked to go to Paris 150 years ago. Well fed, groomed a shade too carefully and clearly revelling in the power over lesser mortals that he had earned by siding with the right candidate in the last presidential elections.

He listened with an indulgent smile as I explained my predicament, took my passport and went to consult with his boss. Five minutes later he returned, announcing that this was all perfectly routine and that I was free to cross the border into Nicaragua wherever I liked, whenever I liked.

I grew instantly suspicious. "Could you give me a letter saying that, please, so I can show it to the soldiers on the border?"

"No need, Señor Ford, no need. We quite understand what you are doing, and you are quite free to do it."

"But I would feel a great deal more comfortable if I had something in writing," I insisted.

"Really, Señor Ford, I can assure you that everything

will be quite correct. Liza," he called to his secretary, "can you show the next one in please?"

I decided not to get up. This reluctance to put anything on paper seemed highly peculiar, even in a bureaucracy packed with habitually evasive officials. But then it struck me why I was being palmed off.

In a civilian democracy such as Honduras was supposed to be, the deputy director of *Migración* ought to have sufficient authority to resolve a case such as mine. His own sense of dignity told him so. But in fact, only the army could make the decision. We would have to dispose of the army.

"There is no need to consult anyone else about this, is there?" I asked innocently. Of course not, the deputy director told me. But sometimes, I persisted, one came across the occasional soldier who thought that his uniform gave him the right to make the law. So wouldn't it be better, just to clarify the situation as far as possible, to have his signature on a permit that I could show to any army officer who sought to overstep his authority?

Eventually he was convinced, overstamping my visa with the *Migración* seal and adding a handwritten note to the effect that I was duly authorised to cross the Honduran-Nicaraguan border at any frontier post I chose. It was as much as he could do. I was foolish enough, at the time, to believe that it was enough.

I was sorry to be arriving in Trujillo by air. It looks its best from the bay as you run outside the breakers under the parade of cannon pointing out towards Roatan from a bluff that dominates the beach below.

Trujillo was one of the first towns the Spanish built in

Central America, and the nascent settlement, strategically placed in the lee of an enormous sandy bay, received an early boost when the conquistador Hernan Cortes paid a visit in 1525. While the Franciscan founding fathers built three convents, soldiers got on with the construction of a fort. But as the premier Spanish port on the Central American coast and the gateway to the goldmines of Honduras, Trujillo took a terrible beating from the bucaneers who swept down in such numbers that by 1596 one English freebooter described Trujillo as "the poorest place in the Indies." Fifty years later the Spanish garrison abandoned the town when Dutch pirates burnt it to the ground yet again.

There was not even much left of the fortress, rebuilt in 1780 during another unsuccessful attempt by the Spanish to colonise the coast, when I went to visit this sorry symbol of Spanish colonialism. But the view was superb, overlooking the wide expanse of the barely ruffled bay, beaten a steely grey by the midday sun, and a feathery blanket of green-gold palm trees shading the town below me. Sweeping round the bay, a thin strip of creamy sand held back the mangrove forest from the sea.

In a plywood shack built against one of the fortress walls I found the *wotcheman*, who waived the twenty-five-*centaro* entrance fee and insisted on giving me a personally guided tour. All he knew about the place was that it had last witnessed a real battle in 1910, when an exiled and disgruntled Honduran general had landed here with a force of Nicaraguan mercenaries in an unsuccessful attempt to topple the president.

The custodian was a Spanish-speaking black, and as we sat down on one of the cannons to enjoy the sunshine I asked him if he was Garifuna.

"Why yes," he said, with a broad smile. "How come you've heard of the Garifuna?"

I explained that I had travelled through a number of Garifuna villages since the beginning of my journey in Belize, and that I intended to visit the furthest-flung settlement his people had founded, in Nicaragua. He grew excited. "Nicaragua? I've got family in Nicaragua. Cousins of mine, I just found out the other day. I've never seen them, though. You tell them hello from me." I asked him his name. Rolando Sambula, he told me.

Sambula. Sambula. The name echoed like a Garifuna *dugu* drumbeat. It is the oldest name in recorded Garifuna history. And it had first been written down on the very spot where we were sitting, in the fortress courtyard, where a Spanish lieutenant had lined up the Garifuna castaways that his governor had rescued from Roatan in 1797. He had taken a roll call of the principal chiefs. Among the names he had recorded was Sambula.

Before my eyes Rolando literally swelled with pride as he surveyed the grassy forecourt where his noble ancestor had identified himself. "I've always liked this job a lot," he told me, "and I've always wondered why. So old man Sambula was a *chief.* Well, well, well."

Rolando was worried about his people's traditions under the pressures of Spanish society, but he thought that all in all Garifuna culture would continue to flourish against the homogenising odds. "Governments," he snorted, "governments, what they do mostly is try to set us apart from our culture. When a Garifuna boy goes to school the teachers laugh at the *dugu,* he's taught to lose his faith. But then he sees things happen that teach him otherwise. He sees his grandmother get well when the doctors couldn't cure her. And he finds his faith again."

I rose to leave. "Before you go, you've got to see where William Walker was shot," he said. "You know, the American?"

William Walker was one of the more unlikely villains to enliven the chaotic pages of Central American history. Born in 1825 to a Scottish immigrant who had settled in Tennessee, Walker embarked on several professions as a young man, throwing over medicine for law, then law for journalism by the time he was twenty-eight. Cast into a black depression by the death of his deaf-mute fiancée from cholera, he sought escape through an ill-planned and unofficial expedition to annex the northern Mexican province of Sonora to the United States. When that failed, he cast about for new territories to conquer.

His eye lit on Nicaragua, which for several years had offered the most convenient route from the American East Coast to the goldfields of California. Rather than risk the back-breaking five-month journey overland through indian country, some 20,000 pioneers a year were paying Cornelius Vanderbilt's Accessory Transit Company to take them from the Atlantic Seaboard by ship to the Caribbean coast of Nicaragua, up a river by rowboat, across a lake in a steamer, over to the Pacific shore by horsedrawn carriage and then up to San Francisco by another ship. In return for exclusive rights to this route, Vanderbilt had promised the Nicaraguan government $10,000 a year rent and ten percent of the net profits. He never actually paid any rent, however, and when the government demanded its share, he claimed that the operation was losing money. In fact he was making about two million dollars a year, but Nicaraguan inspectors who sought to take a look at his books were easily rebuffed.

By 1855 Nicaraguan politics had degenerated into chaos,

with the Conservative government based in the lakeside city of Granada facing the rival claims of a Liberal government installed in the northern town of Leon. Since the Conservatives were threatening to confiscate Vanderbilt's ships for nonpayment of dues, the robber baron simply decided to recognise the Liberals.

He was thus all in favour of Walker's decision to set sail on 5 May 1855 to aid the Liberal cause. The filibusterer's fifty-seven followers were a bunch of ruffians and fortune seekers, but they were armed with repeating rifles the like of which the Nicaraguans had never seen, and within six months the "Immortals," as they styled themselves, had seized Granada. Colonel Walker had made himself a general and a compliant Nicaraguan was found to fill the titular role of president.

Recruits to Walker's army were promised free land in the fertile tropical lowlands on Nicaragua's Pacific coast, and they flocked from America to join up. Walker thereupon arranged perfunctory elections, won them by a landslide and declared himself president. English was made an official language, and Walker issued the decree for which he is most infamous in Nicaraguan memories: he introduced slavery.

He was never able to implement the decree, however, for he was too busy staving off disaster. Even before assuming the presidency he had sealed his fate by stripping Vanderbilt of his rights to the interoceanic transport route, and giving them to two friends. In revenge Vanderbilt suspended sailings to Nicaragua, thus depriving Walker of new recruits who were desperately needed in the face of a Central American alliance between Costa Rica, Guatemala, Honduras and El Salvador, who had all declared war on the American invaders.

Scourged by tropical diseases, outnumbered and regularly running short of ammunition, the "Immortals" could not hold out forever. After razing Granada and holing up in the southern town of Rivas, Walker finally surrendered in May 1857 to a US man o'war lying off the coast. He returned home a hero. Wherever he went the "grey-eyed man of destiny" was hailed as a visionary conqueror, and his reception only strengthened his resolve to try again.

One shortlived expedition to Costa Rica ended in another humiliating surrender to the US navy, and then he set off on his last adventure in 1860. Seeking to attack Nicaragua overland from the north, Walker sailed for Trujillo. On his way there he put in at Roatan, where he found the islanders—British subjects almost to a man—in high dudgeon about London's decision to abandon the Bay Islands colony and hand the territory over to Honduras. Some of the islanders were planning an armed revolt, and Walker, setting aside his Nicaraguan ambitions for a while, saw an opportunity to promote the interests of "the white race" against the slovenly and decadent half-caste Central Americans there and then.

This time he had really overextended himself. Not only did he have the Honduran army to deal with, but the British navy had sent a brig to the Bay Islands to ensure a smooth transition to local rule. Walker was soon run to ground by HMS *Icarus*, and he had no option but to surrender to her commander, Captain Salmon. Salmon immediately handed the adventurer over to the Honduran authorities. Walker was given a preremptory trial by a military court, refused to claim the American citizenship that might have saved his life ("The president of Nicaragua is a Nicaraguan citizen," he told his judges), was put up against the wall I was now standing before, and shot. A stone slab on a low plinth reads simply "William Walker 1825–1860."

Not far from the fortress lies the graveyard where Walker was buried. I walked through the town, past the thick, secretive windowless walls of its grander buildings, their white plaster wash crumbling in places to reveal their simple adobe structure of dried red clay and laths. Through the occasional heavy oaken portal hanging ajar I snatched glimpses of courtyards ablaze with flowering bushes, but these were not the splendid colonial residences of Spanish grandees that one finds in the great cities of South America. These were modest imitations in a port already long past its prime when they had been built. The cobbled streets soon degenerated into concrete and then dirt paths on their way out of town, lined by low adobe walls sheltered by ochre tiled eaves and broken only by narrow doorways leading into bare-floored cottages.

I found the arched entrance in the cemetery wall blocked by a pile of gravel, scrambled over it and came across a scene of absolute abandonment. Walker's grave alone was still cared for, marked by a beige plaster slab blotched with black moss, with the adventurer's name carved in capitals and the date of his execution, "19th September 1860," scratched beneath in a nineteenth-century scrawl. I was the only visitor in the dead-hot hours of the early afternoon. As I wandered in the stillness from grave to grave, Trujillo's immigrant history unfolded before me. Of the inscriptions that were still legible, barely half marked the resting places of those born in Honduras; the rest had ventured to the New World in the nineteenth century and died here, many of them at a very young age.

Smothered by columbine, a rock grotto gaped open, smashed by grave robbers who had nonetheless left a granite plaque. Milosh M. Ceyowich, born in Dulcigno in Montenegro in 1894, died in 1918. An iron cross nine feet high rose from the undergrowth: *"Ici repose Victoria Lacassagne, Française, décédee le 16 Juillet à l'age de 22 ans."* A baroque marble headstone leaned drunkenly against the cemetery wall. Julia Lafitte *"natural de Bajos Pireneos, Francia,"* who died when she was twenty on 22 September 1888.

By the time these young immigrants had been buried here, Trujillo's ties with Spain and England had been largely superceded by burgeoning commercial links with the United States. Where the marble and granite for their headstones had come from there was no way of telling, but the manufacturer of the wrought-iron railings around each abandoned plot had left his imprint on the gateposts. "Hinderer's Iron Fence Works, 1116 Camp St., New Orleans."

I discovered the reason for the graveyard's desolation later. It had been closed in the 1930s and then sacked by grave robbers. Few descendants of the pioneers buried here live in Trujillo anymore: in the early years of this century most of them sold their land to the United Fruit Company for sums they had never dreamt of and retired rich to their native countries. This I learned from Prospero Castillo, who I had mistakenly been told was the British consul in Trujillo. That turned out to be an exaggeration— the consulate had been closed for thirty years, but his great grandfather had indeed been the consul once upon a time and Prospero was the zealous guardian of a collection of consular relics.

I found him at his desk in the damp and peeling office

of the inspector of customs, where he seemed to have little enough to do. He had been made inspector, he told me frankly, simply because he had supported the president's election campaign, and when the next president was elected he would be turned out of office. It was unclear why he had accepted this sinecure: it paid next to nothing, Prospero told me, and the job looked to me like nothing more than an opportunity to get rich through corruption, the prime Honduran reward for political loyalty. Yet Prospero Castillo struck me more as a university lecturer or amateur historian than your average venal officeholder.

Prospero's family history, the story of three brothers and their descendants, was a cameo of the coast's own history over the past 150 years. Prospero was descended from the Melhado family, Portuguese Jews who fled from persecution to England in the seventeenth century and then settled in Scotland. Around 1841, as far as Prospero had been able to establish, William Melhado and his two brothers, Joseph and Henry, set out for Central America to seek their fortunes.

William settled in Trujillo, Henry went inland to a town called Cedrus, and Joseph set himself up in the coffee business in neighbouring El Salvador. Henry married a Honduran woman but moved to Belize when a cholera epidemic threatened, and there he raised his five children. Aurelia, his eldest daughter, married a rich Bahamian and moved with him to the Bahamas, taking with her an unmarried sister. Two sons drank their inheritance away, moved to the United States and were never heard from again.

But the third son, Henry II, turned alcohol to his advantage. His coconut export business was flourishing, but when the US Congress imposed Prohibition he saw a quicker way of making money—emptying his coconuts of their water, filling them with rum and bootlegging the liquor into the United States.

Only at the end of his life did Henry II marry Candelaria, the mulatto servant girl who had been his mistress and who had bore him one son, Arthur. Prospero regretted that he had never met his great aunt Candy, easily the family's most eccentric figure. Persuading her new husband to sign over all his wealth to Arthur, who did what Mummy told him to do, she packed the boy off to school in America, waited for Henry to die and then joined her son in New Orleans. There she lived for many years in a hotel on Canal Street in tremendous style, flaunting her riches and exoticism under the noses of the city's white gentlewomen and financing her extravagant tastes by gradually selling off her son's investments. She died, completely mad, in the early 1960s.

Prospero's great grandfather, meanwhile, the original William Melhado, had built up a prosperous trading company and a solid reputation in Trujillo, becoming the English consul there, which he remained until his death in 1904. He sent his four daughters to convent schools in Belize and America and packed his sons off to boarding school in England, whence they returned to join the firm of "Melhado and Sons." By the turn of the century they were the richest men in town, investing heavily in US stocks and shares and particularly in the new railway that the United Fruit subsidiary, the Truxillo Railroad Company, was building.

One of his sons, Alfred, took over the consulate when William Sr. died, and ran it until his own death, by which time he had still not learned to speak Spanish well. Until the British Foreign Office decided in the middle of the 1950s that they really did not need a consul in Trujillo, the post was filled by Alfred's accountant, a Bay Islander of British parentage named Albury Tatum. Prospero remembered one favourite phrase of Mr. Tatum's wife, Mildred. Her most violent insult, he recalled, had been to call whoever had crossed her "a Spanish Spaniard."

That evening Prospero invited me to come and inspect the family's mementoes. His home, which had once housed the consulate, had the airy elegance of affluent tropical architecture, the walls of cream clapboard set off by bottle-green shutters, a second-floor verandah running round two sides of the house protected from the sun's last rays by delicate trellis work, an air of gin slings and wicker rocking chairs.

The dining room, however, belied that atmosphere, full of dark and heavy Victorian mahogany furniture. It had been saved, Prospero explained, from the officers' dining room of the *Elly Knight,* a merchant ship that had sunk off Trujillo in the 1880s. Great grandfather William, as the local representative of Lloyds, the shipping agents and insurance company, had enjoyed first pick of the ship's contents before putting the rest up for auction.

Standing on the monumental sidetable was a statue of the Virgin Mary. Swathed in a blood-red velvet cape, a beatific smile on her baby face and more golden sun rays around her halo than a Louis XIV clock, she was wrapped in a plastic bag, for Prospero valued this icon highly. Not for artistic reasons, he was quick to tell me, but because it had once belonged to Adela Proudhoth de Martinez, wife of the governor of Trujillo who had sentenced William Walker to death. As British consul, Great Grandfather William Melhado had helped Captain Salmon to hunt Walker down. This was the statue of the Virgin that Señora Proudhoth de Martinez had taken with her to Walker's cell on the eve of his execution, to pray with him and comfort him.

But the centrepiece of Prospero's collection of artifacts was the consular study, a cramped, dusty room lined with shelves that groaned under the weight of the collected works of Thackeray and Longfellow, George Eliot and Balzac. On one wall a grim-faced Queen Victoria stared out from a lithographed portrait that she had graciously signed for her servant in such a distant corner of the empire. And on the uppermost shelf, thick with dust, sat a top hat, a ceremonial sabre, a set of gold-braided epaulettes and a cream topee with the royal lion and unicorn emblem embossed on a badge pinned to its front. I rather hoped Prospero would try it on for me, but he was too serious minded to make any move that I might interpret as mockery of Great Grandfather William.

A mechanic at the garage by Trujillo's municipal wharf poked his head out from under a truck that looked well past repair and laughed at me when I asked if he knew of any boats leaving for Limon, the next village of any size down the coast.

Departures, he told me, were *altamente irregular*, and it wasn't worth taking a boat anyway because there was a perfectly good bus. I explained that I preferred to travel by sea and he looked at me dubiously. If I was ready to wait around for a few days I might find something, he supposed, and disappeared again beneath his truck. At another stage in the journey I might have hung around, but now I had a firm deadline—to cross into Nicaragua.

The Sandinista Interior Ministry had given me permission to enter Nicaragua with returning Miskito refugees on one condition: that I give advance warning of my arrival so that the immigration officials at the border could be alerted and told to let me in. The UNHCR ran its repatriation shuttle to the Coco River once a week, and my wife had carried a message from Tegucigalpa to Managua that I would be crossing the frontier in two weeks' time. If I failed to arrive on time, the chances were that I would be turned back. To complicate matters, there was no road beyond Limon, no public transport to fall back on in case improvisation failed. Reluctantly I decided to follow the mechanic's advice and take the bus. It was a mundane way to go, but it was the last stretch of coast road until I reached another town called Limon, 700 miles away in Costa Rica.

It was not much of a road, dusty and rutted when it ran straight through lush cattle pasture but faltering at the first sign of water, degenerating into a mudslide at each stream it crossed, stiffened just enough by branches and strips of tree bark to allow the bus some traction. A scattering of black faces and headscarves among my fellow passengers indicated that our final destination was a Garifuna village, but the seats were mostly occupied by *ladino* peasant farmers and their families. As the bus emptied at each halt, my sense of excitement mounted. These people might live isolated lives, I thought, but all the same they lived within reach of a regular bus service. I was going to The End of the Road and beyond.

On my map of Honduras, the east stretched away an empty green expanse, unbroken by any of the reassuring red lines that drew a network of roads throughout the rest of the country. The dots that marked villages grew more scattered, Cocobila, Mokobila, Tabacunta, Clacura: Miskito names for clusters of homes lost among the wilderness of swamps and marshes and rivers and lagoons through which I hoped to find my way over the next six weeks. In

Limon, however, I was still within the Garifuna sphere, and still within the reach of government development schemes. Thanks to a team of surveyors—the advance party of a project to pave the road to Trujillo—there was a hotel in Limon. An enterprising shopkeeper had partitioned one of his clapboard huts into eight cupboards, knocked together some basic beds and a signboard and offered lodging. I found a room there and went to enquire about boats.

Searching for Mr. Goff, who I had been told ran a packet boat service up the coast, I soon lost my way among the maze of sandy tracks that ran between the scattered thatched huts. It was a barechested man in a pair of ancient blue trousers who told me that I was way off track for Mr. Goff's house. But when he told me that he was Limon's sole weaver of *rugumas*—the snakes made of dried creeper that Garifunas use to make their cassava bread—I decided that the boat could wait.

Keri Bernardez faced the same problem as Octavio Magdaleno in Hopkins: he could not find any young men interested in learning the *ruguma* trade because it brought in so little money. He agreed with me that this was absurd, because Garifunas up and down the coast are crying out for *rugumas* and turning away from cassava bread simply because they don't have the kitchen implements they need to make it. Yet Keri could only sell one of his *rugumas* every three months in Limon for a paltry ten dollars. The traditional trade routes that Miskitos and Garifunas once plied along the coast in their canoes have withered in the face of new national economies, centred in national capitals inland. My difficulties in following the coast from Belize to Panama were illustrating this point; fifty years ago I would have found boats of all shapes and sizes and I could have made the journey without the slightest delay.

As Keri showed me round his two-room home, extolling the medicinal virtues of a ball of beef suet that hung in the smoke from a mud stove, I thought I understood snatches of the conversation he was carrying on with his wife in Garifuna at the same time. At any rate I understood some of the sounds, without comprehending why. I asked him to repeat a phrase he had just spoken and to translate it for me into Spanish. I had caught the word *"trays,"* and Keri explained that it meant "thirteen." And how do you say "twelve" in Garifuna? *"Dooz."* He was counting in French! The Garifunas' old alliance with the French against the English on St. Vincent, 200 years ago, still echoed in everyday speech but went unheard.

"No, man," said Keri, "that's Garifuna language. That's how we count."

"But it's French, too," I insisted. "I'll count in French and you count in Garifuna and we'll see. *Un deux trois.*"

Keri looked sceptical. *"Abba biyama uruwa."*

Oh shit. Maybe I had misunderstood. But I ploughed on. *"Quatre cinq six."*

This time his eyes widened with surprise. *"Gadu senku sisi."*

This was unbelievable. I knew that the Miskitos counted in English, but I had had no idea that the Garifunas used French. I could not control my excitement. *"Sept huit neuf dix onze douze treize."*

Keri followed suit. *"Sedu widu neffu dis oonze dooz trays."* He called to his wife, sitting outside as she chipped pieces of sharp stone to make a coconut grater, and when she came to listen we broke into a chant.

"Quatorze quinze seize dix-sept dix-huit dix-neuf vingt."
"Katorz keinz disays dised diswidu disneffu weng."

By this time Keri's children had crowded into the kitchen and we had to start again for their benefit. Then a neighbour came to see what all the commotion was about and again I went through my numbers in French. The sight of an Englishman counting fluently in badly accented Garifuna was hilarious, and soon a crowd had gathered by the hut, clapping and laughing as I counted over and over. When I explained that I did not know how to count in Garifuna, that I was speaking French as far as I knew, this was cause for even louder laughter.

Going over the numbers with Keri later I found that the French word for "fifty"—*"cinquante"*—has been lost and converted into *"demisa,"* but there is logic to that change. *"Sa"* is the Garifuna corruption of the French *"cent"* meaning "one hundred," and *"demi"* in French means "half." Thus the numeral fifty is expressed literally as "half a hundred."

A weaver of basketry, Keri was proud of his role as a cultural standard bearer and keen to explain to me every detail of the Garifuna way of life. Yet to him, as to the group of barflies back in Bajamar, his people's history was an enigma. No schoolteacher had ever taught him more than Honduran history, and the "old people" who might have known where the Garifunas came from and how they got here had all died. As I recounted what I had read about the Garifunas' origins he listened raptly. The counting game, it seemed, had transformed me in Keri's eyes into a bearer of unknown wisdom.

Teddy Goff, when I found him with the help of one of Keri's small sons as a guide, was bent over a handmade workbench at the bottom of his coconut grove, recon-

structing an obscure piece of machinery from his boat with
two rusty nails and the ingenuity born of isolation. He was
originally from the Bay Islands; his leathery face bore an
uncanny resemblance to the lugubrious, pitchfork-bearing
farmer standing with his wife before a barn in Grant
Wood's painting *American Gothic,* and his manner was
grave and courteous.

"*My boat a fine one, save dis little engine trobble I gaat here,
bot dat soon fix, mon,*" he told me. "*She corry you anyplace
when she leave. I joss waitin on a loada saaf drink from Trujillo, so we be leavin out mebbe tomarrer night, mebbe de night
aafter.*"

I wondered how long it would take me to walk to Punta
Piedra, the village for which I was heading.

"*Waalkin faast you mebbe get dere in a day if you leave out
at dawn,*" he said. "*Bot I hope you naat so foolish as to go
waalkin down dat side. A boncha Spainyards got demselves fix
op at a place dey caal Farallones an dey real goodfernuttins.
Coupla years back dey kill two black fellers from here, cot dere
troats right open. I doan say dey kill you bot dey steal you fer
sure.*"

I had heard about the cutthroats at Farallones from a
Garifuna in Trujillo, but I hadn't been sure then whether
to believe him. I decided to wait for his boat however long
the Cokes took to arrive.

They came in the following afternoon, and at one o'clock
the next morning I was awoken by Mr. Goff's grandson,
Ray, who was captaining the *Alpha 1* on this trip. He
preferred to leave at this hour, he explained, because the
tide made the passage across the sandbar at the mouth of
the lagoon less perilous, and because this way he didn't
have to travel so long in the heat of the day.

In the darkness I squeezed my way on board the boat,

a cigar-shaped vessel forty feet long but less than six feet wide, lying low in the shallow water at the end of a jetty. Three inches of deckspace ran along either side between the gunwhales and the raised roof of the hold, and towards the front a plywood box sheltered the engine but did nothing to isolate its deafening roar. As we pulled away I lay down on the forward hatch with my fingers in my ears and tried in vain to get some sleep. But the engine's shudder jarred my bones relentlessly, and as we approached the lagoon's mouth Ray edged me aside to inspect the bar more closely. Against the dull silver glow of the starlit water, creaming breakers indicated the sandy shallows that shift with every tide and every change in wind direction. As we approached cautiously, Ray crouched at the bow squinting into the gloom, waving a torch first in his left hand then in his right to indicate to his assistant which way to steer for the narrow passage of dark water where the wave tops did not break. We crept forward into the channel, Ray pointed his torch upright, and the engine slowed to a neutral chug as we wallowed in the swell, waiting for a break in the wave pattern that would allow us to slip into the open sea. It came, the engine screamed, and we shot out beyond the treacherous confusion of the choppy bar into the steady roll of the ocean.

We turned east to follow the shore, a heavy black line drawn between the moleskin sea and the pearly night sky. The boat's wake churned a ghostly grey, illuminated by thin starlight and lit from within by handfuls of diamond points of phosphorous luminescence, seeds of light that sparkled as they rose to the surface. In the sky shooting stars flared and ahead of us the freshest of new moons cut an icy sickle as it rose. I was glad I had not slept.

At around four o'clock the sky began to brighten before

the dawn broke a muddy orange through the clouds that hung low over a spur of hills. The sea seemed reluctant to acknowledge the sunrise, developing a sullen leaden sheen before picking up the pink and orange glow of the spreading day.

A couple of hours later we hove to off Punta Piedra, dropping the anchor two hundred yards offshore as a group of heavy dugouts, each paddled purposefully by seven men bending rhythmically to their work, headed out from the beach to the nets that they had set before dawn. In the surf, small boys manouevred miniature canoes through the waves in imitation of their fathers, not caring that they might fall in. Two of them spotted us at anchor and paddled out, bobbing wildly as they brought their little canoe alongside so that I could toss my rucksack in and wriggle awkwardly after it. Beside these two diminutive oarsmen, one at the prow, the other astern, both shining like fish from their recent dips, I felt unnaturally cumbersome. It was not my size, however, but their inexperience and heedlessness of the water that slewed us sideways into a wave as we came through the breakers, swamping the canoe and forcing us to abandon ship in waist-high surf.

As I went overboard I grabbed at my pack, tied up in a giant heavy-duty garbage bag in case of just such a disaster, and saved it from sinking. I hoisted it above my head and waded ashore to the general amusement of the village youth who had been watching my arrival. Had I not still been wearing the jeans and heavy jersey that I had pulled on against the damp of the night, I too might have found it funny. As it was, weighed down by sodden clothes and furious to discover that my notebooks were floating in a puddle at the bottom of my shoulder bag, I lost my sense of humour.

I pulled myself up to my full height to tower over the two little tykes who had dumped us in the water, scowled fiercely at them, wagged my finger vigorously under their noses and lectured them on the meaning of responsibility, the inconvenience they had caused me and the advisability of letting their elder brothers do this sort of job next time. Only when one of my victims broke his cowed silence with a stifled snigger did I pause for breath and realise what an absurd figure I was cutting, standing on this palm-fringed beach as the sun rose through the trees, dressed in winter clothes dripping seawater onto the beach, shouting at two small boys who were clearly having difficulty understanding me. I retreated to the line of houses strung along the beach behind the coconut trees, in search of some breakfast and a quiet spot in which to salvage my dignity.

I found something to eat, though scarcely a quiet spot, in the home of a *ladino* widow whose eight children swarmed all over me as I sat at a rough bench in her kitchen eating rice and beans. The kids' noses ran perpetually, their skin festered with open sores, and the youngest three were naked as they sprawled, weak limbed, on the mud floor. Their mother, I gathered later from a local social worker who had hitched his horse outside and also stopped for breakfast, was one of the poorest women in the village, so desperate for money in the absence of a breadwinner that she would probably go without even the little food she normally ate in order to sell it to me.

Over the next few weeks, along the coast of Honduras and into Nicaragua, I was to depend almost entirely on the spontaneous hospitality of people I met and on their scant resources. Most families, I found, harvested, fished or bought just enough to feed themselves and were in no position to provide for a stranger. This meant that for the most part I ate either with the poorest people, who were glad for the opportunity to make some money, or with the wealthiest, who had both enough space in which I could sling my hammock and enough extra food to give or sell to me. More often than not, I found that the better-off families among the Garifunas and the Miskitos felt a social obligation to act as host on behalf of their village and refused to take payment for the board and lodging they had offered me.

Strengthened by my plateful of rice, beans and salt fish, I strapped my wet jeans to the back of my rucksack to dry them in the sun, and set off down the beach. It was a glorious morning with a light breeze off the sea. Along this stretch of the coast the villages are often no more than half an hour's walk from each other, and down at the water's edge where the sand was firmest there was regular intervillage traffic. A solitary man would approach, a hand-line stuffed into his waistband, swinging a bunch of fish that he had strung through their gills on a reed; a knot of women and girls would trudge past me, bent under loads of firewood strapped onto their backs by a piece of cloth around their foreheads, hands clasped behind their heads to support their necks. A dozen or so young men, laughing and shoving each other playfully, told me they were re-turning home from the successful launch of a dugout, which they had clearly celebrated at some length despite the early hour.

Everybody that I came across stopped to talk, to find out what I was doing on this empty beach, regarding me with a look of mildly gratified surprise when I explained. And in between these brief conversations I ambled on, stopping when I felt like it to splash in the softly lapping waves, scaring up flocks of pelicans with my approach and seeing how close I could get to the skittish little grey wading birds as they darted along the sand ahead of me, their heads half turned to keep a watchful eye on the intruder, before jumping into the air and flapping madly for a few moments to put another twenty feet of safety between them and me. This was beachwalking as I had imagined it. The purgatory of my forced march up the beach to Tela three weeks ago had been a false start.

I spent the whole day on this lazy jaunt, stopping at noon to eat a fist-sized ball of *machuca*—a mixture of green and ripe plantain boiled and pounded into a tart rubbery mass—and a bowl of spicy fish cooked in coconut milk. The woman who prepared me this standard Garifuna dish served it in her kitchen, a traditional mudfloored thatched hut, but she was anxious to show me around her new home next door, built of breezeblocks and corrugated iron. The money for this house, she said, had come from her sailor brother living in New York, whose remittances had opened up a style of life unthinkable for a subsistence fisherman and farmer. The brother had sent more than money to brighten up his sister's life: the walls were plastered with colourful photographs of Jerusalem, and pride of place had been accorded to a beach towel woven in electric blue and hues of silver, depicting Elvis Presley at his podgiest and gaudiest.

By midafternoon I reached La Punta, a village tucked behind the sand dunes, and found the primary school teacher whose name I had been given by a friend of his that morning. Although he said I was welcome to sleep in the empty house his grandparents had lived in until their deaths, he seemed surly and suspicious of me. My interest in Garifuna culture, it seemed, troubled him. Claudio

Mejia had dealt with government officials and foreign anthropologists and students of Caribbean folklore, but he
had no teaching materials on Garifuna history and culture.
The only play he had ever seen about his people's origins
had been written by a *ladino,* and none of the anthropological studies to which he had contributed had ever been
translated into Garifuna, or even found their way to the
coast. Claudio, like countless other people to whom I had
explained that I was writing a book about the coast, wanted
to know one thing: when would it be published in Spanish,
and where would he be able to find a copy?

I could give him no answer, nor even an assurance that
this book would ever be translated into a language that he
could understand. I felt ill at ease, like a parasite exploiting
the exoticism of the coast with little or nothing to offer in
return. It was some time before I won him over with accounts of Garifuna communities in Belize. As his interest
grew he warmed to me, and stopped examining me as if I
were just another visitor exploiting his people.

The next morning's walk brought me to Sangrelaya,
whose name—as far as anyone can tell anymore—is a corruption of Zachary Lyon, an eighteenth-century English
settler who lived an isolated existence there at the time
that Black River was flourishing a few score miles down
the coast as an English commercial and military centre.
Today Sangrelaya almost bustles with activity, if, between
the torpid sun and the scorching sand, anything Garifuna
can be said to bustle. Workmen were building a graceful
new church under the direction of the local priest, a (real)
Spaniard, a health centre was distributing basic medicines
and sensible advice on hygiene to young mothers, and two
nuns were handing out free food and clothes to the poorer

families—but only, I was told, to those who had turned
their backs on traditional Garifuna religion to worship God
rather than their ancestors.

Living in quiet retirement in Sangrelaya was, I found, a
major in the Honduran army, a figure of some authority
yet removed from daily life, respected in the village as the
only Garifuna ever to reach such a high rank. The story
of racial discrimination and persecution that he told would
doubtless ring familiar to many black American military
officers who began their careers, like Major Justino Fernandez, in the 1950s. But Fernandez persevered, and he
was particularly proud of a distinctively Garifuna footnote
that he and some compatriots had written to the "Soccer
War" between Honduras and El Salvador that broke out
in 1969.

The world attributed this seventy-two-hour flare up of
hostilities to a disputed result in a World Cup–qualifying
soccer match between these two "banana republics,"
though it had more to do with Honduran resentment at
the growing number of Salvadoreans who were sneaking
across the border and settling on Honduran territory. Sitting in a rocking chair on the patio of his crude breezeblock
home, the major recalled how as the prospect of war
loomed he had toured the border region, tracked down a
Garifuna radio operator in what was about to become the
front line and had a word in his ear. Back at headquarters
he found another Garifuna radio man and talked to him
too, unofficially. When the war broke out, it became apparent within hours that Salvadorean intelligence was listening to all the Honduran army's radio transmissions, and
had broken its codes, an advantage that was likely to prove
crucial. Whereupon the Garifuna operators switched to a

code they knew that no one in El Salvador could break. They simply transmitted in their own language.

Whether this little kink in the rule book made any difference to the outcome of the war is impossible to tell: a truce was declared within days and the dispute was referred to diplomatic channels, where it was still dragging on twenty years later. But Major Fernandez told the story in a tone of grim satisfaction, pleased that the Garifunas had shown that they could be useful, but resentful that "those boys at the radio sets, they were never rewarded for their initiative, no medals, no acknowledgment, no nothing."

In Sangrelaya I again met up with Mario, the social worker with whom I had breakfasted a couple of days earlier in Punta Piedra, and he was anxious to accompany me up the coast for a day or so to join in a *fiesta* that the next village was organising to celebrate its name saint's day. It promised serious revelry, he said, the glint in his eye heralding the prospect of a major drinking session. And since his ageing parents lived in the village, San Isidro de Tocomacho, he could take the opportunity to drop in on them.

As it was, though, when dawn broke on the day of the *fiesta,* Mario said he had too painful a headache to come with me. To make up for his absence he lent me his dugout and put me in the charge of his old aunt Filomena. A neighbour called Santos, whose hair sprouted extravagantly in a huge Afro and who grinned broadly through an unkempt beard as he pulled up his ragged pair of cutoffs, offered to paddle, since he wanted to go to the party.

There was no need to venture into the open sea to get to Tocomacho; a network of creeks, lagoons and narrow rivers stretched all the way, winding turgidly through the shadows of the forest. As we pushed off from the muddy bank where all the village canoes were beached tightly one up against the other, Filomena launched into a stream of complaints about how she had been waiting for us half the morning at the *landin* (the English word amongst the Garifuna was a hint of our approach to Miskito country), while Santos tried to placate her by explaining how we had waited for her half the morning at his house.

With Filomena up front and Santos in the back we glided dreamlike through the heart of the thick, pulsing jungle that embraced us in its enveloping folds. As the steady splash of paddles pushed the dugout forward, air and water blended into a uniformly warm and green amniotic fluid. Mario had not provided me with a paddle, and I leaned back on my pack in a lazy wallowing trance rendered even more sensual by Santos's small son occasionally running his curious fingers up and down my back, tickling me as he explored my peculiar colour and feel.

From time to time we would round a bend and come out of the shadows into the bright sunlight of a natural clearing. Long-necked jabiru storks with viciously spiked beaks regarded us superciliously from their perches on the riverbank while nervous moorhens splashed through the shallows on their stilted red legs to hide amongst the mangrove roots at the water's edge. Santos was keen that I should taste the cat-plums growing on a moth-eaten looking tree that overhung the creek. They were a particular delicacy of these parts, he said. I narrowly avoided overturning the canoe as I stood up to grab a handful of the purple, gooseberry-sized fruit, passed them around to my fellow passengers and feigned appreciation as I sucked on the microscopic portion of white woolly flesh that separated the fruit's skin from its pip. It was slightly sweet but quite without taste.

After three hours we came out into a broad lagoon, its water tepid under the sun, fed by a river that in this dry season did not have the force to break through the narrow sandbar of the beach that blocked the way to the sea. On the far side, under a grove of spindly coconut palms reaching into the sky, a score of dugouts were beached in Tocomacho's equivalent of a municipal carpark. Santos, who had been paddling patiently in silence for the last hour or so, pointed them out to me with a grunt of satisfaction and evidently decided that now, as our journey's end approached, was the time to divulge the folk secrets of his race. He made me turn around in the canoe so that I was facing him, and stared gravely into my eyes as he hitched his trousers up again. Apparently simply to exclude Filomena from the revelations he wanted to share with me, he broke into a barely intelligible English, scraps of which he could still recall from a distant boyhood spent on the Bay Islands.

"We Garifuna, mon, you know where we staart?"

I asked how.

"We staart when won creole mon, dis block mon him morry a white woman," Santos told me. *"Dem childern wot dem have, dem is de first Garifuna people."*

I wondered how long ago this had happened, and Santos looked perplexed. *"Laang, laang time baack,"* he said. *"In dem days when dem Inglond mens fighting a waar all over de world, in aal de countries, gainst won Spainiard caal Hitler. Dem Inglond mens win, and we Garifuna people live safe."*

That afternoon the village of San Isidro de Tocomacho celebrated Garifuna traditions and roots through a less distorting lens than Santos's garbled version of his people's origins.

The village was in a state of high excitement when I arrived. For the first time ever, they were going to play out a Garifuna ritual that some of the elders remembered from other times and other towns, and everybody had turned out to watch. Especially the children—squealing crowds of small boys and girls danced and skipped and shoved their way down the sandy path that constituted the main street between two rows of thatched huts, yelping that the show was about to start. Then from around a corner came the beat of a drum. The procession that followed was a little ragged at the edges. At the head came an elderly man in wellington boots with a bass drum strapped around his waist, banging away steadily. Beside him ambled a snare drummer and a young man in swimming trunks blowing snatches on a saxophone, each of whom were pretty much following their own dictates when it came to the rhythm. This was the band, and from the irregular progress they were making up the path it was clear that all three of them had spent a good part of the morning at the rum bottle.

Behind them, led by a high-stepping young girl wearing a pointed cardboard dunce's cap and bearing bouquets of red plastic flowers in each hand, filed seven young women all dressed in red. One, her hair cropped short under a red-and-white baseball cap, wore a thigh-length crimson shift over puce plus fours that reached down to cherry-red football stockings. Another, shambling down the path rather self-consciously, had topped off her outfit of red plastic sandals, maroon ankle socks, ruby wraparound cotton skirt and fuchsia T-shirt with an enormous Mexican mariachi hat, all burgundy velour and gold braid. But the leader of the pack brought up the rear, a bulky young woman swaying and shuffling to the erratic music coming from up front, glorying in a pair of orange slippers, baggy scarlet harem pants and an Eastern-looking blouse of vermilion satin as she glared at the spectators from behind a pair of intimidating mirrored aviator shades. A machete scabbard hung from her belt, and she threateningly brandished a wooden sword as she boogied along at the back.

These women, I was told, were the *Moros,* the Moors against whom the knights of Christendom once battled from Andalucia to Acre. The musicians led them to an open space at the end of the village that served as a basketball court, where an extraordinarily drunken man—a red-and-white tea towel draped around his neck and a cardboard top hat decorated with red paper ruffles tied onto his head—was having considerable difficulty staying on the back of an irritated horse. He was playing the part of the Moorish Prince Fierabras, the principal baddy, and when his troops arrived he spurred his nag into a gallop to greet them with cries of "Up with the Moors" and "Now is the Hour."

As the *Moros* spread out at one end of the patch of sand, beneath the basketball hoop nailed to a backboard that was mounted on an old coconut palm trunk, the musicians sloped off to fetch the opposition. Ten minutes later they returned, the saxophonist blowing increasingly freeform improvisational jazz at the head of another procession, this time of girls and young women dressed in virginal white with straw boaters trimmed with white paper. A little girl led the way with a makeshift bamboo cross indicating that here came the Christians. As they approached the basketball court a horseman galloped up behind them. It was Fierabras, but he had ditched his red hat and turned his tea towel in for a white sheet, and was now playing the part of the Christian general.

An ancient man sitting beside me in the shade of one of the huts at the edge of the court puffed on a homemade pipe constructed of a bamboo stem and a palm-nut bowl. "This is the first time we've played this game here," he explained apologetically. "They're not too well prepared, and it's all a bit improvised." The old man had first seen this game, which he called "tira," in Trujillo, more than fifty years ago. It was about Carlos Magno, he said, the French emperor Charlemagne, and his efforts to convert the pagan Moors. Garifunas acted out the story on special occasions, such as feast days.

The two "armies" of young women were now formed up at either end of the open space, divided by a rope that someone had strung across the court. A red-and-white flag hung from it, advertising "Flores." I recognised it as a leftover campaign decoration from a losing presidential candidate in the last election. While the drummers sat in the shade passing a bottle between them and the saxophonist experimented rather as I had once done with my mouth organ until he found the skeletal outlines of the melody to "John Brown's Body," the women shuffled from foot to foot—clearly beginning to wonder what they were doing there—as they watched the chief Mooress and the chief Christian make a few desultory passes at each other with their wooden swords from time to time.

This went on for some time, and nobody seemed quite sure what ought to happen next. Fierabras had abandoned his disguise as a Christian and had gone back to wearing red as he hung onto his horse's neck for security, but a new Christian general, who had attracted loud cheers from the villagers on his arrival, resigned his commission after a few minutes on the grounds that he could not control his horse. While he went back to a circle of friends watching from the sidelines, the *presidente* of the fiesta went off to find a new leader for the Christian army.

After twenty minutes or so he came back with a volunteer to play the part of Oliveros, only to be presented with a new problem. Fierabras was short of a weapon, having broken his wooden sword on the flanks of his horse trying vainly to beat it into submission. A Moorish footsoldier was persuaded to give up her sword to her prince, who was then inspired to gallop round the field shaking it at all the spectators and roaring anti-Christian insults at the top of his voice. After a couple of circuits he pulled his horse up, reached into his back pocket for an eighth of a bottle of *sini,* homebrewed firewater, and was taking a swig when his mount bucked and threw him to the ground.

Matters were rapidly getting out of hand, and the girls awaiting battle were growing restless after an hour of standing around in the sun. The *presidente* gently shooed a stumbling drunk off to the sidelines and ordered a piece of rush matting and a red blanket to be laid out in the centre of the court. Fierabras lay down under the blanket and then, remembering something, jumped up again and went to have a word with the organiser, who then disappeared into a hut and came out with a slim book.

Fierabras lit a cigarette, consulted the book, stumbled over to his blanket and struck up a challenging pose. "Come on, Christians," he shouted, "hear this, Christians, any Christians that come near to this land will be destroyed by Fierabras of Alexandria." Taking another puff on his cigarette he lay down under the blanket and feigned sleep.

With a lighted cigarette in one hand and the book that

clearly contained his words in the other, Fierabras was not very convincing as a sleeping giant, but that did not seem to worry the crowd gathered around the grassy edge of the acting area. They booed him not for his failings as an actor but because he was the Moor, the way children at pantomime shows hiss the baddy whenever he appears onstage. And they cheered wildly at the reappearance of Oliveros, the knight from Charlemagne's court who was to do battle with the infidel, as he charged up on his pony and sprang from the saddle, pausing only to readjust the grey cloth cap he was wearing.

Oliveros was not satisfied with the words that he had been given to speak. "Pagan, take up your arms and do battle," he declaimed, standing over the inert Fierabras. Then he repeated the line, and then he began to extemporize. "I've been sent here to uphold the law," he shouted. "I represent the authorities and I don't want any trouble. Hear me, you Moors? You can just pack up those swords and clear out of here. I'm the one giving orders around here, okay, so just break it up and get out."

Fierabras peered out from under his blanket looking deeply confused. He was relying on the text in his hand to guide him through his performance, and Oliveros's adlibbing had left him adrift. Luckily the defender of the faith ended his speech by returning to the script.

"Rise up and do battle, you who have called on the Christians so often to fight," he cried. "I stand before you ready to answer your scornful challenges." Fierabras snuck a surreptitious look at his lines, rose groggily to his feet and addressed himself to Oliveros. "Who are you, who come to certain death?" he asked, but the knight would not identify himself.

Their dialogue went on for a minute or so, Fierabras

casting his eyes down to his script each time that Oliveros
spoke his lines, and the crowd much more absorbed in
their own shouts of "Viva Carlos Magno" or "Down with
Fierabras" than in what the actors were saying. Suddenly,
with no apparent warning, the two men launched into a
mock swordfight, flailing their wooden sabres around their
heads in exaggerated circles, blocking and parrying each
other's slow-motion thrusts, until Fierabras decided that
he had had enough of this and, the book still in his left
hand, sunk to the ground in defeat.

The onlookers roared with approval, the drummers
banged loudly and excitedly on the yellowing hides of their
instruments, and the saxophonist reached deep inside himself to come up with the first few bars of the triumphal
march from *Aida*. Oliveros baptised all the women in the
Moorish army, and then actors and spectators mingled in
a tumultuous procession up and down the basketball court.
The show was over.

Fabiano, the old man who had been sitting next to me,
retrieved the booklet that Fierabras had been using and
came back to show it to me. It was a stained and faded
little paperback, published thirty years earlier in Mexico,
nibbled at the corners by mice and missing a number of
pages. It was a Spanish version of a story that Fabiano said
was French, and as I read through the stolidly translated
verse some half-familiar names—Oliveros, Roldan, Ganelon—stuck in my mind.

Slowly it began to dawn on me what this knockabout
drunken performance under the coconut palms on a forgotten Honduran beach had been all about. It had been
taken from a *chanson de geste,* an early medieval epic French
poem about the exploits of Charlemagne and his knights—
Olivier and Roland and Ganelon. I thought perhaps it was

La Chanson de Roland, the first work of literature in modern French, but discovered later that in fact it was *Fierabras,* a twelfth-century poem written in 6,000 rhymed Alexandrines about the Saracen prince's robbery of holy relics from Rome, and Charlemagne's campaign to retrieve them.

Fabiano could not remember where he had come across his copy of the poem, and had even less idea of how or where the play we had just witnessed had originated. Had this poem survived long enough in French popular culture to have been well known among the French settlers on the island of St. Vincent, alongside whom the Garifunas fought against the English and from whom they learned to count? Had they learned it from those settlers and made it a part of their own culture, a tale of good defeating evil even if it was set in a totally meaningless context?

Here was a group of fishermen and manioc farmers, descended from Africa and Amazonia, living on a Caribbean beach, acting out in the sand their version of a mythical combat from the depths of Europe's Dark Ages nearly a thousand years before. If they had been Spanish-blood Hondurans on the other side of the coastal chain of hills, the cultural links would have been easy to trace through the conquest, but the play would probably have been a sad and alienated performance of a story that belonged to someone else. Here on the isolated shore, in the furthest flung of the string of Garifuna villages I had walked through, the mystery of how the epic reached these people made it theirs. Unexpected, unexplained, it was pure Garifuna.

SEVEN

As I lounged in a hammock strung between the treetrunk piles that lifted Mario's parents' house above potential floodwaters one morning, a small girl asked me for help with her English homework. How did you say in English "*Qué tal, amigo?*" she wanted to know. Still half asleep, I did not stop to think that if she could not speak English she certainly could not write it, and simply told her. "How are you, friend."

Laboriously she pencilled it into her exercise book, and brought the results over to show me. I took a moment to recognise what I had said in what she had written: "Habba u bren."

Instant creole. One schoolgirl's attempt at mimicry illustrated at a stroke a process that I had always thought took years—the corruption and dissolution of a language spoken only on foreign tongues, and the growth of a new idiom from the skeletal remains.

As I left Tocomacho, walking under heavy skies into a stiff breeze that whipped the beach sand into flurries around my feet, the map showed my next destination as a hamlet called Palacios. But the people who live there know the area as La Criba, a creolised name that barely retains an echo of its origins.

The sorry little straggle of clapboard huts along the lagoonside, tucked between the muddy water and the encroaching tropical forest, was once the hub of England's occupation of Central America's Caribbean coast, the settlement at Black River. In the mouths of Spanish speakers 200 years ago—the soldiers manning their fortress in Trujillo or the colonial administrators in Madrid to whom the settlement was a dangerous canker—Black River soon became "Lack Reever," and then "Lacreeva," and then, through the endemic Latin American confusion between Bs and Vs, "Lacreeba," and eventually "La Criba."

La Criba is a bastard name for a bastard child. Black River flourished at the heart of a profitable English contraband and plantation adventure for fully half of the eighteenth century, but London never did properly acknowledge fatherhood. The settlement was founded in 1732 by the same William Pitt who gave his name to what is now known as Pizza Lagoon on Roatan, himself the bastard offspring of a famous political family. A distant relative by illegitimate birth of the English Prime Minister William Pitt the Elder, he had first established himself as a logwood trader in Belize but soon tired of being repeatedly harrassed by the Spaniards.

After one particular flight to the refuge of the Honduran shore, Pitt resolved not to go home. He married a shipwrecked Spanish woman whom he had rescued from the Miskitos, and founded a settlement on the banks of a lagoon protected from the sea by a long spit of land and a shallow bar at the river mouth that hostile ships would have difficulty negotiating. The site he chose was a Miskito indian village that a shipwrecked English sea captain had visited twenty years earlier, discovering that the natives spoke a sort of English and were trading tortoiseshell with Jamaica in return for guns and ammunition.

Fostering a friendship between the English and the Miskitos that had been born in the days of pirate visitors a hundred years earlier, Pitt gradually built up the little village into a vigorous trading centre. More and more white settlers came to join him, drifting from Jamaica and Belize, and they brought slaves and servants with them to cut logwood, clear the forest and plant sugarcane, or gather the sarsaparilla root that was once said to cure every ill up to and including the clap and is today used only to flavour root beer.

For a settlement that caused so much trouble in its day and eventually required a special international conference to dismantle, Black River is a tiny place. Indeed the influence that the English exerted over the coast as a whole, and the fond memories that people such as the Miskitos have of that influence today, are hugely out of proportion to the number of Englishmen who ever lived in the area, scattered in a narrow fringe between the Spanish interior and the sea, The Shore. Bare of any Spanish settlement in the eighteenth century, this 500-mile coastline was home to several thousand Miskito and other indians and just a few hundred Englishmen. Eight years after Pitt founded Black River, the governor of Jamaica reported that about 100 Englishmen were living on The Shore. Seventeen years later, when the local superintendent made a stab at a census, he came up with 1,124 inhabitants that he counted as "British," only 154 of whom were white. The overwhelming majority were indian and African slaves, and the remainder were mestizo or mulatto freedmen. In 1787, when England abandoned The Shore and at Spain's insistence evacuated all British citizens, Royal Navy ships took about 2,650 people on board. Well over 2,000 of them, though, were slaves or mestizo freedmen.

Though Black River's residents were the same sort of ruffians as those who lived in Belize, Pitt had a calming influence on them. While in Belize no one had built anything but shacks, Superintendent Robert Hodgson reported in 1757 that at Black River

> the houses in general . . . are of wooden frames, thatched, and the sides of lathe and plaster, whitewashed. But there are some that make a good appearance, built entirely of wood, two stories high.

Black River and its satellite settlements such as Brewer's Lagoon, Nasty Creek, Plantain River and Cape River thrived on trade. By the middle of the eighteenth century, The Shore was exporting £25,000 sterling worth of goods a year to Europe, Jamaica and New York, shipping them in twelve locally owned merchant vessels. William Pitt and his fellow traders also found a ready market among Spanish settlers ill-served by Madrid's claim to a monopoly on commerce with the New World and happy to buy what they needed on the English black market. In return for cloth, tools, firearms, powder and other English manufactures they traded sarsaparilla root, mules, silver, indigo, cacao, animal hides and tallow back down the river through indian middlemen. Closer to the shore, Miskito indians offered deer and tiger skins, cochineal and tortoiseshell for Jamaican rum, powder and shot, while the English settlers themselves raised cattle and employed slaves to cut logwood and mahogany from the forest, or to plant and refine sugarcane.

As I wandered among the scattered huts that make up Palacios today, I came across occasional remnants of that past activity strewn meaninglessly around the village like objects that had dropped from outer space. Beside a path under a spreading mango tree, partly embedded in the sandy soil, sat a terminally rusted round-bottomed iron cauldron, eighteen feet around its rough beaten lip. I peered inside, but the dead leaves and dust that had gathered in the bottom for 200 years had robbed the gargantuan cooking pot of any trace of the heady fumes of bubbling molasses that I tried to imagine.

A young man passed, prodding a cow ahead of him down the path. I asked what he thought of having such a relic lying about his village. It had always been there, he said. His familiarity and disregard showed how clearly the cauldron belonged here. It had sat under this mango tree for as long as anyone could remember. But as well as belonging here, it was also entirely out of place, and even more markedly out of time. It was an object without purpose, a pointless presence left over from another existence. In my mind the cauldron became a metaphor for Black River, and Black River for the coast as a whole, both past and present, ambiguously balanced between two worlds and eventually ignored by both of them. Just as the cooking pot belonged where it sat and yet reflected nothing of its surroundings, the settlement whose inhabitants had boiled their sugar in it had been a strange and foreign presence.

Even though London's interest in the coast faded in time to mere curiosity, the influences imprinted by English pirates and loggers and traders and smugglers faded far more slowly, leaving a fringe of people and places along the coast that belong in Central America and are yet wholly out of place. Physically they are located on the Spanish American mainland, but like the cauldron, they reflect little of their surroundings. Nor was the giant pot the only reminder of the past still visible. The cowherd told me that down at the other end of the village, if I was interested, I would find some cannon.

I walked back a few hundred yards along the edge of the lagoon until the scattering of houses petered out. Sure enough, half buried and covered with fallen leaves behind a rickety palm-thatched cattle shed lay three eighteenth-century British guns. Two were scarcely visible, but the third rose proud enough from the earth for its embossed insignia to be read clearly. Beneath the jewelled crown of England swirled the royal initials in gracefully twined script: "G R," the number "3" threaded in amongst the curlicues to identify the king who ruled when the cannon was forged as George III. Someone at the foundry had carved the date into its thickening base, "23–3–62," and a little closer to the mouth was stamped the arrow that marked all War Department property. I felt a pang of homesickness: that same distinctive arrow had branded every cup and saucer, knife and fork, blanket and bed of the childhood I had spent in air force quarters around England, where the Ministry of Defence was as meticulous as it had been 200 years ago in identifying its assets.

The three guns lay where they had been abandoned two centuries earlier, and looking closely at the ground I could just decipher the outlines of the fortress that had once stood here, faint undulations in the earth. For Black River had been founded as a trading outpost only a few years before it was transformed into an English military stronghold.

The War of Jenkins's Ear against Spain had hardly begun in 1739 when Governor Edward Trelawney of Jamaica sent a young army captain, Robert Hodgson of the Forty-ninth Regiment of Foot, to organise the defence of the coast. He started by cementing the English alliance with the local Miskito indians, agreeing with the Miskito king on a document by which England became The Shore's effective owner, and then set about building defences at Black River.

When the war ended in 1748 with an agreement to return to the territorial "status quo ante," England removed the Port Royal battlements on Roatan and William Pitt came home, but London refused to give up Black River. Indeed, England strengthened its hand; the Board of Trade named Hodgson the first superintendent of the coast, to safeguard British commercial interests.

Protected by the bar across the river mouth and by an improved and extended fortress, Black River survived the next outbreak of Anglo-Spanish hostilities when Madrid joined France's Seven Years' War against England in 1760. But when that war ended with the Treaty of Paris in 1763, the wording concerning the Central American coast was ambiguous enough to lead both the English and Spanish settlers there to think that they had won.

A Spanish colonel turned up at Black River in February 1764 to check that all the fortifications had been pulled down but found nothing had been done. The superintendent showed him a letter from London, signed by the secretary of state for the colonies, reassuring the English settlers that their village did not fall within the scope of the Treaty of Paris, and the colonel and his accompanying patrol only escaped with their lives thanks to William Pitt's protection; the Miskito indians were keen to slaughter the

"Spainyards," but Pitt put them up in his fortified stockade and persuaded the Miskitos to have mercy.

For the next fifteen years, unmolested by Spanish attack, Black River got on with doing what it did best, trading and smuggling, shipping 800,000 square feet of mahogany and 10,000 pounds of tortoiseshell a year. But in the absence of a military threat, the settlers created their own problems amongst themselves, working up their jealousies, rivalries and petty squabbles to such a pitch that the colonial authorities in London eventually lost patience with them. The trouble seems to have started when Robert Hodgson, Jr., the son of Black River's first superintendent, undiplomatically attempted to impose his authority. He had taken over the job from his father in 1767 and married William Pitt's daughter Isabel.

A number of prominent settlers, growing wealthy from the proceeds of their trading activities, in the late 1760s began to buy huge tracts of land around Black River from their Miskito indian owners in order to plant sugar, indigo, cacao and cotton. Hodgson tried to control the purchases, arguing that the Miskitos complained of being cheated and that the deals were poisoning Black River's relations with the indians, so essential for the settlement's existence. His neighbours felt that Hodgson was interested only in protecting his own sizeable land investments, and the dispute sparked a running battle that lasted several years.

Hodgson's father had not bothered much with the running of Black River; he had concerned himself with defending the settlement and keeping the indians happy and left the administration of justice to the men vested with such authority by the governor of Jamaica. Young Hodgson, however, tried to set up a formal governing council on which he had considerable powers, prompting a minor revolt led by one of Black River's largest landholders, Captain James Lawrie, another officer of the Forty-ninth Regiment of Foot who had profited handsomely from his several postings on the coast. When Hodgson asked the governor of Jamaica to fire his opponents from their positions as magistrates, Trelawney refused to do so, but by the time his answer reached Black River it was irrelevant. Captain Lawrie and his supporters had begun to elect their own judges, regardless of Jamaica's decision, and to hold assemblies—the first steps towards independent government—which gave Jamaica considerable cause for alarm.

By this time, William Pitt had died. Perhaps he might have mediated in the dispute between his son-in-law and the rest of the settlers. Perhaps too, before he died, he had foreseen how the internal strife that had broken out would eventually destroy the village to which he had devoted his life. But it was too late to avert that fate.

Hodgson's rivals began writing malicious letters to well-placed friends in London and even dispatched a delegation of Miskito chiefs to London to support their allegations. In August 1775 Hodgson was recalled. The order bringing him back to London, however, acknowledged that he was not entirely to blame for "the disorder and distraction that now prevails on the Mosquito Shore," which was

> chiefly owing to the restless and ungovernable spirit and temper of its inhabitants, which have manifested themselves in acts of usurpation, very little short of open rebellion against the King's government.

The rights and wrongs of Hodgson's arguments with his fellow settlers were of scant interest in London, where officials were losing patience with the fractious pioneers in distant Black River and beginning to wonder whether the commercial and military benefits to be derived from English occupation of The Shore really compensated for all the trouble it caused with Spain.

The extent of that trouble became clear in 1779, when Madrid allied itself with England's rebellious North American colonies and declared war. The English governor of Jamaica, John Dalling, decided to use the hostilities as an opportunity to cut the Spanish empire in half by launching a major assault up the San Juan River and across Lake Nicaragua to the Pacific coast. He drew forces from the whole region for this attempt, which not only failed, but left Black River without its local British army detachment and empty of Miskito warriors, who had all travelled south to join Dalling's expedition. Sure enough, in April 1780, Spanish troops from Trujillo attacked and burned Black River, sending settlers and slaves fleeing into the jungle.

Even though Superintendent Lawrie retook the settlement at the head of a small army of Miskitos, North American loyalists, mestizo freedmen and local settlers, Black River's days as an English village were all but over. Under the Treaty of Versailles in 1783, which confirmed the American colonies' independence, London was keener to recover the West Indian islands she had lost and to maintain control of Gibraltar than to defend the Shoremen, and English negotiators promised to evacuate all settlements except Belize from "the Spanish continent." One last time the settlers tried to argue, as they had done after two other wars, that they did not live in Spanish territory. But in July 1786 a special conference was convened in London to prevent "even the Shadow of Misunderstanding which might be occasioned by Doubt, Misconceptions, or other causes of Disputes between the Subjects on the Frontiers of the two Monarchies, especially in distant Countries, as are those in AMERICA." England agreed to evacuate The Shore once and for all.

The decision provoked remarkably little fuss in Black River itself. A few Shoremen decided they would stay on anyway and live under the Spanish flag, but the overwhelming majority of the 2,650 men and women who were taken off the coast simply packed up whatever they owned and left, without noisy complaint. It was as if they recognised in their heart of hearts that they really had no right to be in Black River. They had been living an anomaly for the past half century, and now their time was up. Most of them went to Belize, whence William Pitt had arrived for the first time fifty-five years earlier, the rest dispersed to try their luck in Jamaica, Roatan or the Cayman Islands. On 29 August 1787, Pitt's grandson, William Pitt Lawrie, formally handed The Shore over to Spain. His grandfather's dream had died.

Nor were the Spanish able to revive it. They shipped in forty settler families from Spain and the Canary Islands, but the new inhabitants lived in constant fear of being slaughtered by the surrounding Miskitos, and Rio Tinto, as Black River had been renamed, did not flourish. Relations between the settlers and the indians deteriorated, until, just before dawn on 4 September 1800, the Miskito General Tempest lived up to his chosen name. At the head of a flotilla of canoes paddled silently up Black River in the darkness, he descended on the unsuspecting village, massacred the *"Spainyards"* and put the whole place to the torch.

———

Though I was sorry not to be in Garifuna territory anymore, Palacios made me grateful for one aspect of Hispanic
life in this little island of *colonos*—a change of diet. The
sour cream that Don Felix Marmol's wife served me with
my tamales as I lunched in a cramped room behind her
grocery store had never tasted so sharp and fresh.

Don Felix's *hotelito,* in reality just three cardboard-walled
rooms above his general store, was the social centre of
Palacios. At dusk, as bats flickered around the outer edges
of the dim light cast by a naked bulb hung above the front
door, a knot of men would gather to enjoy the fruits of
Don Felix's generator—cold beer. As I listened in the
shadows one evening to a boastful conversation about the
size of the tarpon that one of the villagers had fished from
the lagoon, a portly man with several days' growth on his
face came up to me and introduced himself diffidently as
Reynaldo, "in charge of the biosphere."

I was unsure quite what this responsibility involved. Indeed I was unsure quite what a biosphere was until Reynaldo explained that it was the ecologically correct term
for a nature reserve. His job was to conserve the wildlife
over a forty-mile stretch of the coast, which he was simply
unable to do without any help. His main concern when I
met him was to protect the nests of eggs that mother turtles
were laying at that time of the year high up on the beach.
Though it is illegal to take turtle eggs, the law certainly
doesn't dissuade anyone in Honduras from seeking out
this delicacy, and Reynaldo didn't constitute much of a
dissuasive force either since he couldn't do anything except
patrol a limited sector of his beat each night, when the
turtles were coming ashore, until he grew too tired to
continue. Whereupon the nest robbers would sneak out,
find a turtle laying, and simply wait for her to finish before

scooping all her hundreds of warm eggs into sacks for their next day's breakfast.

As the only representative of government authority in Palacios, Reynaldo had stretched his job description to involve the protection not only of the animals and plants in his biosphere but of anything he considered of interest. In the village, he told me, he was proudest of his guardianship of the cemetery. Reynaldo led me to a shack at one end of the village, sitting in the middle of a fenced-off patch of scrub beside the long stretch of rough pasture that doubled as Palacios's airstrip. "There," Reynaldo announced grandly, gesturing to the dusty grass at our feet. *"El cementério de La Criba."*

As I stood there looking bewildered Reynaldo ducked into the thatched hut and emerged with a shovel in his hand. "Go and dig over there, but carefully," he suggested, pointing to a patch of shade beneath a skinny tree. Digging up an alleged graveyard struck me as a pretty dubious proposition, but Reynaldo nodded again in the direction of the tree, and with the blessing of the biosphere chief I decided I might as well see what was exciting him so much. I took off my T-shirt under the early afternoon sun and began to dig.

I had shovelled only a few inches of dry earth away when my spade scraped against a rock. "Go gently now," Reynaldo cautioned, and I dug with shallower sweeps, realising with each spadeful of earth that I had hit not a rock but a plaque of some sort. Reynaldo handed me a piece of dried thatch and I dropped to my knees, using it as a makeshift broom with which to sweep away the dust. I could make out some sort of carving on the stone, but only when I had brushed away all the dirt did I understand what I had uncovered.

HERE
LYETH THE BODY OFF
WILLIAM PITT . . .

I couldn't believe it. I looked up over my shoulder to Reynaldo, whose smile had broadened to a grin at my excitement, and turned back to brush away the earth that was obscuring the rest of the gravestone.

HERE
LYETH THE BODY OFF
WILLIAM PITT SON OF MR
WILLIAM PITT WHO DEPARTED
THIS LIFE JANUARY THE 31
ANNO DOMINI 1741–2 AGED
3 YEARS 8 MONTHS AND 9 DAYS

MOURN NOT FOR ME FOR I AM BLESST
AND IN CHRISTS ARMS I TAKE MY REST

So this was not actually old Pitt's grave, but that of a young son. His father did not see him die, and perhaps did not hear of his death for many months, for in January 1742 Pitt was on the island of Roatan, fortifying it against the Spaniards. I told Reynaldo, a little disappointed, that this didn't seem to be the grave of Black River's founder after all. "There's another one just next to it, I think," he said. "Try there."

I dug again, and sure enough quickly came upon a second grey granite stone, smaller and less deeply carved, but still just about legible.

To the memory of the Honrble WILLIAM PITT
who died March 20 1771 Aged 76 years
Also Willm. . . . Lawrie Hewlett. . . . Aged
a year and Ann Pitt Hewlett
who died March 1 1771 Aged . . . yrs and
10 months . . . Love Hewlett . . . children
Honrble Wm Pitt

That was where the old man lay, his bones mixing with
those of his grandchildren beside a mangrove-fringed lagoon, protected by a stone that might have been carved
for an English country churchyard. His memorial had lain
covered by brush and jungle for nearly two centuries of
abandonment. Now, exposed again to the tropical sunlight,
the tombstone lay, forgotten, nearly indecipherable and
matchlessly eloquent.

Black River's history has an extraordinary epilogue.

For twenty years after General Tempest's attack, the
settlement rotted. The boards of its shingled houses fed
termites, cauldrons rusted in the undergrowth and the
sugar plantations reverted to bush. And then, in 1820,
Gregor MacGregor showed up.

Born in Edinburgh in 1786, MacGregor had fought with
the British army in the Spanish Peninsular War and then
become a general in Simon Bolivar's army fighting for
South American independence. In 1817 he went freelance,
sponsored by English merchants to launch a series of attacks on Spanish possessions in Florida, Colombia and Panama. The last his band of mercenaries saw of him he was
urging them to fight to the last man in defence of a beseiged
fortress in Panama. MacGregor himself, however, slipped

away in a rowing boat, regained his ship and sailed away leaving his men to their fate.

He headed north until he reached Cape Gracias a Dios, where the Miskito King George Frederick held court. Playing on the king's well-known weakness for the bottle, the Scottish adventurer plied him with rum and friendship, and weaseled in return an enormous land concession in the west of George Frederick's kingdom, centred on the mouth of Black River. Armed with the necessary papers, MacGregor set sail for London to play an outrageous confidence trick on the City of London.

During his stay at Cape Gracias a Dios MacGregor had undoubtedly heard tales of the Poyers, a tribe of indians living in the Black River region. The people themselves were of no interest to MacGregor, but they inspired the name for his scheme. Arriving in England he announced to the world that he had established a new nation on the Central American coast, that its name was Poyais and that henceforth he would be obliged if people would address him by his rightful title, His Highness Gregor I, Cazique of Poyais.

He used this absurd invention, however, for more than just his personal glory. On Dowgate Hill, close to the City, he opened a Poyaisian embassy, entertaining politicians and financiers lavishly and selling plots of Poyaisian land at one shilling an acre to would-be colonists. These he attracted through a massive public-relations campaign, causing ballads in praise of his newfound paradise to be posted and sung in the streets of London and Edinburgh. He also enlisted a friend, Thomas Strangeways, to consult all the available literature on the Miskito Shore and concoct a guide to the area extolling its potential.

Strangeways, who styled himself "Captain, First Native

Poyer Regiment and aide-de-camp to His Highness Gregor," published his *Sketch of the Mosquito Shore, Including the Territory of Poyais, Chiefly Intended for the Use of Settlers* in 1822. It was a tissue of lies from start to finish, opening with a reassuring promise. Any idea readers might have gained from the coast's name that it was infested with mosquitos, Strangeways wrote, "would be a very unjust conclusion, for there are perhaps few countries under the tropics so little troubled with these disagreeable insects."

Young men jilted by their brides-to-be, traders fallen on hard times, mill hands impatient with a life of drudgery, tricksters anxious to evade the law, anyone with a spark of adventure must have dreamed of bright new opportunities as they read Strangeways's account of this unknown country, his imaginative descriptions of its tidy English villages, friendly natives, prosperous plantations and busy sawmills. "The land is everywhere fertile in a very uncommon degree, and capable of producing in the utmost perfection whatever is produced between the tropics," he lied blithely. Strangeways dedicated much of his book to apparently convincing but entirely fictitious calculations of the return on investment a settler might expect from a variety of crops. Picking figures out of the air for such items as wages (twenty-five shillings a month for a Miskito indian but sometimes payable in clothing) and land, he concluded that a sugar planter could easily make "a clear income of £1,200 sterling per annum, free of all taxes whatsoever."

Some sceptics found these blandishments a little too juicy to be true. MacGregor's propaganda, one satirical critic commented, portrayed a paradise "where all manner of grain grows without sowing and the most delicious fruits without planting; where cows and horses support themselves and where roasted pigs run about with forks in their backs crying 'come, eat me.' "

Over 200 men, women and children were nonetheless convinced enough to set off for Poyais. Some had bought land, others embarked as indentured servants pledging to work for the Poyaisian government, and their numbers included teachers, clerks, shopkeepers, cabinetmakers, jewellers and a City of London banker who had been engaged as manager of the nonexistent Bank of Poyais.

As the would-be pioneers approached the coast of Honduras, MacGregor launched a £200,000 loan, secured by the credit of Poyais, to finance the colony. With a respectable firm of City stockbrokers handling the issue, Poyaisian bonds sold well, and MacGregor earned himself about £160,000 before news began trickling back from the Caribbean about the settlers' fate.

The first colonists had arrived in Honduras at the end of 1822, in the middle of the worst of the rains, and as soon as they came within sight of the shore they saw how badly they had been deceived. The fertile plantations and active mills, the bulging warehouses and bustling streets, the civilised Garden of Eden that Strangeways and his balladeers had conjured up was an unbroken spread of jungle. Hardly had the unfortunate adventurers cleared enough land by the edge of the lagoon to erect a few feeble wigwams of sheets, blankets and leaves than foul weather set in. The captain of their ship weighed anchor immediately, taking with him most of the colonists' dry and unspoiled weapons, powder, merchandise, medicines and spirits.

Few of the colonists were fit for this sort of ordeal. The wind blew their tents down, the rain soaked them day and night, and they were astonished to discover that the indians who found them huddled miserably on the beach would not accept the Poyais banknotes that they offered in return for food. Instead the settlers were forced to trade the rum, powder and shot that they had, and soon even that was not enough. Undiplomatically they refused to swear allegiance to King George Frederick, who promptly ordered his people to do nothing to help these lost and luckless foreigners.

Eventually news of their plight reached Belize and a ship was sent to bring them to safety. She found fewer than fifty survivors.

MacGregor himself, however, was undeterred, moving to Paris and selling 480,000 more acres of Poyais land to a colonisation company. He went on selling land certificates for nine years after his first unfortunate victims had perished on the beach at Black River. He served a ten-month jail sentence in France but was never prosecuted in England, perhaps because several highly placed financiers and politicians had been involved in his swindles. Eventually MacGregor retook his general's rank in the Venezuelan army and retired to Caracas. He died there in 1845 and the president, the cabinet and the diplomatic corps attended his burial in the cathedral. Not a drum was heard, not a funeral note, from the First Native Poyer Regiment.

EIGHT

I took to Rodolfo Sandoval immediately, but it was only after an hour or so of conversation in the shade of his porch that I realised what it was about him that I found so engaging. One of his eyes was slightly smaller than the other and when he grinned it almost disappeared beneath a drooping eyelid. My own right eye, always partially closed, does exactly the same thing whenever I smile. The familiarity of Rodolfo's features unconsciously bred a quick rapport.

He had been recommended to me as the oldest man in Cocobila and the village elder most likely to recall the Miskito people's origins and traditions. By his own rough reckoning he was eighty years old, his angular face was creased with age, and his high cheekbones, broad forehead and dark coppered complexion revealed his indian ancestry.

Among Miskito indians, that is unusual. They have mixed so freely over the past 400 years with so many of the visitors to their coast that tribesmen run from nearly black to blue-eyed Scandinavian. Where the Miskitos came from originally is not entirely clear. Rodolfo was by no means certain himself.

"I always wondered about that, you know." He shook his head. "But an *Ingles de color* who lived with my aunt, he used to say, though I don't know if it's true or if he was lying because he was here before I was born, he used to say that Moses was a Miskito."

Many theories have been advanced to explain the Miskitos' origins, but since none have suggested that they are the lost tribe of Israel, Rodolfo's scepticism about that fanciful version of the Old Testament seemed justified.

Whether the Miskitos and the other indians of the Caribbean coast came down from North America with the main tide of settlers when Central America was peopled for the first time, or whether they slipped back up the coast much later from Colombia and Venezuela, is a matter of dispute among linguistic historians. Nor are anthropologists entirely agreed on whether the Miskitos really existed, as such, before 1641.

Legend has it that in that year, a Guinea ship washed ashore near Cape Gracias a Dios and deposited a cargo of West African slaves who had risen up and taken over their vessel, tossing the crewmen overboard and with them all knowledge of navigation. The winds and the currents brought them safely to land in Central America, where they proceeded to settle amongst the indians they found there just as a similar shipload of slaves mixed with the Caribs on St. Vincent at about the same time, creating the Garifuna people.

The question that divides the academics is whether the indians that the slaves found were Miskitos already, or whether it was the fusion of indians—perhaps Sumus— and blacks that created the Miskito race. Enough English pirates and other adventurers in the seventeenth century wrote accounts of indians whom they called Miskitos, describing them as pureblood indians, to make it seem more likely that the Miskitos were Miskito already before the slave ship was wrecked. But that does not explain where their name came from.

For most of the 400 years or so since Europeans first came across the Miskitos they have been called "Mosquitos" and there has been little doubt in the mind of anybody to whom the question occurred that the name derived from the biting insects presumed to infest the coast. The region's endless mangroves are indeed often impenetrable, and its swamps and creeks, if not pestilential and foetid, can be on the rotten and stagnant side. But on the question of mosquitos I find myself in embarrassingly close accord with Thomas Strangeways, who wrote Gregor MacGregor's propaganda for Poyais and claimed that "there are perhaps few countries under the tropics so little troubled with these disagreeable insects." That was putting it a little strongly. But I certainly had no more trouble with mosquitos on my journey along the coast than I have had, say, with midges in the highlands of Scotland or with horseflies in the southern Andes.

The coast is, however, infested with sandflies, so minute as to be invisible and with a bite that itches beyond the wildest dreams of a mere mosquito. Early travellers driven insane by these vicious insects, known in coast English from Belize to Panama and in Miskito as "no see'ums," may well have simply mistaken them for their less potent cousins. Immune to all known insect repellents, sandflies threatened to make my journey miserable on many windless evenings, until a friend in Tegucigalpa offered me a bottle of bath oil. For reasons that science has yet to fathom, Avon's "Skin So Soft" bath essence, spread liberally over all exposed skin, provides cast-iron protection against sandflies.

Whether the prevalence of sandflies mistaken for mosquitos explains the name of the coast and of the indians living along it is by no means certain. Nowhere are the sandflies as insufferable as in Belize, and Belize was definitely not part of the "Mosquito Coast"; nor was Costa Rica, where they also terrorize tourists. The label was only applied to the part of the coast where the Miskito indians lived, which suggests that it derived from the indians themselves.

Why then did the area come to be known as the "Mosquito Coast" almost as soon as Europeans began writing about it? One possible explanation emerges from one of the first accounts of the Miskitos ever published, comprehensively titled "THE MOSQUETO INDIAN AND HIS GOLDEN RIVER; Being a familiar DESCRIPTION of the MOSQUETO Kingdom in America. WITH A True RELATION of the ftrange Cuftoms, Ways of Living, Divinations, Religion, Drinking-bouts, Wars, Marriages, Buryings, &c. of thofe Heathenifh People; together with an ACCOUNT of the Product of their Country."

No one knows who wrote this brief essay at the end of the seventeenth century—it was mysteriously signed only M. W.—but his spelling of "Mosqueto" opens up an avenue of speculation with its similarity to the Spanish word *mosquete* meaning "a musket." Could it have been the Spanish who baptised the indians allied with English pirates and traders—and from whom they had secured firearms—*los Indios con mosquetes*, the indians with muskets?

Today Miskitos are anxious to emphasise their indigenous origins and to cast off the names that foreigners have given them. They prefer to be known as "Miskitos." But even this name is not free of foreign taints; in fact it is the spelling devised by German missionaries from the Moravian church in the nineteenth century who implanted the Teutonic Christianity that still holds sway amongst the indians.

A century earlier the Miskitos, or some of them at least, were called "zambos" or "sambos." That was what the English called the darker Miskitos with the curlier hair, the ones with slave blood in their veins, who developed a reputation for ferocity that far outstripped that of their pureblooded brothers. Where that name originated is not clear either, but its use in the United States in the nineteenth century suggests that it was a general appellation for blacks. Englishmen writing about the coast tended to assume that the "sambos" came from "Samba country" in West Africa, but John Holm, an expert in linguistics who has studied Miskito Coast English, suggests another more interesting derivation. "*Nzambu,*" he explains, is the word for "monkey" in the Congo, whence many of the slaves shipped to the New World came. Was it the slang that seventeenth-century Portuguese and Spanish slavers picked up in West African ports, the word they used amongst themselves to dehumanise their cargo, that gave the title to the storybook *Little Black Sambo?*

The Miskitos' history since their first contact with Europeans has been dominated by their extraordinary relationship with the English, a close and lasting affiliation that for two and a half centuries made them the undisputed masters of their land and a holy terror to their neighbours, but left them rudderless and nostalgic when London abandoned its strategic concerns in Central America a hundred years ago.

Although English buccaneers may have put ashore amongst the Miskitos earlier, in search of food and water, the first documented contact between the two nations occurred in 1633 when Captain Sussex Cammock, a trader with the Providence Island Company, approached Miskitos living at Cape Gracias a Dios. English Puritans had founded a colony on Providence Island, off the Nicaraguan coast, a couple of years earlier under the sponsorship of the Earl of Warwick, who had a royal charter from King Charles I to grow indigo and sugarcane. Cammock explored the coast with the help of a Dutch pirate, Abraham Blauvelt, who gave his name to the present-day town of Bluefields at the southern limits of Miskito territory, and the Providence Island colonists probably introduced their new trading partners to firearms, using what must have been one of the first "pidgin" English tongues ever spoken. The tools they brought with them in return for tortoiseshell and animal hides left the first English marks on the Miskito language: *ámar* for "hammer," *páyal* for "file," *áyan* for "iron."

The Spaniards stormed Providence in 1641, breaking up the Puritan colony. (Three years later the Earl of Warwick was given a new charter to reestablish Providence on Rhode Island off the coast of Massachusetts.) But pirates preying on the Spanish empire built upon the foundations that Captain Cammock had laid found the Miskitos ready recruits for the raids they staged on Spanish cities deep inland. Acting as scouts and hired guns for the pirates, the Miskitos launched a long tradition of fighting alongside Englishmen against Spaniards, or indeed against anybody else the English happened to be fighting at the time. Fifty Miskitos sailed to Jamaica in 1720 to help put down the Maroon rebellion by runaway slaves, and in 1774 the Miskito King George pledged 5,000 of his warriors to the English King George should they be needed to put down rebellious colonists in North America.

In the meantime, London had taken formal possession of the Miskito Shore by means of a little-noticed ceremony at the edge of a lagoon behind Sandy Bay, just south of Gracias a Dios. On 14 March 1740, Captain Robert Hodgson had gathered an assembly of Miskito dignitaries and proclaimed an agreement transferring the coast to Great Britain. He read it, he reported later to the governor of Jamaica,

> in a solemn manner under the colours, and at the end of every article fired a gun, and concluded by cutting up a turf and promising to defend their country and procure for them all assistance from England in my power.

Whether everybody in the audience understood the full import of Hodgson's declaration is doubtful, but the young captain overcame any reservations by making a handful of the more prominent luminaries admirals and generals.

In their joint campaigns and sea voyages, pirates and indians had learned to speak each other's language, after a fashion, developing a mutual confidence in which the pirates learned to trust the Miskitos and the Miskitos learned to hate the Spanish. The pirates and the Miskitos, after all, had much in common. They were both nomadic sorts of people, with the hunter's love of the chase whether they be running down a turtle or a well-laden galleon, and they both lived in highly democratic and egalitarian societies that vested authority in captain or king only in time of war. The pirates were not interested in buying or seizing land; they settled into an indigenous indian way of life while the Miskitos became the pirates of the coast both literally, as crewmen for the Europeans, and figuratively, using English tools and weapons to impose themselves on every other tribe the length of the coast.

The Miskitos' habit of waging almost constant war on all their more peaceful neighbours, the Twacas and the Uhlwas and the Panamacas and the Kukras and the Poyers and the Ramas (known generically in Miskito as "alboa-winneys"—"uncivilised indians") made them a permanent menace. In the seventeenth and eighteenth centuries the Miskitos raided other indian communities for slaves, either for their own use or for sale to the English who came in sloops from Jamaica. When slavery was abolished in the British empire the bottom fell out of the slave market, and the Miskitos took to extorting tribute from everybody in the vicinity.

The results were predictable and are still visible on the coast today. While the non-Miskito tribes, known now as Sumus, shrank from around 7,000 to 3,500 over the course of the eighteenth and nineteenth centuries, and withdrew from the coast itself to more protected and isolated riverside settlements, the Miskitos spread out and multiplied fivefold to number perhaps 10,000 by the beginning of the nineteenth century. They owed their supremacy not only to their more aggressive and expansive nature, but more fundamentally to their alliance with the English, which gave them an enormous advantage in firepower over any rivals armed only with arrows and spears. And the Miskitos' view of both this world and the next was coloured by their dependence on this alliance.

English travellers from the earliest times commented on the friendliness Miskitos had shown them as soon as they

had established their nationality. Writing of the Miskito-
men who sailed with the pirates as fishermen, William
Dampier reported that

it is very rare to find Privateers destitute of one or
more of them when the Commander, or most of the
men, are English; but they do not love the French,
and the Spaniards they hate mortally.

Two hundred years later Thomas Young, manager of an
ill-fated attempt to set up a British colony on the coast in
1840, found that

any Englishman could traverse from one end of the
country to the other without the expense of a yard of
cloth, for the king's orders were to feed and lodge
them and provide them with horses when they
wanted.

But no account of the Miskitos' feelings towards the English reveals the depth of their admiration and gratitude
so well as a passing phrase in M. W.'s sketch of the people
he came across when he visited the coast sometime around
1690. Describing their religious beliefs he wrote that

most of them believe the immortality of the soul, that
when they sleep or die their spirit goes to another
place or world; but they say they do not know what
sort of a place they will find of it, but believe they
shall be always among the English there, and not the
Spaniards or Alboawinneys.

Greater love hath no man, than he who believes that heaven is exclusively populated by the English.

England's formal absence from the coast after the 1787 evacuation did not entail any serious disruption of her patronage of the Miskitos, nor did it discourage settlement schemes such as Gregor MacGregor's swindle, or the more straightforward but equally ill-fated project that Thomas Young was involved in twenty years later, to build a colony to be called Fort Wellington on the site of the Black River settlement. But by then the Spanish had abandoned their Central American empire, crumbling in the face of independence movements, and a new rival to British interests in the western Caribbean had emerged, the United States.

When Christopher Columbus had sailed down the Nicaraguan coast in 1502, seeking a way through the landmass to what he thought was the "coreland" of India, he had anchored off the mouth of the San Juan River, which today marks Nicaragua's southern border with Costa Rica. He never realised, though, that the river winding its way into the wet green forest was the nearest passage that existed to a strait through the isthmus. Over the 300 years that followed, the Spanish developed the river into a major trade route linking Lake Nicaragua in the interior with the natural harbour on the Caribbean coast, and by the middle of the nineteenth century the river, the lake and the narrow strip of land that blocked the way to the Pacific Ocean on the other side had become the obvious route along which to build an interoceanic canal.

That potential was of extreme and equal interest to Great Britain, who already ruled the waves and intended to rule any channel between them, and to the United States, keen to develop its west coast. Ignoring the newly independent Nicaraguan government's claim to sovereignty over the country's eastern shore, London staked its claim promptly in 1843 by announcing the creating of the "Mosquito Kingdom," a protectorate under British sway that stretched from Cape Gracias a Dios down to San Juan del Norte, at the mouth of the eponymous river.

The next half century marked the apogee of the Miskitos' unequal alliance with the English, their leaders under the tutelage of an English royal agent who doubled as consul general and effectively ruled the territory. Even if American pressure forced London to end the protectorate in 1860, recognising Nicaraguan sovereignty over what became a "reservation" and demoting the Miskito king to "hereditary chief," it was only in 1894, when the Nicaraguan army stormed the port of Bluefields and hauled down the Union Jack, that the English finally abandoned their trustiest servants in the hemisphere. There are many old men on the Miskito Shore who still cannot bring themselves to believe that the Miskito Royal Standard will never again flutter in the trade winds above the king's palace.

Rodolfo Sandoval was not one of them, though. He was happy enough to recall the old days for me—his life in the 1920s as a teenage "*lodermon*" in Belize, helping the "*troctormon*" load logs, the traditional indian herbs that cured the two-year attack of diarrhea that brought him home in 1934, the good and evil spirits that inhabit the trees and the rivers of the Mosquitia. But he answered all my questions with a bemused air and found it curious that I should want to know so much about how life used to be. "The past is important, why not. But so is the present," he chided me. "The old times don't exist anymore. They are forgotten."

The "present" manifested itself in Cocobila in the shape

of a small maroon Hyundai pickup truck, an inverted crate bolted to its sides to form a roof, whose presence in this roadless hamlet tucked between lumpish sand dunes and the leaden waters of Ibans Lagoon served the single purpose of distinguishing its owner, Domingo, as a man of means. The vehicle spent most of its life parked in the sand under a mango tree for lack of fuel, but every now and again Domingo would start his precious status symbol up and collect a fare from passengers going anywhere along the few miles of beach passable by a truck.

Twenty-one of us wedged our way into the flatbed that afternoon, including a small boy tucked between the back of the driver's seat and the cab window, four youths precariously perched on the rear bumper, and an arthritic old man clutching a sack of cassava, hoisted bodily onto the roof and left there to hang on as best he could. It occurred to me to offer to swap places with him, but I was so firmly jammed between the spreading hips of two large women on either side of me and beneath the small daughter that one of my neighbours had dumped on my lap that any further movement was impossible.

Cramped sweatily in the enclosed gloom, we set off as Domingo ground along in first gear at little more than walking pace, weaving between the trees that grew just inland from the beach, behind the sand dunes. Not far out of the village the woods thinned, giving way to broad, open savannah backed with stands of spindly pine in the distance. We jolted over this rough land, past a handful of morose cattle with dusty concave flanks, following not so much a track as a partly worn ribbon through the scrubby tussocks of parched grey grass. Stopping every few minutes at the command thumped urgently by a passenger wanting to get off, we crawled past several scattered collections of stilted, split bamboo-walled huts cowering under the glare of the sun and sheltering nothing but the bare essentials of poverty—a sheet and blanket on a raised platform of planks, a few patched and dusty clothes hung over a rafter, a faded postcard-sized image of Christ holding his bleeding, thorn-entwined heart left by some Catholic missionary years ago and now pinned to a cornerpost in some semblance of interior decoration.

After an hour or so of this tortuous progress the truck ran up against a belt of tangled mangrove trees and stopped. This was as far as it could go, a scant three miles from Cocobila, and I was glad of the chance to get down and stretch my twisted limbs.

Beyond the mangroves lay a half-hour walk to Rio Platano along a tideline that was almost busy. About fifteen of us had stayed on the truck to the end of the line, and there was also a steady flow of pedestrians heading up the beach towards Cocobila. Groups walking in either direction would hail each other and stop for a chat as if they were out doing their Saturday morning shopping on an English high street, but while they dawdled I set a more determined pace. With a large rucksack on my back, ambling was simply too uncomfortable.

Rio Platano, at the mouth of the Plantain River, is a sizeable village of stilted huts in various stages of disrepair strung out on either side of a wide grassy strip that is unnaturally flat and well tended, as if it has been levelled to serve as a landing strip. In the early evening, as I walked up it in the quickly gathering dusk, the air was acrid with woodsmoke drifting from the ramshackle outhouses behind each home that served as kitchens.

To me, Rio Platano meant only one thing: a radio set that I could use to contact Patuca, thirty empty miles up the coast, to confirm that a tramp steamer with which I had arranged a ride three weeks earlier was indeed putting in on time and could carry me on down to Lempira and the Nicaraguan border. I was growing increasingly anxious about the logistics of arriving at the border on the day I had indicated to the Sandinistas, the only day I would be authorised to cross. I had six days until the Tuesday deadline fell. In two days' time, on Saturday, the *Amy J.,* whose owner I had met in Cortes, was due to put in briefly to the Miskito refugee settlement at Patuca, off-load some cargo and sail for Lempira with me aboard. That gave me Sunday and Monday to make the short drive to the United Nations camp at Mocoron, where I was to hook up with the Miskito refugees returning home to Nicaragua. But in those two days I also had to track down the leader of the anti-Sandinista Miskito guerrilla army, who used Lempira as his rearguard headquarters, and persuade him to write me out an authorisation to travel through the Nicaraguan territory that his forces controlled, which included a large swathe of the coast. I was confident that I had the time I needed, but I was cutting it close, and there was no room for anything to go wrong.

Things went wrong as soon as I found the grocery shop that housed the village radio and made contact with Patuca. I was told that the *Amy J.* was not running on schedule, and that in fact she was in Patuca right then, preparing to leave for Lempira. I swore loudly and foully—one of the pleasures of a life abroad where your language is not spoken—and all the male customers in the shop turned sharply towards me. I was in the Mosquitia, I realised, and though my language was perhaps not spoken as widely as it once had been, it was still understood.

The radio operator in Patuca, though, assured me that

another coastal steamer bound for Lempira was due to put in on Saturday morning. He would talk to the captain, who would surely take me, he said. I was not to worry.

The grocery store that housed the radio was the most substantial structure in the village, a squat wooden shed radiating prosperity from its corrugated iron roof, the blue and white paint protecting its clapboard walls and the throaty chug of a diesel generator round the back that promised electric light and cold soda in the fridge. As I struggled to communicate with Patuca through the radio static, clumsily pressing the button on the mike when I wanted to listen instead of when I wanted to talk, forgetting to say "over" and hearing only hiss as Patuca waited for me to continue, a score of young men milled around in the shop and on its verandah.

Dressed for the most part in shorts and unbuttoned shirts they ranged from a skinny little African-looking boy to a hulk whose hairless indian body was hung about with a heavy gold necklace, a thick golden bracelet that kept getting snagged on his gold watch strap, and two preposterously outsized gold signet rings on his stubby fingers. The whole crowd appeared to be pestering Señora Castillo, looking stern behind the counter, with four fat ledger books and her spectacles, to give them more credit. It was hard to see how a scant community such as Rio Platano, where subsistence farming and the occasional fishing trip kept the villagers alive, could generate such consumer frenzy. Señora Castillo's shelves ranged from floor to ceiling, crammed with tinned meat and fish and peas and peaches, medicinal tablets and capsules and creams and unguents, printed T-shirts and polyester trousers, trainers, a wide choice of gaudily coloured shampoos, deodorants, Taiwanese sewing kits, cornflakes, pop music cassettes, cigarettes by the thousand and crates of rum. One enormous freezer chest stored nothing but beer while another was packed with Sprite, Fanta, Coke and knotted plastic bags containing fist-sized chunks of frozen-fruit cordial, the local model of ice lolly.

Offering me a beer and settling his bulk into a tattered hammock on the verandah, the bejewelled man gave me a thin smile that barely creased his battered features but revealed that even two of his front teeth were made of gold, and asked what I was doing there. He watched me with flat, expressionless eyes as I explained the journey I was making, and although he did not seem to think it made any more sense than had anyone else to whom I had explained it over the previous month or so, he concluded that at any rate I was harmless. When I bought him a beer and asked what *he* was doing there, he grinned slyly. "Spending money," he said, taking a long draught at his bottle.

Even if I was harmless, it clearly was not the custom in these parts to tell strangers more than elliptical half truths until one was quite sure of the reason for their curiosity. And even then, I was to discover, Miskitos are often not much more forthcoming.

The respectful way in which the youths around us treated the older man as they stood just within earshot of our conversation suggested that he was a figure of authority, and over the course of several more beers that evening he explained to me that he was the captain of a pirate lobster boat, sailing out of the Bay Islands but fishing almost exclusively, and entirely illegally, in Nicaraguan waters, where the lobster was more plentiful. The boys around us were his divers and canoe paddlers, thirty-eight of them in all, who would bring in about 4,000 pounds of stolen lobster, worth $40,000, during the two-week trip on which they were to embark the next morning after taking on stores.

The ship's owner paid half of that money to the captain, his divers and their canoe handlers, and they spent a good portion of it at Señora Castillo's, not least because she was the paymistress for the boat. The captain, he explained, would hand over to her all the money due to the crew-members, and she would pay it out to them, less what each one owed her for the rum and other goods he had bought. The origin of Señora Castillo's prosperity, then, was not hard to understand. Handling five boats like this, each making two trips a month, and taking a $500 commission from each trip for her duties as paymistress, she was earn-ing $5,000 a month even without the profits from her shop. And as the owner of the only store in town, with a captive clientele of about 200 free-spending, high-living young men with a taste for rum, those profits were extraordinary.

I spent the night in Señora Castillo's "guest house," the hut next door to her shop that she had filled with greasy mattresses and evil-smelling blankets for the use of boys too drunk to find their way back to their boats lying at anchor a couple of hundred yards off the beach. There were plenty of them that night, their last evening ashore for a fortnight, and they ensured that I slept little as they stumbled in one by one, tripping over their prostrate fel-lows in the clammy dark, crashing heavily into the walls or crawling back out again to retch into the ditch at the bottom of the steps.

Just before dawn a sudden gust of wind slammed a win-dow shutter back, freshening the foetid dormitory night in a rush of cool air, and as I started awake an immense thundercrack exploded overhead. Torrential rain dinned on the corrugated iron roof, sheets of lightning hung from horizon to horizon for seconds at a time and I gave up on sleep, stripping naked and stepping outside to drench myself in the sweet new water running off the eaves. I was glad that I was not putting to sea that morning with a hangover.

The rainclouds had blown over and the wind died to a steady draught off the sea as I set out later for Brus, but the sun lacked its customary ferocity. The sand was covered in delicate pinks, purples and cream by fragments of shell that stretched in a carpet, damp and firm underfoot. The waves fell gently and predictably, and I soon found myself in cruising mode at an even pace that seemed to replenish rather than sap my strength.

Brus, squatting at the end of Brus Lagoon and surrounded by forest and swamp, could not be reached on foot, but on Señora Castillo's radio I had arranged with a boatman from Brus to pick me up from the bar at the mouth of the lagoon, and we had agreed on a price for a *viaje expresso.* I reached the bar an hour or so before the midmorning rendezvous we had set and went for a swim. Splashing naked in the shallows and surveying the creamy length of the deserted palm-fringed beach from the turquoise water, I saw the coast for the first time as it would look later in my photographs, as the essence of a tropical paradise. Walking its length, hunting down canoes, haggling over the fare in a passenger dory, I had been living this journey from the perspective of the shore's inhabitants. Only now, with some time to spare and my journal up to date, with no one in sight and a strong urge to laze, did it occur to me that when I got out of the water I would crave an iced rum and coconut water with a trace of lime juice.

Two women approached, their outlines blurred by the shimmer of the heat now rising off the beach, and I shook off my tourist fantasies as I scurried up the sand to my rucksack to pull on a pair of shorts. They had walked from Rio Platano, they explained, because they had heard that I had called up a boat from Brus and wondered if they could come with me. They were lucky that the faceless voice who had identified himself on the radio as Juan Membreno and who promised to pick me up at half past ten was not a man of his word. *Viaje expreso,* I gathered, did not mean "express journey" in the sense that it was quickly accomplished, but rather that the journey was being made expressly for one passenger. We found some shade, pulled up some dead branches in the sand and sat down to wait by the side of the fifty-yard cut through which the sea raced into the lagoon as the tide came in.

The older of the two women, Josefina, was taking advantage of this unexpected opportunity to visit Brus to go and see her daughter, in secondary school there, and was clearly enjoying the prospect of a few days in town. She had pulled back her bush of African hair, sun-bleached an orange blonde at its frizzy ends, into a tight bow, and sported a bright yellow floral print frock that she swept out behind her as she lowered herself so as not to dirty it on the branch she was sitting on. From the plastic bag she had been carrying on her head she pulled out to show me the leather sandals she would start wearing when we reached Brus and a dozen sweet-bread rolls that she was bringing to her daughter.

"Maria's staying with her auntie," Josefina explained to me in simple-accented Spanish. "She looks after my little girl good, but she can't bake even a loaf of bread and Maria she just loves this *pan dulce.*" Josefina's companion, a sallow-faced, thin-lipped girl with lank black hair, had no shoes to put on when we arrived in town and was less ebullient. It turned out Sandra, barely out of her teens, was from Puerto Cabezas, way down south in Nicaragua, and was going to Brus to see the local judge. In Puerto, she told me, she had met a man who had moved in with her, and they had had three children in the space of four years. Then suddenly the man had upped and gone home to Rio Platano. Leaving her infants with their grandmother, Sandra had made her way up here, too, to see what he intended to do about his family. Nothing, it had transpired, so Sandra was going to complain to the judge about him. I wished her luck, but the chances were remote that a young single mother, and a foreigner to boot, could persuade the Honduran judicial system to force the father to pay any sort of maintenance.

Around one o'clock, in the stillness of the midday heat, we heard the approaching chug of a *toog-toog*, a long narrow dory named for the sound of its two-stroke inboard engine. A stubblefaced old boatman grinned at us from under his greasy blue denim baseball cap, introduced himself as Francisco and apologised for being late. Juan Membreno had not been able to come, he explained, and it had taken him all morning to find any petrol in Brus.

We sat in single file in the boat and set off across the grey-green lagoon. About twenty minutes out the engine spluttered, revived, choked again and died. The wind blew up as we wallowed, the sky darkened with new storm clouds, and from the back of the boat came a good deal of muttering, some vicious banging with a spanner and then Francisco's cheerful announcement that he had forgotten to check the oil before setting out and we appeared to be out of it.

Since forgetting to check the oil is a failing of mine, I would have been disposed to tolerance, except that as soon as Francisco did coax his engine back to life the waves, whipped by the freshening wind into whitecaps at the prow, began crashing over the gunwhales each time we dipped into a trough and breaking over my rucksack, which I had carelessly left out of the plastic trash bag I normally wrapped it in for journeys by sea.

Every quarter of an hour or so the engine would shudder to a halt again, and Francisco would spend five minutes tugging ineffectually on the starter cord, muttering and banging until for no apparent reason it consented to cough into a little more life. Josefina and Sandra launched into a double-barrelled barrage of abuse against Francisco's incompetence, and when I reminded them gently that they would not have been able to go to Brus at all if Francisco had not kindly agreed to fill in for Juan Membreño they rounded on me, saying forcefully that if they had known this was going to happen they would have walked back to Rio Platano and waited until another day.

I appreciated their anxiety. No aid was in sight: we were alone on the increasingly choppy lagoon surrounded by unbroken forest, and the periods when the engine was working were growing alarmingly short. Eventually, though, we limped into Brus through reedy channels of mustard-coloured water and slipped up alongside a short wooden jetty set into a yellow mudbank.

Brus Lagoon had once been known as Brewer's Lagoon before its eighteenth-century English residents had been forgotten and their name corrupted. Certainly no trace of anything of the least interest was to be found in the squalid collection of rundown houses, perched on their pilings amongst a sea of litter that made up the present-day town.

After an hour of enquiring about boats heading further down the coast, I found a gangly Miskito youth in a pair of ragged denim cutoffs sitting crosslegged on a pile of coconuts at the bottom of an enormous dugout. He said that his name was Douglas and that he worked on the boat. They would be leaving at midmorning the next day for Patuca and I was welcome to come along.

That evening, I celebrated my good fortune in finding just the boat I needed to put me in Patuca just in time to catch my ride to Lempira and give me the two days I needed to reach the UN camp on the eve of the date I had fixed with the Sandinistas to make the most delicate border crossing of my whole journey. At a newly built planking hut smelling strongly of creosote that had just opened its doors as a restaurant I ordered several beers. The Chinese-Miskito girl who served me was very sorry but the *bote* had not come in for over a week so there was not much food left. But by the same token they were serving shrimp that would normally have been sold to the merchant owner of the *bote*, and I gorged myself. I spent all evening drinking beer, as the restaurant owner sat by his boom box going through his collection of tapes. Caribbean rhythms predominated, the lilting, swaying thump of reggae, the Latin-influenced charge of *soca*, the more clipped, chirrupy beat of calypso. But in amongst these songs, smiling to himself and closing his eyes dreamily, the would-be deejay slipped in the occasional wailing lament of a Country and Western number, and the whole restaurant would sing along.

As the toads burped in the benighted swamps outside and the howler monkeys roared in the distant forest, I found the music that reached right to the Miskito soul. And it was sung by Conway Twitty.

"Dat son shine haat, mon," a voice called over to me as I stood at the end of the jetty the next morning, disconcerted to find neither Douglas nor his boat tied up there. I looked around and noticed an old man, wearing the inevitable baseball cap. I walked over and asked if he knew anything about my supposed ride. He didn't, but I sat beside him against the wall of a collapsing warehouse and wondered where he had learned his English.

"I com from Roataan, mon, bot I tek cold one night, ronnin dat toog-toog up de river, and dat trow me right down," he said. Dicky, as he called himself, had once owned a coconut grove out on the dunes beyond the lagoon, *"bot I had a woman an I got two little childen now an I caant raise dem childen out dere for de sanflies,"* he explained. *"Dat a lonely place for a man on him own, night aafter night, day aafter day, no one to taalk to. An den I come acraaas one Canadian feller an he juss crazy to buy my cocal so I sell it and now he SUFFRIN from dose sanflies."* Dicky was in town sorting out his business and putting the two houses he owned in Brus in his childrens' names. *"I got to straighten dat out good at de aafice, cos my plan, you see, is I not gonna forsake my little childen."*

I wondered about the children's mother. *"Well she a Miskita woman, see, an I don't rightly know whaat she'll do. Som time she say she want to com wid me, som time she say she stay wid her mother here. Right down to braas tacks, I don't know what her plan is."*

Meanwhile, Dicky was nursing his cold with plenty of rum in the evenings and plenty of rest in the shade in the daytime. In no hurry himself to return to Roatan he could not comprehend my anxiety at the absence of Douglas and his boat. *"He com by soon nuff, mon, doan fret. Probly ronning errands som place, bot he leave out today."* Since Dicky had told me earlier he had no idea who Douglas was I had little faith in his apparent familiarity with Douglas's whereabouts and plans, and unless I made Patuca that night I would miss my boat to Lempira and God knew what sort of problems that would entail. After a while I went in search of my missing boatman.

I asked at the general store, a long, gloomy building set on the largest and least worm-eaten wharf, full of empty oil drums and coils of rope in its dark corners, the creek water gurgling and slapping just below its floorboards. Nobody had heard of Douglas and nobody knew of a boat leaving for Patuca that day. I clambered from jetty to jetty, slipping on the slick mud of the creek banks, hunting for the boat I had seen the day before and asking after Douglas, but the men tinkering with ancient boat engines or bailing out their leaky canoes with old tin cans simply shook their heads, knowing neither who I was talking about, nor why I should be so desperate to find him. My clockwork plans, with each boat ride cogging neatly with the next, had been absurd, I realised.

Eventually, returning dejected to the general store, I was hailed by one of the men I had questioned earlier, who called me over and introduced me to the captain of Douglas's boat, a shifty-looking character with a broken nose and a squint. He explained to me in a matter-of-fact and uninterested manner that Douglas was merely the bowman, and slightly simpleminded at that, who did not know what he was talking about. There was no petrol in town and there wouldn't be until the *bote* came in, so he could not leave. Perhaps tomorrow around three in the afternoon. Why didn't I come by then to see.

That was no use to me. The Lempira boat was leaving Patuca at dawn the next day, and I was trapped in this decrepit bloody mudhole; the only escape was by boat, and nobody had any fuel. In mounting despair I did the rounds of the jetties again, this time asking after anyone who had enough petrol, and a boat seaworthy enough, to take me to Patuca on a *viaje expresso*. My enquiries were just as futile as my earlier efforts had been, and then a thought occurred to me. There was one man in Brus whom I might convince that he owed me a favour: Juan Membreño, who had agreed to pick me up at the bar the day before but who had not come, and instead dispatched a tardy and ill-prepared substitute.

I found Juan at home on his verandah overlooking a bare dirt yard, a dull-eyed man in a tattered string vest, sitting in a crudely made wooden rocking chair as he played with his infant grandson. He seemed ill at ease when I introduced myself, perhaps expecting me to chastise him for the events of the previous day, but he relaxed when I explained that I had come to ask for his help. He was clearly unwilling to interrupt his lazy morning, but the urgency of my need to get out of Brus made me insistent. Standing at the bottom of the steps up to his house, striking a despondent pose, I pleaded and cajoled and implored him, driving him back to his last line of argument, that he had no fuel. But he had had enough fuel the day before to make the trip to the bar, a journey he had not actually made, so didn't he still have that petrol left? Yes, he conceded. Then couldn't he at least take me back across the lagoon to the seashore, to a point from which I could walk to Patuca? He thought about this, pushed his baseball cap back from his forehead and acknowledged that he could, at a price.

The price was quickly agreed upon and an hour later we pushed off, poling the canoe down the creek until we came out of the reeds into the wind and the open water, turned northwards and headed towards the distant sand dunes. The clatter of the *toog-toog* engine made it impossible for either Juan or me to understand the few attempts we made at conversation so we soon gave up trying, and I lay back against my pack in the prow, revelling in the smell of salt on the wind. As we approached the far side of the lagoon, though, I began to worry. I could see only an unbroken wall of reeds, behind which undoubtedly lay swamp, and I could not see where Juan could possibly let me off.

He wasn't going to. Instead, taking a sighting from two palm trees to left and right, he nosed our boat into the reeds, cutting back the engine as we gently bottomed on the mud beneath and taking up his barge pole. For five minutes we nudged our way through a barely decipherable channel that scarcely admitted our width, until we came out into another lagoon, reedbound, windless and clogged with water lily pads. We continued to edge forward, picking our way between shoals of black mud, rotten treetrunks and the peaty banks of putrified water lily that glistened just above the surface. Juan would rise to his feet every now and again, his eyes seeking out the faint ripples on the water that indicated a trickle of current and a channel more than twelve inches deep as we crept our way across this stagnant rotting lagoon. When we reached the far end, Juan nudged the boat through a gap in the reeds and grounded in the soft mud. This, he explained, was as far as he could take me, and he pointed down a barely raised causeway that led through thick, swampy grass. That would lead me to the beach, he said.

I followed the path for a few hundred yards until it petered out into sand dunes. I clambered to the top of them and found myself leaning into a strong and scorching wind that blew hard into my face. Screwing up my eyes against the sand and the sun, I set off down the beach. The hop and skipping mood that had lightened my walk to Brus Lagoon bar the day before had deserted me. I had thought then that I would have to walk no further, that I would find boats all the way to Lempira. My body was protesting. My socks and hiking boots, which I was wearing because prolonged barefoot walking had blistered my heels, grew heavy as they filled with sand and water from the waves that foamed at my feet. The unrelenting wind blew steadily but brought no relief. Bent under the weight of my pack and of my self-pity, I plodded down the broad corridor of beach.

Two hours later I came upon a solitary man on the beach, a dark and motionless speck in the glaring desolation of the blasted sand, gravely regarding the waves. He swivelled his head as I approached, and stared at me levelly, but otherwise did nothing to acknowledge my presence. His tightly muscled limbs were black, but with the gaunt cheek-bones of an indian, he resembled an Australian aborigine, and he had an unsettling glint in his eyes. I stopped to talk to him, not because he hailed me or nodded a greeting but because he looked as though he might assault me and I felt that if I established even a tenuous thread of human contact he might decide not to.

He lived alone in this wasteland in a thatched hut behind the dunes where he had scratched away the scrub and planted a patch of spindly manioc plants. He ate fish and manioc, and spent his days on the beach, either squatting or holding a hand line, his only possession apart from a smoke-blackened pot, a pair of shorts and a singlet. This solitary savage was not at all surprised to see me, and knew perfectly well what I was doing there.

"You've come to mend the lighthouse, haven't you," he told me. "They've been waiting for you for months."

I had been mistaken for many things on this journey—doctor, missionary, spy, fishing-boat captain from the Bay Islands—but this was the first time anyone had taken me for a lighthouse repair man. The idea seemed doubly unlikely in view of the fact that there wasn't a lighthouse anywhere in sight. I agreed with him quickly that indeed I had come to mend the lighthouse. I had better be getting on now, I humoured him, if they had been waiting for me for so long. I hoped urgently to myself that the lighthouse in this crazed hermit's imagination lay in the direction of Patuca. It seemed to, for he did not call me back as I set off.

It was not long before I looked up from my dragging footsteps and saw, quaking in the distance and the heat haze, a lighthouse, striped red and white as a barber's pole. Whether or not it was in need of repair I could not tell, but I knew it was going to be a bloody nuisance. It obviously stood in or near Patuca, marking the rivermouth, and with a visible goal I could no longer fool myself that the village was just around the next point, only to chide myself for being overly optimistic when I had rounded the point and found nothing but more beach in front of me. On these long walks I would talk to myself constantly, no less mad, perhaps, than the fool on his lonely beach.

As I slowly drew nearer to the lighthouse, the beach broadened into a wind-whipped lunar surface, pitted and craggy, dotted with dead fish left by a receding tide and piled with the carcasses of treetrunks and branches that the sun and the salt had bleached silver. I picked my way wearily through this fallen driftwood forest until the beach ran out, choked by tangled thickets of mangrove spilling down to the waterline. However oily and uncomfortable the tramp steamer that would be picking me up the next morning, I thought, however noisy and boneshaking and smoky, I had had enough of nature's bloody profusion. Too exhausted even to remove my socks and boots, I waded through the breakers, dragging my aching legs, until I reached the next point and a view of the red roofs and whitewashed clapboard of Patuca, a mile or so away.

I was close to exhaustion as I collapsed onto the steps of the refugee agency depot that had become the hub of village life since the United Nations had set up a camp nearby for Nicaraguan Miskitos. A young man appeared in the doorway, looking somewhat disconcerted to find a sweaty and enervated Englishman lying prostrate at his feet, and introduced himself as Flavio, the local *jefe* for World Relief, the agency administering the UN camp.

It was Flavio with whom I had talked by radio from Rio Platano, and as I pulled myself into a chair on his porch I thanked him for having arranged my passage to Lempira on the next morning's boat.

"Ah," he said, hesitantly.

"Ah?" I asked back at him, my stomach sinking.

"Well, you see, in Ceiba it's carnival and the captain's from Ceiba and it's the weekend too . . ."

"The boat's not coming." I stated it as a fact, leadenly.

"No."

Already physically shattered, I felt all the hope drain out of me. This was it. This was where my journey ended, at a silted rivermouth lost among mangrove swamps with rain coming on. Between Patuca and Lempira lay a four-day walk, two uninhabited bars that I could not cross without a canoe and a thirty-mile stretch of lagoon. Impossible. I cried.

Flavio was aghast that a grown man could cry merely because a boat was not arriving on schedule on a coast where boats never arrived on schedule, especially when the boat was only going to Puerto Lempira. Puerto Lempira was a dump, he consoled me. I didn't want to go there anyway. I explained how the boat had been my last chance to reach Mocoron in time to cross the Nicaraguan border on the day I had been authorised to do so, and how it looked now as if I was stuck. Flavio, whose job comprised little else but solving logistical foul-ups to keep several thousand refugees fed and housed, was confident that somehow or other I would find a way out. Meanwhile dusk had fallen, there was nothing to be done until the next morning, and he was grateful for the presence of a stranger. We bought a bottle of rum and half a case of Coca-Cola and in the flickering glow of his paraffin lamp discussed the relative iniquities of each of the Central American governments until I had drunk myself to sleep.

Early the next morning, after searching fruitlessly throughout the village for somebody with a boat, a functioning engine and a drum of petrol, it became clear that I was not going to reach Lempira by sea. Since it was unreachable by land, that left an aeroplane as the only possibility. Patuca did have a length of relatively flat grassland that could be used as an airstrip, and Flavio knew a man in Lempira with a light aircraft, Mr. Osman, who ran an aerotaxi service when he wasn't flying for the CIA, the contras, the United Nations or any other organisation with business in the jungle and dollars in cash. The problem was how we were going to find him and persuade him to fly to Patuca.

All morning I sat by the radio, chanting Flavio's call sign into the microphone, *"del cinco, del cinco, Barra Patuca; del*

cinco, del cinco, Barra Patuca," trying to reach Osman's office
and hearing nothing but static in reply. When suddenly a
woman's voice did break through the crackle it was to tell
me that she did not know where Osman was, that he was
out with his plane somewhere and that she doubted she
could find him on a Saturday afternoon. The disapproval
in the voice was palpable even through the whine and hiss
of the radiowaves: Osman was almost certainly on the piss
in some godforsaken jungle clearing with some of his dis-
reputable friends.

My hope that she might be able to track him down was
a pretty forlorn one, but forlorn hopes were all that I had
left. Shouting in desperation I urged her to do her best to
find Osman and to tell him he could name his price for a
viaje expreso from Patuca to Lempira. She said she'd try.

What happened over the next few hours I never really
understood. Every fifteen minutes the woman's voice came
back to me over the air, squeezed into a squeak or drawn
out into a growl by whatever climatic conditions control
such distortions, and each time she plunged me deeper
into confusion, ignoring or unable to hear my pleas for
an explanation. First she told me the flight had been arranged. I was exultant, and asked her when it would arrive.
No answer. Then she called to say it had been cancelled.
I was downcast. I wanted to know why. Silence. Then
she was back, to say the price had gone up. I said I didn't
care. Had she heard me? No response. She had lost contact with Osman. She was confirming that the plane had
taken off for Patuca. No, her last message had been
wrong. The plane had not taken off at all and would not
be coming until Monday. This was all she had to say. It
was getting late and she was going home for the weekend.
Over and out.

I raved into the microphone, but I never heard another word from her. Dispirited, frustrated and helpless, I slumped into a hammock and sulked. My plight was too miserable to contemplate. I slept. I was woken by Flavio, shaking my shoulder. "The plane, the plane," he shouted. I heard a distant buzz, grabbed my rucksack and raced through the village. Rounding a corner, I caught sight of the plane at the end of the airstrip, its engines running, and as I approached it pulled around, ready to taxi away. Had Osman lost patience so quickly? I screamed above the clatter of the propellers, waved my arms madly and sprinted. Reaching the plane, I yanked open the door, piled my rucksack in and jumped after it, but Osman, sitting in the pilot's seat with a beery grin on his face, was not in a hurry after all.

"*Tek it easy, mon,*" he told me cheerily. "*You pay dis passage, I wait on you. Juss dat de battery doan work too good so I keep de engine ronnin and dat way I doan have to start her op agin.*"

As we bumped our way down the makeshift runway I strapped myself in and banged the door, trying to close it. Osman laughed. "*Dis old plane, mon. Need new battery, new door, new everyting. Dis door stay open, bot doan fret. De breeze kip it close.*"

Puerto Lempira was named after a heroic indian chief whose noble features glare proudly from Honduran banknotes, but there was nothing noble or heroic about the sweaty, sullen town skulking on the edge of Caratasca Lagoon. A few low municipal buildings of breezeblock and corrugated iron elevated Lempira from the status of village to regional capital of the Honduran Mosquitia, and its potholed roads were covered with gravel, but such pretentions could not disguise the town's self-conscious embarrassment at lying at the end of the world.

Its inhabitants all had the air of being up to no good, sidling suspiciously about their business with mistrustful looks on their faces, and the hot stagnant air, unmoved by a breath of wind, was heavy with intrigue. This was the headquarters of the eastern front of the US CIA's war against the Sandinistas.

The local CIA man's home was pointed out to me. Known as "Chuck Norris" to townspeople scornful of his self-importance but impressed by his helicopter, he lived in the middle of the dusty parade ground of the Honduran army barracks. There, surrounded by open space across which no one could creep without being detected, sat a ship's container, painted a dull red with a line of once-significant code letters stencilled in white. At one end of this squat box an entrance had been cut out with a blowtorch and filled with a heavy metal door. Onto one side an air-conditioning unit had been bolted. In that windowless tomb, certain of his security, lived the luckless American charged with organising the Miskitos into an effective armed struggle against Managua.

One way or another the Miskitos had been waging war on the Sandinista government since 1982, fighting what many of them saw as merely a renewal of their people's historic hostilities with the *Spainyards*, using American rather than British guns. Because while the Somoza family that ruled Nicaragua for forty years had been content to leave the coast alone and let its indians get on with their isolated lives, the Sandinista authorities had stormed in in 1979 full of revolutionary fervour and plans to incorporate the coast into the new Nicaragua they dreamt of.

Predictably this was not welcomed by a people who

hankered for their British colonial past, believed strongly
in the conservative precepts of the Moravian church and
never trusted anyone from Managua. Nor did the Sandinistas' passion for land reform and agricultural cooperatives
have the slightest relevance to traditional Miskito systems
of land tenure. The government's efforts to bring doctors
and teachers to the coast did not earn any praise either.
Many of them were Cubans, from Fidel Castro's hated
Communist stronghold, against which the Bay of Pigs invasion had been launched from this very coast, and even
if these socialist missionaries were well intentioned, their
comrades setting up the state security service were not,
and the latter were much more in evidence.

Nothing could endear the Sandinistas to their unwilling
citizens, not even the creation of their own organisation,
which the government had thought might help. Three
young Miskitos with secondary education, ambitious and
articulate, were put in charge of MISURASATA, which
stood for "Miskitos, Sumus, Ramas and Sandinistas Asla
Takanka," or "Working Together." They didn't work together for very long. While Brooklyn Rivera, Steadman
Fagoth and Hazel Lau got down to working out an autonomy charter for the Caribbean coast the Sandinistas began
worrying that the indians were going to secede. On the
coast itself, mutual incomprehension between the people
and their new masters was growing dangerously intense,
and in early 1981, when the MISURASATA leaders began
looking up old maps to see where the borders of the Miskito kingdom had been drawn and what the British protectorate had looked like, the Sandinistas threw them in
jail.

Scarcely had they been freed, after an outcry on the
coast, than Steadman Fagoth made a beeline for Honduras,

where he had heard that the Americans were secretly organising an anti-Sandinista guerrilla army. Brooklyn Rivera, slightly more wary of the former Somoza guardsmen
who made up the core of that army, went south to Costa
Rica. Hazel Lau was talked into cooperating with the
Sandinistas.

War broke out in earnest in 1982 when Sandinista
troops, enraged by the hit-and-run attacks that Fagoth's
men launched from Honduras across the Coco River, resorted to the brutal strategy of razing the earth, which is
the conventional army's wisdom in the face of guerrilla
insurgency. Government soldiers swept down the Coco
burning villages, killing cattle, hacking down fruit trees
and trampling crops. Twenty thousand Miskitos fled from
this rampage, scrambling to the opposite bank of the river
to become refugees. Another 10,000, not forewarned in
time, were trucked 50 miles south and herded into relocation camps that the Sandinistas had christened *Tasba Pri*,
"free homeland" in Miskito.

The CIA, at that time in the process of creating the
contras, was handed a golden opportunity. An entire people, living along several hundred miles of the Sandinistas'
poorly defended eastern flank, in ideal country for guerrilla
warfare, had become the government's sworn enemy. The
flood of refugees provided a ready pool of young men eager
to take up arms. The Honduran government was ready to
let them organise and train on the pine-studded plains
north of the Coco and to seek refuge there after sorties
into Nicaragua.

The opportunity was lost. Over the course of six years
of bribes and threats and pressure and manipulation, CIA
operatives were never able to overcome the violent rivalry
between Rivera and Fagoth, nor create a credible leader

who would do Washington's bidding, nor put many more than a thousand men into the field at any one time. For it was not long before it dawned on even the slowest-witted Miskito footsoldier that the United States knew little and cared less about indian rights in the Mosquitia and was interested in the Miskitos only as pawns in their greater battle against Managua. As manifesto after manifesto from contra headquarters in Miami failed to say anything about Miskito rights, as the contra leadership repeatedly failed to find room for a Miskito representative, as the anti-Sandinista *Spainyards* proved themselves just as racist as the Sandinista *Spainyards*, the Miskito warriors' morale sunk and their keenness to engage in battle wilted.

By 1985, the government had had plenty of time to rue the results of its cruel and disastrous policy towards the coast, and more importantly had wrenched itself away from the Latin American Left's tradition of regarding all problems with ethnic minorities as a question of class.

The Sandinistas concluded that the coast could be quietened only with political concessions, and set about drafting their own autonomy statute for the region. Meanwhile they began ceasefire negotiations with individual guerrilla field commanders, letting them keep their guns and stay in place if they promised to stop attacking the Sandinista army. Unit by unit the government neutralised the military threat and in 1987 unveiled a plan that gave the Miskitos, Sumus, Ramas and blacks limited but significant control of their political and economic affairs.

By the time I arrived in Puerto Lempira an uneasy temporary truce had been declared the length of the coast, leaving YATAMA, as the anti-Sandinista guerrillas were known, in control of the lower Coco River and a large stretch of country running south from the border. To travel in that area I needed permission from YATAMA, and in Puerto Lempira I hoped to find someone of sufficient authority to issue me with a *laissez-passer*. I had been given a rough address and a *nom de guerre;* I was looking for *Tigre 17*, who could be found three blocks west and one block south of the Moravian mission school.

I found five decrepit houses on that block set back from the street in a patch of rough grass. In the flaccid empty hours of mid-Sunday afternoon the shutters on all the houses were closed. Nothing moved. I strolled up the street trying to look nonchalant, eyeing the houses as I went and wondering which was most likely to be home to a Miskito guerrilla commander and his family. As I reached the corner and turned to walk round the block two dark-skinned youths ambled towards me, their arms around each other's shoulder. They wore grubby T-shirts and old jeans, but their feet gave the lie to these civilian clothes. Both boys wore US Army-issue combat boots, heavy, thick-soled black-leather jobs that all the YATAMA fighters used. I asked them which house "the Nicaraguans" lived in.

"Nicaraguans in Puerto Lempira?" one of them asked with faked surprise. "All the Nicaraguans are in the refugee camp in Mocoron."

That was the official line; the Honduran government insisted vigorously at every opportunity that it did not allow Nicaraguan guerrillas to operate from its territory, but it was scarcely a secret that Lempira was teeming with YATAMA troops who could do as they liked so long as they kept their weapons out of sight. I dropped my voice to a conspiratorial whisper.

"I'm from the agency. I have a message for *el Tigre*."

The teenage soldiers pointed to one of the dilapidated huts I had just walked past. I retraced my steps and called softly to announce my presence. After a moment an unseen hand twitched aside the cotton sheet that was hanging in the doorway and a woman's face appeared. I told her who I was looking for, she frowned and withdrew. From inside the house I heard agitated whispers. The woman poked her head back out again and asked who I was. I told her my name and said I had been sent by *Comandante* Blas, the YATAMA military operations chief. I hadn't seen Blas in a couple of years, but I knew he was the most widely respected of the military commanders across a broad spectrum of feuding warlords. His seemed the safest name to drop.

More whispering followed, until I was beckoned in surreptitiously. I stepped into the darkness of the hut and could feel several pairs of eyes on me as my own grew accustomed to the shadows. The inspection felt curious rather than hostile, though, and as soon as I could make out something other than silhouettes in the gloom my heart leapt with surprise and relief; sitting on the bed was a man I recognised, a bearlike *comandante* I had interviewed a year or so earlier. Raul Tobias remembered me, too, with an enormous grin. His hefty handshake was open and warm, and as he introduced me to his colleagues as *"mi amigo periodista,"* everyone relaxed. Nobody opened the shutters, though.

When I explained what I was doing and that I needed a *permiso* to travel freely through YATAMA-controlled territory, Raul insisted that the man I ought to talk to was Wycliffe Diego, a man whose Godfearing parents had christened him after the medieval Bible translator and who himself had taken to the cloth as a Moravian pastor before the Americans had made him YATAMA's political leader.

The CIA had picked Diego primarily because as a pastor

he commanded respect from Miskito civilians and was internationally palatable when he was needed to lobby Congress in Washington—and because he was submissive. His authority over military commanders in the field—the men whose help I would be counting on inside Nicaragua—was minimal. But none of the YATAMA high command were in town, Raul told me, and Wycliffe was. He would take me to see him.

It was hard not to feel sorry for Wycliffe Diego. Although I had heard him harangue his followers at a public meeting, speaking in the manner of a tetchy schoolmaster berating wayward pupils, in private conversation he suffered from an excruciating stutter. A short, mousy man, he was painfully deferential towards foreigners and always oddly anxious to help reporters. Having been plucked from his life as a backwoods preacher in the wilds of Nicaragua, he was horribly out of his depth in the treacherous currents of international diplomacy and he knew only too clearly that he was being used. In every word he spoke you could hear his apology for having allowed himself to be manipulated in such an undignified manner.

I found him that evening in a small plywood-walled hotel room bare of any furniture but a bed and a stool, and he was only too happy to help me. Since all the lights had gone out in the hotel, and he didn't have a table at which to write, we went across the road to a bar, and there he composed my permit.

"*Naha waitna na, witin periodista kum sa England country ba wina,*" it began. Whether anyone to whom it was addressed would pay any attention I had no idea, but at least it would reassure any suspicious and nervous guerrillas I might come across that I was known to their leader. I hoped.

NINE

T hat Monday morning at the UN camp in Mocoron
I found the administrative building besieged by
refugees waiting to hear their names called out by
the brisk young woman from the capital who was distributing money. Tomorrow these families would be returning
to Nicaragua, and if they faced an uncertain future, so many
years of homelessness and a life without purpose had finally
numbed them to the hazards they were about to confront.

The women were gathered to one side. Some of the
younger ones suckled infants, looking defiantly about them
and hoping that they had made the right decision. A few
old crones, their long grey hair tied up in headscarves,
were going back to ensure that they died in their ancestral
villages and not as strangers in an artificial town set in a
distant plain run by foreigners. The men stood separately,
their worn and dirty trousers tucked into wellington boots,
their eyes shaded by the visors of baseball caps, cautious
from so many years of trouble. They had come to confirm
that they had indeed decided to go home, and to collect
the fifty dollars that each adult was entitled to and the

twenty five dollars per child. After years of indignity and dependence, this was the last handout they would have to suffer; the money was their own bridge to a life they would at last be able to build themselves.

Inside, in the thatched and shuttered cool of the office of the local representative of the UN High Commissioner for Refugees, a sense of order prevailed. The Frenchman in charge, with the eyes of a spaniel accustomed to regular beatings, quite understood that I wanted to cross the border, and why, and when and how, and would be perfectly happy to put me on a truck tomorrow with the refugees. Except that he did not have the authority to do so. Only the colonel, he told me regretfully, could permit such a passage across the frontier. It was clear from the manner in which he referred to the colonel that the Frenchman had suffered only arbitrary injustice and humiliation at his hands, and that I could expect nothing less myself. The colonel, head of the Fifth Battalion of the Honduran army and the local military authority, liked to call himself the new king of the Miskitos, I was told, for the power he wielded in his autonomous fiefdom. He also enjoyed a reputation for liking to make other people's lives miserable.

I said that in that case I had better ask the colonel's permission to accompany the refugees the next morning. The Frenchman looked mournful. He had himself been hoping to talk to the colonel for three days but had not succeeded in securing an audience. I was welcome to try. And if I did manage to see him, would I mind passing on the message that the UNHCR chief would like a word?

I walked the three miles down the gravel track through the pine forest that led to the Fifth Battalion headquarters until I came to a brightly painted red-and-white striped wooden pole stretched across the road. A pair of suspicious eyes peered at me through the gun slit in a sandbagged sentry post. I explained that I had come to see the colonel and could I kindly pass. The eyes did not change their expression, but I heard a snigger. I hesitated. Sometimes, I had found in dealing with half-witted Honduran soldiers, it was worth adopting a tone of authority, hoping they would respond to that rather than to the sight of a scruffy foreign journalist. The snigger, however, did not suggest a half-wit. It sounded more as if the colonel had instilled his taste for arbitrary power into even his lowliest sentry. I decided to be polite.

An explanation of who I was and what I wanted elicited only a hand stretched through the gun slit and a curt order. *"Pasaporte."* I complied, and heard the sentry crank up his field telephone. "Post number one to the colonel's office," I heard him shout. "Request for audience with the colonel. Ford, Peter. British. Journalist." He waited for a response. Outside the sentry box, under the sun, feeling very alone in the emptiness, I waited for a response. It arrived, a throaty crackle over the primitive phone line. The hand reappeared, proffering my passport. I took it. The eyes reappeared. "Request refused."

It was spoken so definitively that further enquiry seemed futile, but I could scarcely leave it at that. Could I perhaps return at an hour more convenient to the colonel? "I don't know." Could he ring the colonel's office again to find out? "No." Was I unable to see the colonel because he had refused to see me or merely because he was not there at the moment? "I don't know." Could he ring the colonel's office again to find out? Even as I asked I guessed the response. Out of principle rather than hope I wrote a note addressed to the colonel explaining who I was and what I wanted from him, and pushed it through the gun slit, asking that my message be passed on. The sentry just grunted.

For the next four days I laid siege to the colonel, dogging his imagined footsteps, pouncing on every jeep that emerged from his headquarters from dawn to dusk one day and never setting eyes on him. I had lost the chance of crossing the border on the day I had appointed with the Sandinistas, and very possibly I had lost the chance of crossing altogether. As I lay on my bed between sorties, suffocating in the cell that Don Charlie, a baggy-faced Chinaman and owner of Mocoron's sole restaurant, had rented to me, my goal of reaching Nicaragua developed into a monstrous obsession, fed by my mute, helpless fury at being so capriciously frustrated.

I learned from a UNHCR official who had spoken to the colonel's deputy that he had definitely received the note I had left for him. He knew I was in Mocoron, he knew I was desperate to get out, he knew he was the only person who could authorise my departure and he was being very careful to do nothing that might be construed as helpful. He was not avoiding me; it would have been beneath his dignity to go out of his way to avoid a straggling Englishman in need of his favour. But he was confident that his movements were sufficiently unpredictable, his subordinates sufficiently secretive and his means of transport sufficiently varied (one day he flew to Tegucigalpa by helicopter from his army base, thwarting the guard I had mounted on the refugee camp airstrip) to make him well nigh impossible to track down.

Until Thursday morning. As I sat outside my room watching Don Charlie's mongrel dog worrying at a tired old sow that lay in the dust of the yard, Charlie emerged from his kitchen, threw a stone at his dog and told me

casually that he had seen the colonel driving towards the
army post by the landing strip. About half an hour ago.
He hadn't told me earlier because he was eating his breakfast. The colonel was probably gone by now. But it was
worth a look, he thought. I bounded out of the yard and
raced the 500 yards to the airstrip. Bumping towards me
up the track from the army post came an open-topped
jeep. I stood in the middle of the path and the jeep pulled
up. At the end of the gravelled landing strip, shimmering
away into the distance, we were alone. At the wheel sat a
dour flat-faced man in mirrored aviator shades and camouflage fatigues. No rank insignia or name patch indicated
his identity.

"I'm looking for the colonel."

"Why?"

"To ask him for a permit." The driver looked at me
impassively and left his engine running, but he shifted the
gear into neutral. *He's going to listen to me.*

"To do what?"

"To cross the border with the refugees at Leimus."

"There's no customs post here. Foreigners are obliged
to go through customs." My mouth went dry.

"*Migracion* in Tegucigalpa gave me preliminary permission." I showed him the scribbled authorisation I had secured in the capital after so much cajoling. "But they said
the final decision would be the colonel's."

He grunted. He clearly liked his butter laid on even
thicker.

This was my only chance to continue my journey, I
pleaded. The book I planned to write depended on his
magnanimity, I grovelled. He was the only man who could
help me, I beseeched.

I had leaned one hand against the bonnet of the jeep.

It seemed too familiar. I removed it and shifted to a more respectful stance, my hands behind my back. That was too abjectly schoolboyish. I folded my arms across my chest. The colonel merely stared silently from behind his sunglasses, revelling in my discomfort. On one of his fleshy fingers resting on the steering wheel a large purple stone set in a bulky bronze graduation ring caught the sun. He pushed his forage cap back. "You need a UNHCR permit," he parried.

"I have it." I handed him the letter that the UNHCR chief in Tegucigalpa had written for me. He grunted again.

"But they know they have to send a note to the Armed Forces Public Relations office and they have to give their permission for this."

"At the Public Relations office they said the decision was yours," I insisted.

"Who told you that?"

"The people in the office," I said lamely. I hadn't actually visited the PR office, and it seemed wise to be as vague as possible.

He shifted one booted foot onto the jeep's running board and stared at me. I stared at my reflection in his sunglasses.

"When would this border crossing take place?"

I'm winning. "As soon as possible. There's a special repatriation tomorrow morning at seven-thirty."

"But I have an office and it's not here."

"If you did give me permission, a UNHCR driver has told me he could pick it up from your headquarters this evening," I pressed.

He snorted, but not a muscle moved in his face. He asked for my full name. I handed him my passport and he read it. "Give the permit to Lieutenant Ballesteros at the frontier." He put his jeep back into gear and drove away. He had never told me directly that he would give me a permit. He had never actually acknowledged that he was the colonel. But that night, my permit was duly written, stamped, signed and sealed. I would be allowed out of Honduras. Would I be allowed into Nicaragua?

I added an unexpected word to my skeletal Miskito vocabulary the next morning, helping a family load its sacks of belongings into the open-topped truck that would carry us the fifty kilometres to the Coco River. One sack, tied firmly at the neck, wriggled and meowed as I passed it up. The Miskito word for a cat, I learned, is *poosi*. That is the English word too, I said. A woman loading her own possessions looked at me as though I was simple. "What do you mean?" she asked. "The English for *poosi* is 'minnie.' "

The returning refugees were beginning their lives again with pitifully little. One boastful fool had spent his family's repatriation money on a showy radio-cassette player and was playing it loudly for all to hear. When the batteries he had bought ran out he would have no more use for his expensive toy: batteries were all but unobtainable in Nicaragua. Most had been more cautious, settling for new clothes, wellington boots, kerosene lamps and sacks of vegetables as their defence against uncertainty.

The refugees who were staying behind, still too wary of the Sandinistas' promises to risk another trauma, stood around the six trucks looking sceptical, stretching out their hands uncertainly for a farewell clasp as one by one the engines choked into life. On board, the atmosphere was charged with noisy excitement. Never had I seen a group of Miskitos in such a good mood. When the convoy stopped at a military checkpoint on a rise we all looked out over the pine tops into the grey distance. "That's Nicaragua," someone said, and the truck fell silent for a moment as everybody stared.

The Coco is a sacred river to the Miskitos, especially to those who live along its shores, a focus of their culture and a unifying myth signifying plenty. Only on maps is it a dividing line, spelled out as the frontier adjudicated by the International Court of Justice at The Hague on 18 November 1960. When we arrived, a torrential rain was whipping the muddy current into a froth and shrouding the far side from view, but that was the least of my troubles. The UNHCR official from the Nicaraguan side told me that I could not cross with the refugees in the giant canoes (although I could pay a boatman later if I liked), that he would not give me a ride to Puerto Cabezas, that as far as he was concerned I had no right to be there and that he had had too many "tourists" entering Nicaragua like this.

An arrogant, beaky-nosed Spaniard who insisted on speaking to me in his pitiful English under the impression that he spoke it fluently, Jorge Delamotta had an extremely high opinion of himself. In his egocentric imagination he had sloughed off his identity as a lowly bureaucrat trying to organise five canoes in the rain in the back of beyond, and had become singlehandedly responsible for the resettlement of the entire Miskito people. This was tiresome, but there was nothing to be done about it except be patient. I sat under a dripping tree and watched him sliding around in the mud dispatching his canoes until the last one was about to leave, half empty. I suggested, in as reasonable a voice as I could muster, that I would not be causing him any difficulties if I jumped on too. He relented.

My appearance at the end of a queue of Miskito indians

filling out their entry forms in the chaotic gloom of the Nicaraguan customs post clearly struck the immigration officer behind the counter as irregular. And if there was one thing that a low-ranking Sandinista official disliked more than anything else, it was an irregularity that might call for some initiative to be taken. Lieutenant Ricardo Zuniga knew what to do with irregularities: send them back where they came from.

All my efforts to alert the Sandinista authorities to my plans had been in vain. Lieutenant Zuñiga had never heard of me. No, he had not been expecting me last Tuesday. No, he had no orders to let me pass. No, foreigners were not authorised to enter Nicaragua here, especially when they had no Honduran exit stamp in their passports as I did not. No no no no no. He had not even deigned to look at the letter that I was intending to use to open every official door on the coast in Nicaragua, a letter of support from the top two Sandinista officials in the region. I had been given it just before leaving Managua three months earlier, and I had been counting on it as a passe-partout in an area where normally every foreign visitor was obliged to register his every step a week in advance.

1988: POR UNA PAZ DIGNA, PATRIA LIBRE O MORIR

read the letterhead, the 1988 slogan that introduced every official Nicaraguan document that year.

Dated 2 March and addressed to me, *Comandante* Guerrillero Lumberto Campbell, the top Sandinista at the southern end of the coast, and *Subcomandante* Jose Gonzalez, the boss in Puerto Cabezas, the letter announced that they "support your project of writing a book about the Atlantic

Coast of Central America and do not doubt that the results of same will be important study material for our work.

"Before entering Nicaraguan territory it would be helpful if you could inform us of the date and of the route you intend to follow in order that we can issue the appropriate instructions to facilitate your mission."

I forced Lieutenant Zuñiga to read this missive and looked at him triumphantly. He could scarcely turn me back if I had Campbell and Gonzalez's blessing.

"But you didn't inform anyone of the date you were coming," he said truculently.

"Oh yes I did. My wife told the Interior Ministry in Managua that I would be arriving last Tuesday, and when I was delayed I sent a note with the UNHCR officials for *Subcomandante* Gonzalez telling him I would be coming over later in the week."

"Well we didn't hear anything. And anyway, it's expired."

"What's expired?"

"This letter. It's dated March 2nd. That's nearly three months ago."

In vain I tried to explain that this was not a permit valid for a certain length of time, it was a letter written on the eve of my departure from Managua and its contents did not go stale over time like the corn tortilla that Lieutenant Zuñiga was chewing on as he heard me out. My arrival was all highly irregular and that was all there was to it. But he did not appear eager to send me back into Honduras, at least not immediately, so I thought it better not to force the issue until I had come up with some more arguments. I was trapped in a no-man's-land on the frontier and in the no-man's-land of Lieutenant Zuñiga's indecision as he wrestled to match my unexpected and troublesome presence to the rules and regulations he lived by. It was the meticulous care with which I saw him inspecting each of the 245 immigration forms the refugees had filled out that suggested an argument that might make sense to him.

I sidled back up to the counter. "If you won't let me into Nicaragua," I asked innocently, "what do you suggest I do?"

"We could find you a boat across the river," he told me.

"Back into Honduras?"

"Yes."

"But the Honduran authorities on the other side are only there for the refugees and they are only allowed to let people out of the country, not into it," I said.

"Really?"

"And that means that they don't have any entry forms at their immigration post. I couldn't possibly get past them."

That clinched it as far as Lieutenant Zuñiga was concerned. If the Hondurans didn't have the right forms then there was no point at all in sending me back. I would have to come into Nicaragua, but he would have to talk to his superiors in Puerto Cabezas to ask for further instructions. That was all I wanted.

In Puerto Cabezas, I was confident, Chepe Gonzalez would be able to sort everything out. But Lieutenant Zuñiga's radio was out of action and Jorge Delamotta said he could not possibly allow anyone other than UNHCR personnel to use the radio in his jeep. Up until then their common reluctance to let me pass had made allies of Delamotta and Zuñiga, but now that the Lieutenant had decided I could not go back to Honduras he began to see my presence as an opportunity rather than a problem. If I had to go to Puerto Cabezas I also had to be accompanied.

For Lieutenant Zuñiga Puerto Cabezas was home, and a great deal more attractive than the woebegone, rain-sodden customs post he was stationed at. His indecision vanished.

"You are being detained," he told me. "You will be taken under escort to Puerto Cabezas." I almost held out my hands to be cuffed, I was so glad to be arrested. Lieutenant Zuñiga did not feel such dramatic gestures were called for, but he did unholster his pistol and kept it on his lap as we jolted down the track. He kept his weapon at the ready not for my benefit, I found, but for fear of ambush, as we drove past a gutted military transport rusting in the ditch. Too many government vehicles had been set upon by Miskito guerrillas, and Lieutenant Zuñiga had little faith in the truce that had recently been declared.

Nor did Sublieutenant Mario, who ran the Interior Ministry post at La Tronquera where we halted to radio Puerto Cabezas. Installed as the chief of internal security in this remote village full of surly Miskitos who talked behind his back in a language he didn't understand, the Sublieutenant had surrounded himself with the familiar and reassuring symbols of the revolution he served. Hung on the walls of his clapboard office, as he sat behind a monstrous ancient typewriter and a pile of snub-nosed M-79 shells, were an AK-47 assault rifle, a bunch of olive-drab knapsacks and ammunition belts and a banner in the red and black colours of the Sandinista Front depicting a youth brandishing a book in one hand and a rifle in the other. Below a photograph of the nine supreme Sandinista *comandantes* he had written down the three cardinal rules that succoured him during the long nights of uncertainty about whether enemy assassins were prowling outside his window.

"Philosophers have only interpreted the world in various ways. The point is to change it." —K. MARX.

"The great cardinal problem of all philosophy, especially of modern philosophy, is the relationship between thinking and being."　　—F. ENGELS.

"Marx's doctrine is all powerful because it is exact, complete and ordered, and it gives people a monolithic conception of the world."　　—V. I. LENIN.

When the Sublieutenant had finished informing his superiors in Puerto Cabezas that he had in his charge a loose Englishman with an out-of-date letter and we were waiting for instructions, he gravely explained the relationship between being and thinking. How much success was he going to have with the Sandinistas' new "hearts and minds" campaign among the indians if he went on like this?

It was not long before Puerto Cabezas came back on the radio. I was to be taken to the Immigration office there immediately for questioning. Silently I rejoiced. In Puerto I should at least be able to find an official with sufficient authority and sense to concede that letters of introduction did not expire.

Subcomandante Julio Rugama, a slim mustachioed young man with canny eyes and four bright brass echelons on the epaulettes of his newly pressed green uniform, had as much authority as anyone in Special Zone I, as northern Zelaya had become known in Sandinista-speak. He was the senior officer of the Interior Ministry, the minister's personal delegate. What he said, went. He was also the head of the secret police, and he wanted to know what I thought I had been doing, entering the country at an unauthorised border post at a spot adjacent to enemy-held territory.

I apologised, explained and tendered the oft-folded, torn and rather damp letter that Gonzalez and Campbell had written for me. He agreed that it had not expired. I thanked him. He regretted that warning of my arrival had never been passed to his office. So did I. How did I intend to proceed? I explained that I planned to return to the Coco River near where I had crossed, and then follow it downstream to the sea before turning south down the coast and thus back to Puerto, before continuing south towards Bluefields. I wanted his authorisation to make this journey.

"I wish I could help you," he said affably, leaning across his desk to offer me a cigarette. "But we don't have a single soldier anywhere you say you are going. Having my written permission would not just be worthless it would be dangerous. That's all contra territory. What are you going to do about the contras?"

I hesitated. To tell him merely that I would deal with them when I found them was not going to wash. He would not let me drive out of Puerto towards rebel-held areas so ill-prepared: he was, after all, nominally responsible for the whole of Special Zone I and felt partially responsible for my safety. On the other hand, to tell the chief of Sandinista security that I'd cleared everything in advance with the enemy and that they had issued me safe-conduct passes seemed to be inviting suspicion. I coughed. The *Subcomandante* raised his eyebrows. I could not dissemble.

"Well, yes, I'd thought about that," I conceded. "And, umm, to be on the safe side you see, just in case, I umm, went to talk to one or two of them."

"And what did they tell you?"

Reluctantly, I pulled from my money belt the letter that

Wycliffe Diego had written me, and one that the best-known Miskito rebel leader, Brooklyn Rivera, had made out a few months earlier when I had visited him in Costa Rica. I was particularly nervous about showing Rugama the letter from Brooklyn. More than a safe conduct pass it was a warmly expressed recommendation typed on YATAMA-headed writing paper describing me as "an honest and upright person" and urging "indigenous brothers to give him all support and collaboration" on my journey. He could scarcely have broadcast more clearly my sympathy for the Miskito cause, and I had thanked him for his help when he had drafted the letter. Now, sitting across from the *Subcomandante* as he read through it for a second time, I felt that perhaps I had not been wise to show it to him.

Rugama pushed the piece of paper across the desk towards me and tapped it deliberately with his forefinger. I held my breath. "With a letter like that in your possession," he said, looking hard into my eyes, "travelling in Nicaragua at a time when US-funded Miskito guerrillas are fighting an undeclared war against the popular Sandinista government . . ."

He paused. I swallowed.

". . . I would say that with this letter you can go anywhere you want on the coast and you won't have any trouble."

He smiled at the way he had taken me aback. "No, really, I mean it. In the places you are going an authorisation from Rivera is of much more use than anything I can make out. You are free to go."

He rose to leave, but while he was there and in such a flexible mood I wanted to sort out a few details like getting an entry stamp in my passport. And would he mind, just for the sake of it, writing me out permission to visit all the villages I would be passing through? After all, they were officially in Nicaragua, and you never knew when a permit like that might be useful.

"You write out the permit yourself and I'll sign it on Monday morning when I've told the army what you are up to," he said breezily, opening the door and striding past Lieutenant Zuñiga, who had been waiting outside. My erstwhile jailer smiled at me. "No hard feelings?" he asked. I acknowledged that by being an unhelpful bureaucratic bastard he was probably only doing his job. Anyway, he was the only person in Puerto Cabezas that I knew and I felt like company. We went to find a drink.

There was nothing in town to drink except rum and rainwater. The beer truck from Managua hadn't been seen for weeks, and even Lieutenant Zuñiga, hardened to the vicissitudes of life on the Nicaraguan periphery, would not touch the scarlet cherryade, smelling of nail-polish remover, which was the only soft drink left. We argued about where to go. I wanted to find a bar in the part of town where there was no electricity; that way we would be spared the severe neon that stripped a room of every shadow and the deafening music that went with it. Lieutenant Zuñiga's sole priority was ice, and he was intransigent.

I bowed to his singleness of purpose, and he led me through the rutted streets and up some steps into a plain rectangular wooden room with a bar at the far end protected by a heavy iron grille. Under the harsh light, at rows of formica tables the colour of congealed iguana blood, groups of diners scooped up spoonfuls from the mounds of rice and boiled shrimp before them. Lieutenant Zuñiga spotted a knot of uniformed army friends and pulled me over towards their table. I tried to suggest that we could find somewhere less grim, but over the noise of the reggae from the record player on the bar I could not make myself heard. The lieutenant's friends pulled up two chairs and I squeezed in as a waitress brought a bottle of rum, a plastic jug of water, a bowl of ice and two tall beakers. Wordlessly, as I diluted shots of rum into cloudy draughts and drank them down one after the other, all thought of conversation drowned by the music, I wondered whether it would be unacceptably rude to stand up and leave.

I was spared the decision. As I reached for another shot of rum the light overhead flickered, the music ground to a rumble, and the electricity went off. The chorus of cat-calls, whistles and boos that arose to fill the silent darkness did nothing to bring it back. Lieutenant Zuñiga and his friends reasoned that if the power had been switched off from this part of town, perhaps it had been turned on elsewhere. They trooped off in search of more neon. I stayed in the rapidly emptying bar and enjoyed the rest of the bottle in the dim light of a hurricane lamp, listening to the giant frogs in the ditch outside send up their persistent mechanical croaks.

In the days of the English, Puerto Cabezas had been known as Bragman's Bluff, for the low sandstone cliff that held the town clear of the breakers on the stony beach below. But it was the Americans who had lent the town its fleeting prosperity. Digging gold from the nearby mines of Bonanza, tapping rubber from the jungle, cutting timber from the stands of pine, planting bananas on swampy riverbanks or canning turtlemeat from the Cays offshore, American companies had shipped their booty through Puerto Cabezas from the early years of the twentieth century in continuous cycles of boom and bust.

239

The Miskitos had proved willing workers. Slowly they were weaned away from their subsistence lifestyle, developing a taste for the food and clothes and other goods that came from "*de out.*" That they were growing dependent on the imported merchandise, and had to spend their earnings to pay for it, went unnoticed, and in many men's memories, those were glory days. "*Ennyway I waan go work, go, an ennyway you can go work,*" one old man explained to me about the *foss times* of his youth. "*Bushwork, mahaagany, pine, saamill, dese are fishboat work, ennywhere you mekkin sumtin money line. Buy yo clodes, feed yo chilren dem, yo mudders dem, buy cattle dem, haars. Well who want live good live. Bot who waant drink only rom, he no have nottin.*"

By the time I was making my journey there had been no more companies on the coast for the past twenty years. They pulled out when there was no more money to be made, and they left their Miskito workers stranded between the disappearing stern of the last steamer and the remains of a culture they had in large part abandoned.

I went to evensong at the neat little whitewashed Moravian church, a sober wooden structure redeemed from austerity by its red window frames, painted to match the zinc roof and spire. Inside, its only adornment was an ancient clock, whose pendulum marked time with the measured cadence of the Reverend Shogreen's sermon.

The Reverend Andy Shogreen, a moon-faced bespectacled black man, preached in English to his congregation made up mostly of plump matrons squeezed into starched Sunday dresses. It was Mother's Day, and the Reverend Shogreen did not approve of Mother's Day. It led men to think that only mothers were responsible for children, whereas the Bible commanded us to honour our mother *and* our father. Mother's Day was just another aspect of the double standard on virginity from which women in Puerto Cabezas suffered. This all seemed rather advanced stuff from a conservative Protestant preacher, and I flipped through the Moravian hymnal to see if anything like it could be found in the church's approved texts. There, in the Litany, I came across a prayer to be used in times of war. "Grant, O Lord, unto the President of the United States, in these times of danger, Thy gracious counsel, that in all things he may approve himself the father of the people."

With the president of the United States funding a war against the Nicaraguan government, the Reverend Shogreen had found this an embarrassing supplication, and an "erratum" slip had been pasted over it to offer a more general prayer that the Lord might "deliver us from the sins that give rise to war." But it could not disguise the fact that as far as most Miskitos were concerned, God was naturally on America's side, and there was not much the Sandinistas could do about that.

I asked the Reverend Shogreen for a letter of introduction to Moravian pastors I might come across in no-man's-land and in YATAMA-controlled areas. The wider the range of safeconducts I could gather, the more confident I would feel. He gave me one, but it was a member of his congregation who offered me the most practical piece of advice that I had heard on how to handle the next leg of my journey.

To go where I was going it was all very well having permits from both sides in this war, he explained to me when we fell into conversation after the service. But when I came across a patrol in the jungle, how was I to know which army it belonged to? After all, soldiers from both sides carried the same AK-47 assault rifles, and they all mixed and matched their battle fatigues according to what they had pulled off the dead bodies of their enemies and which style of camouflage they favoured. I could get into serious trouble if I ran into the rebels, mistook them for the regular army and produced my letter from *Subcomandante* Gonzalez, he pointed out.

I told him Rugama had said the Sandinistas had withdrawn all their troops from the river and from the coastline. I expected to be dealing only with rebel troops.

"*Dis cese al fuego, mon, it laas joss so laang as de Sondinistas seh so,*" he scoffed. "*Todeh dere no guvvemen soldiers op de Coco side, temurrah dey tek op won helicopter an dey bock dere right den.*"

If I came across soldiers, he told me, I should look at their ankles. The rebels, like the American advisers who had trained them, folded their trouser bottoms tightly into their combat boots. Sandinista troops, on the other hand, tucked their trousers loosely into their socks. "*It joss a liddle deetail, mon, bot it de onliest way to tell em apaart.*"

I was grateful for the tip, but my immediate problem was how to get up to the river in the first place. Even during a truce, I discovered, transport was close to non-existent. Boats lacked either a functioning engine or the petrol to make them run, and by land my choices were limited. The army was confined to barracks, so there were no military trucks leaving Puerto. The government welfare ministry did not dare send its vehicles along roads anywhere near rebel positions; too many had been ambushed in the past. The Swiss delegates at the International Red Cross office were sorry but their charter forbade them to carry anyone other than Red Cross officials in their jeeps. I knew how unhelpful the UNHCR man was.

That left the Moravian relief agency, which occasionally

sent a truck up to the Coco with supplies for the refugees who had come home and were trying to rebuild their villages. First thing on Monday morning, clutching my letter from the Reverend Shogreen, I picked my way across the sticky orange clay forecourt in front of the agency's garage and enquired of a pair of legs protruding from beneath a truck if they knew of anyone going up to the Coco River. This truck would be going, I was told, as soon as it had been greased.

What time would that be?

"Mebbe today."

I sat on a boulder under a mango tree and wrote in my journal all morning, checking occasionally on the garage, but things there looked bad. The grease gun ran on electricity and the power had gone off. This did not seem to surprise anybody else and it did not unduly upset me. For the first time in weeks I was not pressed by a deadline.

At lunchtime a small boy ran up to tell me that someone was leaving for the river. I followed him down a maze of paths that led through palm-shaded backyards, ducking under washing lines and skipping out of the way of angry dogs until we came to a small crowd gathered solemnly around a small white pickup truck. A straw mattress had been laid in the back, and as I approached two youths emerged from a nearby hut carrying a limp old man by his arms and legs. *"El moribundo,"* a bystander explained to me, was being taken home to his ancestral village to die.

Time was clearly short. As we rattled along the track through the fragrant pine forest the grandfather stretched out at my feet under a grubby sheet was jolted from side to side. He was already unconscious and he breathed with an irregular rasp. His daughter leaned over him solicitously, holding a pink umbrella to shade his face from the sun, poking her hand under the sheet from time to time to reassure herself that his fading heart was still beating, or laying the back of her hand against his cheek to feel for his life's warmth. Thankfully the old man was still breathing when we emerged from the gloom of the forest into a sunny clearing where we jerked to a halt before a hut. This was Koom.

Once the grandfather had been unloaded the driver crashed on through the long grass and brush as if following an instinct, and as we lurched over the rough ground the sensation gripped me that we were passing through some archaeological site. Vaguely rectangular patches where the trees were younger and shorter than the surrounding forest, like mysterious weed-choked mounds, suggested a previous existence. I realised then that the driver was following the path that the track had taken once when these mounds and clear patches had been homes and yards, before the Sandinistas had laid waste to the village six years earlier, trucking its people away, and before nature had swiftly reimposed itself.

Now, returning from Nicaraguan government relocation camps or from Mocoron, the people of Koom were gauging from the taller trees where their homes had stood, swiping down the grass that was throttling any fruit trees the Sandinistas had left standing, cutting back the undergrowth with their machetes and building their village anew as near as they could make it to the original they had lost. They had precious little in the way of construction materials beyond what they had gathered from the forest. Some families had got hold of zinc sheets and planking from the Moravians to build themselves a less precarious home; others had helped the village pastor to dismantle the church, whose materials could house another dozen families. Now all that remained of the church was its skeleton, fronted by a broad set of concrete steps that had once been grand and now looked merely foolish as they led up to an empty frame of pillars and joists.

As dusk fell a young man mounted the steps, took up a crowbar and struck the rusting cog that hung as a sub-stitute churchbell. From a hut at the forest edge the chime was answered by the keening wail of womens' voices. A death was being mourned.

Night darkened and new mourners added their cries to the sobbing and yelping, calling up echoes around the trou-bled village. A dog bayed and his howl was taken up by other mongrels. An infant bawled and from scattered hid-den huts everywhere shrieks of sorrow split the sky like lightning. The women were grieving the death of a daugh-ter, I was told, and their lament subsided into a moaning chant recalling her dying days. How she'd been only nine-teen, only nineteen, the women wailed. A bright-eyed girl and a strong one too, a healthy girl just a week ago. How she'd walked down to the river here only last week, she'd gone with her man, a YATAMA man, he'd taken her with him just a week ago. How a message had brought the news today, that the girl was screaming, that her mother should come, how her mother had rushed down the path by the river, how she'd found at the rebel camp her daughter was dead. Dead on a camp bed with no one to care for her. Dead and a baby dead, born prematurely.

All night the women howled, telling and retelling the story of their bereavement. All night the dogs yapped and the babies screeched and they would not be stilled. For the cries that rent the night mourned more than the name-less girl who had died in agonised childbirth that day. They mingled in a collective shriek of desperation from a village mourning its years of homelessness, acknowledging its terror that this war would never end, that it would destroy the Miskito people and that nothing would remain but dead women and their stillborn babies.

Towards dawn the frenzy abated. The dogs' barking died away, the children slept, and the wailing quietened to heaving sobs. Koom had exhausted itself.

I had found Koom in YATAMA's hands, and as soon as I arrived I had been surrounded by guerrillas who wanted to know who I was and what I was doing there. They were more curious than hostile, though, and their doubts were easily stilled by a packet of American cigarettes, especially when one of them, who introduced himself as Hubert the local intelligence officer and took me aside for a few questions, recognised me from a Miskito rebel assembly I had attended in Honduras a couple of years earlier.

The thirty or so teenage soldiers hanging about Koom were enjoying the ceasefire, swaggering around the village parading their weapons before admiring clutches of small children. Some of the guerrillas who had family in Koom were making better use of their time off at home, setting aside their rifles to help clear land or build houses.

Hubert told me bluntly that my hopes of travelling downriver to the coast were unrealistic. There was no traffic, he said, no boats, no engines and no petrol. I mulled this over as I lay in my hammock that night in the Moravian church storeroom while below me mice gnawed their way into sacks of rice seed. If Hubert was right, the only way out of Koom was back the way I had come, when the church truck made its way back to the river. That would quash my main reason for venturing this deep into Nicaragua's northeastern corner: to find the Miskito crown jewels. Historical records speak of crowns and sceptres and orbs sent from London to successive Miskito kings at their coronations down the centuries, and though everybody told me that they had been lost long ago if they had ever really existed, it was those myths that had drawn me here.

I was eating the breakfast that the pastor's wife had prepared for me when one of the guerrillas called me from the kitchen to tell me that *el jefe* wanted a word with me. His tone was sufficiently peremptory to make it clear that *el jefe* was not going to wait for me to finish my rice and beans. I was brought before a burly man with a dark scowl, hung about with every possible accoutrement of war from a spiderweb of straps and webbing, spare magazines for his AK-47, a pistol, a map case and compass, torch, water bottle and his rifle itself slung behind his shoulder. He did not bother to introduce himself as he asked me who I was. He shook his head disapprovingly as he read my letter of introduction. "This isn't Wycliffe's signature," he growled in strongly Miskito-accented Spanish. "Who gave you this?"

There was little I could do except assure him that I had had the letter from Wycliffe's own hand and had watched him sign it just a few days earlier at the hotel in Puerto Lempira. *El jefe* remained unconvinced.

"They're all politicos anyway in Lempira, and I'm a *militar*. There's too much trickery amongst the politicos, all they do in Lempira is fuck around with their half-assed manoeuvering for power. I take orders from Blas and no one else. No one's told me anything about you."

Blas was YATAMA's military chief of staff whom I had failed to find in Lempira. But if this man took orders only from the chief of staff he had to be pretty senior himself. It occurred to me that he might be Siskar, the rebels' top

field commander in the whole area I was hoping to travel
through. I asked him cautiously if that was who he was
and he nodded. My heart leapt. The Reverend Shogreen
had told me he knew Siskar well; triumphantly I pulled
from my money belt the letter he had written me, addressed to all community leaders. Siskar shoved it back
into my hands without even glancing at it. "I don't want
to see anything from a pastor," he snorted.

I suggested that if he didn't believe in my letter of introduction from Diego he should radio his headquarters,
and if he didn't mind I would like to go with him, to be
able to speak directly to the people in Honduras. I was by
no means sure that the radio operator would be able to
find Diego or any of his lieutenants, and if headquarters
replied that no one there knew anything about me, Siskar
might feel inclined to investigate my identity more closely.
It would not take him long to find my letters of authority
from the Sandinistas and then God only knew what he
might decide to do with me.

While Siskar watched me in silence I babbled on nervously about the journey I was making and the contact I
had had with Miskito rebel leaders as a journalist in Honduras. I dropped as many names as I could remember from
the hurried clandestine meetings in Tegucigalpa that contra
spokesmen would call occasionally.

"Have you ever spoken to Brooklyn Rivera?" he asked
me suddenly.

That pulled me up short. Rivera's forces, as far as I knew,
were concentrated in the south of Nicaragua, closer to his
Costa Rican refuge. And the rivalry between Miskito rebel
chiefs was often fiercer than their common hatred of the
Sandinistas. Siskar was loyal to Wycliffe, who hated Brooklyn, I reasoned, so it would be safer to say I had never

met him. But something in Siskar's voice suggested that his question was not a trap. Yes, I acknowledged, I had spoken to Brooklyn. Here was a letter from him.

No sooner had he finished reading it than Siskar plunged into a political discussion. Did I think the ceasefire would last? Did I believe Sandinista troops would really be confined to their barracks? Would the government allow food supplies into rebel-held areas? Were the Sandinistas honestly prepared to recognise indian rights?

I was circumspect in my opinions, but Siskar clearly welcomed the opportunity to discuss with an outsider the questions he was asking himself, tempted as he was to come in from six years in the bush but deeply sceptical of the government's proclaimed good faith. At any rate he decided I could be left alone in Koom while he went downriver to his camp to radio headquarters personally "so that we get things straight."

Whom he talked to and what they said I never discovered, but by the time Siskar returned three hours later he was full of apologies for the way he had dealt with me that morning and was anxious to help in any way he could. I explained that I was trying to reach Cape Gracias a Dios at the mouth of the Coco.

"I've got the same problem myself," he told me. "The gringos dropped us some supplies downriver yesterday and we need to move them to the coast but I've no way to do it because we've run out of petrol." He had a boat, he said, and he had an engine, and he knew of a man who had a drum of fuel that nobody but YATAMA had any use for, but he didn't have the money to pay for it.

He left the solution hanging in the air, and I reached for it immediately. If his men would carry me down to the Cape in their supply boat, I would buy the petrol to get us there. I was not entirely comfortable offering a little personal humanitarian aid to the contras to supplement the $100 million that the US Congress had voted that year, but if that was what it took to get me out of Koom, that was what it took.

As Siskar organised his men to ready the boat, I wandered off in the direction of some plaintive singing I could hear in the distance. In a small clearing amongst the pines I found a group of women gathered around a freshly dug mound of earth, their feet bare, their faces worn, as the pastor led them in a hymn with which to bury the girl who had died the day before. The tune that their thin wavering voices sang was familiar from countless school chapel services when I had belted it out as a boy. So were the words, even though they were in Miskito.

> *Man buram Kristyen sulyar,*
> *Jisus man Kapten sa . . .*

Or, as I had known it,

> *Onward, Christian soldiers,*
> *Marching as to war . . .*

The war was far from everybody's mind as we poled the heavy, square-nosed *pipante*, hollowed from an enormous treetrunk, away from the steep bank and into the current. The four young guerrillas chosen to accompany me were in high spirits at this unexpected break in their routine and behaved as if they were on a school outing, while the boy at the tiller gunned the outboard engine mercilessly to bring the prow out of the water like a speedboat's.

They calmed down a little when a submerged log struck us a glancing blow that nearly overturned the boat, but excitement overtook them again at the sight of a large white goose standing motionless on the sandy shore of a bend in the river. The sergeant in charge of our party, a slight man with a narrow face who had chosen the peculiar *nom de guerre* of Damalupia, which meant "Old Lady," told the tillerman to slow down and took aim with his AK-47. As he fired his shot the bird rose in a puff of feathers, flapped its wings in a few weak beats and dropped into a patch of tall reeds. Hooting with anticipation we beached the canoe and tumbled out in search of the stricken goose. But the reeds were ten-feet tall and grew so thickly together that we found nothing more rewarding than bloodstains. That night, when we stopped at a small group of bamboo huts perched above the river, where YATAMA troops kept some stores, we had only the guerrillas' basic fare for supper: oatmeal porridge.

The next morning we set off to collect the supplies that we were to carry down to the Cape. A US transport plane had dropped them a day earlier by the river, and now they had to be distributed among the YATAMA troops. We reached the drop zone by midmorning, and it was immediately apparent that something was wrong. There were no neatly piled cartons of stores or crates of medicine on the riverbank. Instead we found half a dozen sweaty guerrillas up to their knees in swamp tugging fruitlessly at the corners of sacks stubbornly embedded in the muck.

One of them gave up the task with a stream of foul abuse and explained to me what had happened. It was all, he said, the fault of "Chuck Norris," the CIA man who lived in a shipping container in the middle of the parade ground in Puerto Lempira.

Chuck had flown out a couple of weeks earlier in his helicopter in search of a good place to drop the next batch of supplies. His eye had been caught by this wide stretch of flat, treeless land right by the riverbank, about the size of five football fields. The drop would happen here, he ruled. The Miskito rebel officer to whom he had communicated this decision had apparently voiced some reservations. He knew this part of the river, he had said, and when it rained this likely looking drop zone flooded and turned into an enormous marsh.

Chuck had apparently been unimpressed. Miskitos, he had told the YATAMA officer, did not know enough about air drops to choose the best places to carry them out. That was his job, and this was the ideal drop zone. The goods would arrive in fifteen days' time. YATAMA should make sure they had enough men on hand to gather them up.

Two weeks later, on the eve of the drop, it had rained heavily. Five planes had flown the supply mission, each laden with several tons of food and other essential goods. One by one they had passed over the drop zone and with practiced accuracy offloaded their cargo just where they had been told to. Straight into the swamp. Three months' worth of food supplies for a thousand men were lost or ruined. More than fifteen tons of beans, sugar, rice, lard, oatmeal and soap, and only the soap could be salvaged. When a 100-pound sack of beans is dropped onto dry ground from 1,000 feet without a parachute, it leaves a three-foot-deep crater, but at least the beans can be recovered from their split sacks. When the same sack of beans is dropped from that height into a bog it simply disappears.

A few sacks had not been entirely swallowed up but had left waterlogged craters from which scraps of sacking protruded. It was these that the men were trying to rescue, but it was a hopeless business. Even if they had been able to extricate a sack or two, the beans had been under water for a day already and would soon be inedible. The sugar, oatmeal and rice were beyond even thinking about.

Nobody seemed to know if the Americans would drop them some replacement supplies once news of the disaster filtered back to Swan Island, the Honduran island halfway to the Caymans where contra logistics were organised. So we loaded onto our *pipante* a few cases of powdered milk that had been left over from a previous drop and headed downstream to the nearest radio set to report the foul-up.

Once we had done so, and taken on board a young *comandante* named Ben, the crew decided to take it easy. With one lad up front waving his AK-47 to the left or right to indicate a path through the submerged logs and branches, we followed the looping, sweeping bends of the river, stopping now and again at fruit trees on the bank to pick some guavas or a wild papaya. At one point we pulled in alongside the bank to visit two soldiers manning a small weapons depot in a forest clearing. Their marksmanship had been better than Damalupia's; on a fire by their tent bubbled a pot of stewing duck. We plunged our fingers in greedily, pulling out chunks of rich, dark meat and wolfed them down. Ben grinned at me as he wiped the grease from his chin with his uniform sleeve. *"Dass life on de Coco, mon. Lil by lil you get your lonch."*

The guerrillas seemed accustomed to disasters such as the wasted supply drop, and used to improvising solutions. Because the flat-bottomed *pipante* that had carried us downstream was unstable on the open sea, a small sailboat had been commandeered to take us and our load of powdered milk across the Cape Gracias a Dios bar where Columbus had anchored and down the coast to a YATAMA base at Old Cape.

But there was no sailboat waiting for us. Ben decided to paddle across the river to a settlement on the Honduran bank to see what had gone wrong, but first he had to change into a red T-shirt and a pair of jeans that he pulled from his pack. The Honduran army maintained an outpost in the settlement, and for appearances' sake, since the contras were officially not meant to be in Honduras, YATAMA troops were expected to wear civilian clothes in the presence of Honduran authorities. Pulling on the jeans seemed a strangely comic act of diplomacy in such a remote and hidden corner of this jungle.

While we waited for him, we passed the time by talking about Nicaragua as if it were a foreign country. "How much would this shirt cost in Nicaragua?" "Can you get trousers like these in Nicaragua?" *Subcomandante* Rugama, the Sandinista chief in Puerto Cabezas, had been right; the central government's writ simply didn't extend this far. The only currency anyone ever saw was the US dollar or the Honduran lempira, all the food and goods that found their way here came from Honduras, not from Nicaragua, and as Damalupia insisted "First of all we are indigenous indians and then we are Nicaraguans."

As we lay beneath a tree on the riverbank, brushing ants off our clothes, Damalupia studied closely a ten-dollar bill he had asked me to show him. I had rarely ever noticed more than the denomination on American banknotes; Damalupia pored over the bill intently, insisting on an explanation of everything he saw. No one had any money out here, let alone real American money, and his fascination demanded an exhaustive inspection.

"This note is legal tender for all debts, public and private," I translated into Spanish, skipping over the portrait of Hamilton, of whom I knew little. Damalupia didn't care; his eye had already caught a serious anomaly. The note was signed not only by James A. Baker III, secretary of the treasury, but by the treasurer of the United States, Katherine Davalos Ortega. How could this be? Damalupia demanded. How could a relative of his arch enemy, the evil Nicaraguan President Daniel Ortega, be responsible for the symbol of power and goodness, the US dollar?

The engraving of the US Treasury on the other side of the bill did not engage his attention as much as a few stick figures on the pavement that I had not noticed. "Who are these people?" he wanted to know. "Civilians?" In his world there were just three classes of people: Sandinistas, to be killed; *militares,* his comrades in YATAMA; and civilians. These were civilians, I said. "Going to change their dollars, I suppose," he laughed.

Ben returned with the news that the catboat was nowhere to be seen and that we would have to march three hours to Old Cape. We had already suspected as much, and the men greeted the order to load the powdered milk onto their backs with groans of resignation.

Through thickening darkness we pushed our way along a scarcely visible forest path. Branches whipped into my eyes and caught on my pack, and the coarse sharp grasses cut my hands. When Ben led the way out of the wood onto a beach I cheered under my breath—the afternoon's goodnatured chatter had subsided into dogged silence during the march—but underfoot I found not the sand of a beach but the squelch of a mudflat. The mudflat quickly turned into a lagoon, but we plodded on single file through the dusk and the shin-deep water regardless, disturbing stingrays that roiled up the shallows at our approach, each of their tails leaving an elegant single ripple as its wake in the black water.

We arrived at the base to find there was no food beyond a mugful of oatmeal and water flavoured with sugar for each of us. I forced these down and fell into my hammock, asleep before the mosquitos found me.

I was shaken awake before dawn. I could make out silhouettes of the men around me, sitting in their hammocks, rubbing their eyes. *"Peter, sit op in your hammock and preah,"* Ben ordered me.

Each man spoke his own prayer, out loud, one by one. I could understand little of their Miskito, but I could make out the names of their leaders—Wycliffe, Brooklyn, Steadman, Fagoth. This early morning prayer session was clearly a practiced ritual among Ben's men, but they did not rattle off their invocations in a hurried mutter, impatient to finish an obligatory chore. They spoke forthrightly, simply, directly into the darkness, and I felt an edge to their voices.

As the sky over the sea lightened to a serge grey, Ben told me what he had told the others before I had woken. Two runners had arrived during the night from Bismuna, the next village down the coast, with news that Sandinista troops were on the move.

"Dem invadin dis side, mon, Cape and Bismuna. Now what to do? You nervous?"

I choked on my cold oatmeal, unable to hide my anxiety. I had been caught in a battle between Sandinista and contra troops only a few months earlier and had very nearly been killed. I did not want to be that frightened ever again. I told Ben I had no interest in getting involved in any fighting and that I was not here as a war correspondent. *"You didn't come for dat, mebbe, bot now you have to stand,"* he laughed.

Why the Sandinistas should be breaking the ceasefire I could not imagine. But to Ben and his troops such government duplicity was only to be expected. In fact Ben thought that the soldiers might be hunting for me, to capture me and show that journalists could not travel with impunity with enemy forces. My hands were shaking as I unhitched my hammock and packed my rucksack, wondering what I should do.

The easiest and quickest option seemed to be to retrace my steps to the river and cross into Honduras, trying to keep out of sight of the army patrols there. Ben would not hear of it. If the Sandinistas were attacking Cape, he said, they would surely have sealed off that escape route.

As the sun came up I sat on one of the makeshift benches under the zinc roof that constituted the Cape Gracias a Dios Moravian church, while Ben busied himself on the field radio, his men crowded round him listening for scraps of information.

Such news as we heard of the enemy's whereabouts was garbled and contradictory. If the Sandinistas were indeed attacking Cape, I had no intention of staying. If they were actually attacking some other village it was not at all clear which one. Either way, I decided to accompany the messengers from Bismuna, who told me they were going back down the beach after breakfast. Ben agreed with me that I was in no more danger doing that than doing anything else, and promised me two of his men as guards.

This was kind of him. If there was going to be a fight he would need all the men he had, and sparing two of them just to look after me was almost foolhardy. It was difficult to turn down his generosity and to explain that I would rather travel with civilians only. I was afraid that if we did come across Sandinista soldiers, the first thing they would do on seeing uniforms and guns would be to open fire. It was not an argument that made any sense to Ben. As far as he was concerned, Sandinista soldiers would open fire on us in any case, and the least he could do was to ensure that we had someone with us to shoot back. I could not say no.

Seven of us set off, the two messengers, the two guerrillas, two Bismuna men who had been staying in Cape and me. As soon as we had squelched our way across the mudflats and I had had time to explain that I was heading for Puerto Cabezas, my companions decided that I was a Sandinista spy. Who else would be free to go into Puerto like that? On the other hand, Ben had told them to take care of me until we reached Bismuna, and had given me a letter of recommendation to the YATAMA chiefs down the coast. Confused, they walked in single file behind me until I managed to convince one of the previous night's messengers, a frank-faced teenager with a bush of curly hair and glinting gold caps on his front teeth, that I was there in good faith.

Morland, the brightest of the bunch, soon brought his friends round. He also volunteered to help carry my pack when the beach ran out and we were forced to pick our way through the tangled knots of mangrove roots that ran right down to the sea. Between the labyrinthine red roots piles of bleached driftwood had tangled, and amongst the silver logs and branches lay plastic containers washed up on the tide. I examined this litter closely and with a strange tenderness, seeking comfort in detritus that reminded me sharply of my own world. The familiarity of a bright red tin of Shell lubricating oil gave me unexpected solace. Its yellow cockleshell emblem reminded me of the symbol on the spine of the Shell Book of the Countryside that my parents had kept in the dashboard compartment of our car when I was a boy.

Briefly I coddled myself in such memories, until I was struck by a peculiar realisation. Almost all of this rubbish was French. Square-ridged transparent plastic Evian mineral-water bottles, dark green tear-shaped bottles of Perrier, Johnson *et* Johnson *Talc Bébé* shakers, *Ambre Solaire* suntan lotion dispensers. What strange current had brought this floating litter from Martinique or Guadeloupe, at the other end of the Caribbean? Or had a cruise ship full of French tourists emptied its garbage holds off the Nicaraguan coast?

For several hours I struggled to keep up with the others. Eventually we emerged from the mangrove thickets into a surreal landscape—Ypres in negative. The mangroves and other trees had died, leaving their whitened trunks stripped of branches, blasted by wind and sea, stark in the burning sunlight against black sand and muddy black swamp mould behind the beach.

A strong breeze off the choppy sea revived my spirits, Morland offered to shoulder my pack again for a while and his companions struck up conversation. They were pretty confident now that we were not going to run into the Sandinistas; behind the beach stretched an impenetrable marsh and then a lagoon. This had always been barren and inhospitable land, they told me, but before the war the village of Cape had been wealthy in cattle. Men had once driven herds down from Cape to the Puerto Cabezas market, they said, in a weeklong journey along the coast.

I wondered how they had crossed the rivers that intersected the beach at several points with the fast and tricky currents of the bars. *"Dem cows go crazy, mon,"* grinned an old man who had introduced himself as Morland's uncle.

259

"You gotta cotch em good before you gets to de waater, den you lash em to a big canoe, pive beasts aside, and off you go. You de ferryman, dem cows swimmin, an you gets acraas. Bot dem cows, dem hombog you bad, mon. Dem not made to swim."

Reaching Bismuna as night fell I was taken before the local YATAMA commander, an unkempt older man wearing only a pair of fatigue trousers as he hunched over the bowl of rice and beans on his knees. He waved my proffered letter of introduction to a subordinate who could read, and grunted what I took to be his assent when he had heard Ben's message. He showed no surprise at my arrival, nor did he show any further concern about my presence in the village. The reports of an imminent Sandinista attack, I was told, had been false.

The guerrilla escorts Ben had sent with me from Cape asked where we might spend the night. The *comandante* looked up from his supper, waved the tin spoon he was holding in one fist in the general direction of "anywhere but here" and muttered something through a mouthful of food. I was to be billeted, it was explained, on the family with the biggest house in the village, as was only fair.

The house was a simple enough structure, the standard square weatherboard, balconied affair on high pilings, with a zinc roof, but it reeked of wealth. For a start, the balcony rails were painted red and blue: paint was unknown outside Puerto Cabezas and hadn't been seen even there for several months. I knocked hesitantly on the open door, and while my companions explained to the girl who appeared what was happening, I stared into the living room, lit with the glow of kerosene lamps.

The room was a paean to modern American kitsch. On a crudely made wooden dresser, plaster leopards reclined on yule logs set at either side of a small glass vase stuffed with violently coloured plastic flowers. Behind them was a velveteen wall hanging that depicted a pink Christ with golden halo leading a flock of alabaster sheep to a turquoise river that ran through lime-green hills beneath a scarlet sky. On the opposite wall were pinned gigantic publicity photographs of Daytona Beach and St. Petersburg, reflecting glass skyscrapers stretching between sky and sea of equally impossible blues, while the table—set with plastic lace doilies—boasted an enormous boom box and a battery-powered toy police car large enough to carry a small infant. Between the lamps hanging from the ceiling, the rafters were decorated with fishing net floats, but these were not the folksy bottle-green glass balls that might hang amongst dried starfish and other salty dog curiosities in a seaside pub on the west coast of England. These were giant orange and blue plastic buoys that were so intrusive I had to duck my head as I was shown to my room.

The bed I was to sleep in belonged to one of the family's sons who was, it turned out, in the United States, the third of the five brothers to have gone north and to have come home from time to time loaded with interior furnishings. His mother showed me his photograph, that of a short, squarely built young man with an orange hard hat and a hairless suntanned chest, his arms draped around two buddies' shoulders. The picture had been taken in *"Tekas,"* his mother told me proudly. I asked where the boy was now. She didn't know.

Bismuna had been almost completely rebuilt in the three years since the village elders had first returned from their relocation camp. Only two families remained in Honduras and life had fallen into its traditional rhythms. I met a mechanic from Puerto Cabezas who had come to try to mend the village truck and who didn't think much of Bismuna. *"Dese people live behind time,"* he told me disdainfully, though his real problem seemed to be the amount of fish in the local diet. *"Snook give me trobble in de head business, mek me blackop, mon."*

Even though the community's truck had broken down and the fishermen had no way of carrying their shrimp catch to Puerto Cabezas, the village seemed prosperous. The Sandinistas had cut all the coconut trees down, I was told, but the paths that led through the scattered houses were shady with broad-leafed breadfruit trees, mango, cashew, banana, orange and lemon trees. Mountains of shrimp lay on zinc roofing sheets to dry, and in one backyard a woman shuffled her feet through a carpet of cashew nuts, spreading them more evenly in the sun. Down the path a way, past two small boys hunting iguanas with slingshots, a group of women were throwing sticks up into a mango tree, bringing down the nearly ripe fruit, while another pounded rice in a mortar hollowed from an enormous treetrunk. As she began to winnow the grains from one bowl to another, chickens heard the rattle of rice on tin and scuttled to her feet.

I was looking for the old men of the village who might remember stories of the old Miskito kings, and who might know if any of their jewels and finery still existed in some secret cache. I recalled a story told by Bernard Nietschmann of his arrival in the Nicaraguan coastal village where he was to do anthropological research. Stepping from his boat he asked the first man he came across where he could find the oldest man in the village. The fellow had looked at him curiously for some time, and then had shaken his head. *"Oldest man? Oldest man? . . . Oldest man, him dead."*

The old men of Bismuna were not dead, but they were

pretty confused about their people's past. Three of the grandfathers who by common consent knew most about the history of the coast sat down with me on a verandah and proceeded to squabble amongst themselves in rapid and toothless Miskito each time I posed a question. It soon became clear that if one of them knew something that the others didn't they were so loath to acknowledge it that they simply laughed it off as invention and made up their own instant folklore that they presented as the truth.

They all agreed on only two items of history: that the first Miskito king had been called *"Ulman,"* which I took to mean Oldman, and that Henry Morgan, king of the pirates and king of England, had given Oldman a cannon in return for turtle meat. The cannon lay some four hours by canoe from Bismuna, they told me, and it was all that was left of the *"foss-time people."*

Beyond that, it was impossible to tell truth from fiction. One of them insisted that he had seen a crown once, but that it had been washed away and lost during a hurricane in 1972. Another drew for me a horseshoe-shaped chest-plate he said had belonged to his great grandfather, one of the king's generals. In his shaky hand he sketched two crowned lions bearing crossed swords. Around the edge had been an inscription in English, he said, although he had not been able to read it. He had buried this symbol when the Sandinistas had forced the villagers out of their homes in 1981 and now he could not find it again.

I could not believe that nothing was left of a two-hundred-year dynasty that had come to an end only a century ago. In the late 1920s a Moravian missionary on the Coco River had reported seeing an ebony sceptre that had once belonged to a Miskito king, but no more had been heard of it since. Until the mid-nineteenth century the kings had lived at Big Sandy Bay, just down the coast. I hoped the people there would know more about their ancestors.

"The usual way of holding meetings with the Mosquito indians," Governor John Dalling of Jamaica advised his emissary to the coast in 1780, "is to begin with the King at Sandy Bay, the General Tempest at Patook, the Governor next near Tebuppy, finally the Admiral at Pearl Key Lagoon."

What is one to make of this precise and delicate protocol? Indeed how is one to approach the whole history of the Miskito kings and their courts, undoubtedly the oddest of all the oddities to be found on the coast and in its past? As a string of puppets aping the manners of their English masters? Or a legitimate lineage adopting English customs as outward signs of its authority over the Anglophile Miskitos? While historians write polemical papers arguing their particular interpretations, the Miskitos don't think twice about the matter. Their memory of their kings, faded and distorted though it mostly is, is central to their sense of identity. The kingship is the symbol of their lost autonomy, and the story of how invading troops from Managua forced the last king to flee the coast in 1894 is still told with bitterness.

The first recorded Miskito king was called Jeremy I, which is a clear enough indication of who crowned him and whence he derived his authority. On a visit to Jamaica in 1687, however, Jeremy told the Duke of Albemarle that an earlier king had sent his son to England, where he had spent several years at the court of King Charles I before returning to his own, more rustic throne.

M. W., the anonymous Englishman who travelled the

Mosquitia towards the end of the seventeenth century, also met King Jeremy, who told him that his father, Oldman, had been carried over to London soon after the English conquest of Jamaica in 1655. In England, Jeremy told him, his father had "received from his brother king a crown and commission, which the present Old Jeremy keeps safely by him." M. W. was shown the crown, which he disdained as "but a laced hat," and he read the commission, which he found "a ridiculous piece of writing, purporting that he should kindly use and relieve such straggling Englishmen as should chance to come that way with plantains, fish and turtle." On the strength of that commission, M. W. reported, Jeremy "esteems himself a subject to the king of England," and from that moment on it matters little whether the Miskitos had always had kings of their own or whether the English imposed the idea. Such power as a king enjoyed, he enjoyed because the English crown had conferred it. "On the death of their monarch, the next heir repairs to Jamaica with a few principal men, to certify his claim," explained the historian Edward Long in 1774, "and he is then invested with a commission to be king of the Mosquitos: until this is obtained he is not acknowledged by his subjects, so dependent do they hold themselves on the British government."

From the middle of the seventeenth century to the end of the nineteenth century, the throne passed from father to son or from elder to younger brother within the same royal family, as continuous a line of succession as most European monarchies could manage. But the Miskito kings do not appear to have enjoyed absolute authority even over the area where they lived, except when it came to gathering war parties or to "doing law" at annual dispensations of justice during village-by-village tours.

Councils of elders have always played a leading role in regulating Miskito affairs, and the king was probably little more than a first among equals, relying heavily on his advisers. These courtiers often had ambitions of their own and were not easily controlled. Occasionally they had to be murdered, and at least one king, George II, was himself the victim of regicide.

Assuming the Miskito throne in 1777 at the age of only nineteen, George II emerged from the influence of his Uncle Isaac—who styled himself the Duke of York—to grow into a "cruel, barbarous and vindictive" man, according to the account of an English trader of the period, Orlando Roberts. He treated his many wives so brutally that several died at his hands, and the murder of one of these women "under circumstances of peculiar barbarity" provoked a riot during which the king was shot by his own people.

His son, George Frederic, had been packed off to Jamaica to be protected from such licentiousness, and there Lady Nugent, the wife of the island's lieutenant governor, found the boy dressed in a scarlet uniform wearing a crown upon his head "of which he seemed very proud." The crown, she wrote to a friend in 1804, was of silver gilt, ornamented with mock stones "sent from England some years ago. Both the little king and his uncle seemed to hold it in high estimation."

As far as one can judge, this appears to be the same crown that Patrick Walker found in need of repair some forty years later. Named as resident British representative to the Kingdom of the Mosquitia when London formally declared the area a protectorate in 1843, Walker wrote to Foreign Minister Lord Aberdeen, as he prepared for the

coronation of King George Augustus Frederic, that when
he sent for the regalia of the kingdom

> I received a sort of crown formed of silver gilt and
> studded with crystal ornaments. I have sent it to Ja-
> maica to be cleaned and repaired, but as it is, in my
> humble opinion, unworthy of its destiny, I have most
> respectfully to suggest for your lordship's considera-
> tion, the propriety of government presenting the
> young king with a new crown, and adding thereto a
> sceptre and a sword.

He was granted the sword, but in the lengthy account that
the *Honduras Observer* and *Belize Gazette* give of the coronation ceremony on 7 May 1845 there is no mention of
a sceptre.

The coronation, performed in St. John's Cathedral in
Belize, was an orgy of petty colonial pomp and circum-
stance. The royal procession, gathered behind the sword
of state, made its way through the dusty streets lined by
an honour guard splendidly dressed in red cutaway jackets
with golden frogging and royal-blue harem pants tucked
below the knee into white calf-length boots. Inside the
redbrick cathedral the Royal Honduras Militia brass band
waited in the organ gallery. At the altar stood the Rural
Dean. "Sirs," he cried, "I here present unto you George
Augustus Frederic, rightful king of the Mosquito nation,
wherefore all you that come this day, are ye willing with
due homage to acknowledge him as such?"

"God save King George Augustus Frederic," the people
responded.

And the king, in his British army officer's uniform, knelt

before the altar. His head, his breast and his hands were anointed with holy oil "as Solomon was anointed king by Zadoc the priest and Nathan the prophet," before the indian chiefs helped to gird on his sword of state and the Dean exhorted the king to "stop the growth of iniquity. Protect the church of God. Help and defend widows and orphans." The crown was placed upon the king's head and royal salutes were fired by the cannon at nearby Fort George and the band played "God Save the King." George Frederic "displayed no timidity," according to the *Honduras Observer* correspondent, "but at the same time was mild and quiet in his deportment. His character we understand is most amiable and renders him beloved by all who come in contact with him."

A far cry from his ancestor Jeremy I with his "aspect somewhat terrible and with a harsh voice like a bear" as M. W. had found, George Augustus Frederic was the apogee of his line as the English had modelled it. He wore European clothes with elegance, he spoke English more fluently than Miskito, and a visitor wrote later that

he had acquired a refined taste hardly to have been expected: he was never without one or two volumes of our best English poets in his pocket, and availed himself of every unoccupied moment to peruse them.

At the same time he was "the best shot and canoe's man in the whole country." In other words, the ideal young Victorian gentleman, possessed of all the arts and graces.

But he was the last true Miskito king, for in 1860 the British signed a treaty with Managua abandoning their protectorate and creating instead a Miskito reservation under Nicaraguan sovereignty. The office of king was abolished,

and George Augustus Frederic was downgraded to hereditary chief.

By this stage the Miskitos' influence on coastal affairs
had largely been supplanted by the growing number of
blacks who came to settle as Jamaican owners freed their
slaves. Known on the coast as "creoles" they became the
dominant cultural force in the port of Bluefields, the political and commercial capital of the Mosquitia, where earlier immigrants from the eastern Caribbean had married
descendants of the Black River Hodgsons. When a con-
vention was held in Bluefields in 1861 to draw up a con-
stitution for the reservation, only eleven of the fifty-one
headmen who attended appear to have been Miskitos. The
rest, including nine Hodgsons, were creoles. Forty-three
of the chiefs were named to a General Council; they included all nine Hodgsons but only three indians.

Officials in Managua had never held the Miskito kings
in anything but contempt, and now they felt they had good
reason to ignore their promise under the 1860 treaty to
pay George Augustus Frederic's successor, William Henry
Clarence, a $5,000 a year annuity. He had been elected
by creoles, Managua said, and did not represent the Miskito people. Managua and London argued for years about
who was breaching the treaty, until in 1894 Nicaraguan
President Jose Zelaya lost patience with the dispute and
put a sharp end to it by ordering his troops to descend the
Rama River and to take Bluefields by force.

The town surrendered without a fight, and the Miskito
kingdom turned protectorate turned reservation became,
on paper at least, fully Nicaraguan. Some 600 Jamaicans
who could not face that prospect were taken off by a British
man of war to the Costa Rican port of Limon. So was
Robert Henry Clarence, the last and sorriest of Jeremy's

line, who chose Jamaica as his home in exile. There he lived on a British government pension of four pounds and eighteen shillings a day until 1908, when he died at the age of thirty-five after a failed operation.

In one of the villages on the coast—I am under oath not to reveal which—it had been rumoured that a descendant of one of the kings still guarded some royal relics, a holy memorial to the Miskito past whose very existence was kept a secret.

Even my most indirect enquiries, my most subtle and tangential probes, were met only with empty stares. The presence of the Moravian pastor, who accompanied me to vouch for my good faith, did nothing to help. Villager after villager merely looked at me in pretended incomprehension, recalled vaguely that they had heard once of some such thing but many years ago, or insisted flatly that what I was looking for could be found in such and such a village further up or down the coast. Their evasions convinced me that the rumours I had heard were true, but they also made it abundantly clear that I was not to be trusted. After a day spent knocking my head against the wall I gave up.

The YATAMA *comandante,* as he saw me off, asked if I had found my conversations in his village useful, and I told him I had been disappointed to find that rumours about the Miskito crown jewels had been false.

"They're not false," he said bluntly. "They're here and I know who they belong to. There was a ring that was stolen, a little gold statue of a dog that broke, and a staff. Do you want to see them?"

An old woman stooping under the weight of a bundle of firewood that she carried on her shoulders was coming up the path towards us, and the *comandante* beckoned her over. In rapid Miskito he explained what he wanted, and with a few brusque interruptions he overcame her doubts.

Just as she was leading us to her home, however, her elder sister appeared and demanded to know what was going on. As soon as she had been told, she planted herself squarely in our path. An old blue cardigan wrapped around her head, she set her wide mouth, broadly flared nose and sunken walnut cheeks firmly against me.

The *comandante* explained again what it was that we were after. No, she said, word would get out and the Sandinistas would kill her. He explained patiently who I was and what I was doing. She was unmoved. He stopped explaining and began arguing. No, she replied, she had lost the things that once she had owned. He snapped at her, cajoled, negotiated, while I stood by helplessly. From time to time she would look up at me and give me a hard protracted stare. As our eyes met I filled mine with mute goodwill, pleading with her to believe that I was not here to steal her treasure or reveal its whereabouts but just to look at it, just once, just a glimpse.

For two hours the *comandante* kept up his assault, mixing threats and promises to no avail. The old woman would not be shaken: Somoza's National Guard had come looking for it, the Sandinistas had come looking for it, she had been persecuted, two foreigners who had spoken to her at the resettlement camp had been arrested, no she would not show it to me, no she had not got it any longer, no she did not know what we were talking about.

The *comandante* finally turned away in disgust, ashamed as well that an old woman should so openly flout his military authority. "If only her men were here," he snorted. "These women don't understand anything. The men you can reason with."

At that moment one of his subalterns recognised a man trudging up the path in outsized wellington boots and called him over. The old woman, it was explained to me at last, was a great great granddaughter of George William Albert Hendy, who had ruled the Miskitos from 1884 to 1888, and the man in the wellington boots was her son. Slowly, the *comandante* went over the whole question again, setting out who I was, where I had come from, what I was doing and why I was so curious to see anything that remained of the Miskitos' royal history. In less than twenty minutes he was persuaded. His mother, he said apologetically, had been convinced that I was a Cuban communist.

Before I could set eyes on the royal heritage, however, an elaborate security procedure was set up. I had to stay where I was for half an hour and then follow a prescribed route to a house where I would rejoin the *comandante*. With him, I drank a mug of tepid sweetened oatmeal liquid while we waited for a signal, and then set off together into the bush that surrounded the village. After twenty minutes' walk through thick, dry spiky grass dotted with clumped, thorny bushes, we reached the spot that had been agreed on for our rendezvous. The sun was about to set, casting a warm bronze glow over the savannah, and as we sat waiting for someone to arrive the silence was only heightened by the distant cries of mothers calling their children to supper in the village.

The longer I waited the more certain I grew that the women had changed their minds. Or perhaps they had sent me off into the bush simply to get rid of me? My guts knotted tight with disappointment. And then, a few hundred yards away, a sandy-haired mongrel dog broke through a line of bushes and behind him came the old woman who had proved so stubborn, Carla, and her sister Rosa.

Carla hobbled towards me, a hessian sack slung over her shoulder as she turned her head this way and that in an unwitting parody of someone with a guilty secret. In that sack, I thought, she was carrying perhaps the last remains of a royal ancestry that had once gloried in gifts of gold doubloons from Henry Morgan. Reverently, Carla laid the sack down on the ground and bent over to untie the knot she had made in it.

As she pulled the royal sceptre from the bag she turned and presented it to me with both hands, her open palms upwards. I reached out and took hold of a Victorian gentleman's wooden cane, its gold hilt badly battered, and found it strangely disproportioned, short, snapped off. Yes, Carla explained, once it had been over three feet long, but she had broken it in two a few months earlier, the better to hide it from Sandinista soldiers who were searching the village.

The cane, chipped and scratched, had a finely engraved gold head, narrowing into an octagonal sleeve that fitted onto the wooden shaft. On four of the sides, a London canemaker had carved the owner's name and title: "GWA/ Hendy/Mosquito/Chief." The other four sides were decorated with delicately chased fleurs de lys and rambling roses and lilies framed in Gothic windows.

Such walking sticks must have been made by the thousand a hundred years ago. Antique shops up and down England doubtless still sell them for not very much to anyone who can think of a use for a showy cane. But as dusk fell on the Miskito coast and an old woman—rightfully a princess she reminded me sharply—took back the cane to caress its length and gaze respectfully at its gold adornment, this was not an old broken walking stick. This was a sceptre. This was a crown jewel. Carla wiped it on her skirt, wrapped it in a torn cotton square and carefully slid her treasure back into its sack. I thanked her for having shown it to me. She simply nodded and grunted, turned away, and walked off back towards the village.

TEN

I travelled from Bismuna to Big Sandy Bay by night, the coolest time for a long canoe journey and the safest time to negotiate the marshy lagoons and mangrove-throttled creeks, should the Sandinistas be about.

A powerfully built young man named Fernando had agreed to take me in his dory, glad of the chance to make some money. His story was as absurd an account of the wastefulness of the war and Nicaraguan bureaucracy as I had come across, and he told it with bitterness.

In 1980, as a teenager, he had won a Miskito dance competition and the new Sandinista government had been impressed enough with his talents to give him a grant to attend ballet school in Havana. Fernando had graduated four years later and returned to Managua as one of the country's most privileged young dancers, expecting to be able to help develop Nicaragua's nascent ballet company. Instead, he was drafted into the army as a footsoldier. Since all three of his brothers were already serving in the army, his father was dead and the rules allowed every widow to keep one son at home, Fernando asked that if he had to join up, one of his brothers should be let out. His request was refused, and within three months it became irrelevant. In the space of a few weeks all three of his brothers were killed in action. Sickened, Fernando simply deserted and made his way home to Bismuna. Now he was sitting in the back of his narrow canoe, a bizarre knitted cap resembling a red tea cosy on his head, his jeans rolled up above his bulging calf muscles, paddling a visitor from village to village through the night for a few dollars.

We pushed off from the peaty mud of the landing and were immediately enveloped in the warm night. Beneath the low clouds the darkness was almost tangible, broken every now and again by brief, faint smudges of lightning from a distant storm, or the occasional gentle snap of the makeshift sail, cobbled together from old plastic bags, that Fernando had raised to catch the odd whisper of wind over the lagoon. The wind was not strong enough to carry us, though, and we were obliged to paddle—Fernando from the back, where he could steer, me amidships, and up front Glenn, a fair-haired boy whom Fernando had brought along to help. Each stroke of our short, broad-handled paddles brought the water alive, as fish, startled by our approach, dashed away in foamy underwater wakes of phosphorescence. Paddling like automatons through the blackness, sometimes across the open ruffled waters of a lagoon, sometimes winding down narrow streams where we had to brush away overhanging mangrove branches and bending reeds, we kept our silence, lost in our own thoughts. We did not stop for a rest until the sky ahead of us had begun to turn a leaden grey above the flat unbroken margin of mangrove bushes that lined the natural canal we had emerged into. If I didn't mind walking for a while, Fernando told me as I stepped unsteadily out of the canoe, we could go and look for skeletons at the spot that YATAMA used as a body dump for alleged informers. I declined.

Not until seven o'clock, after nearly twelve hours in the dory, did we catch sight of the coconut palms that marked Big Sandy Bay on the far side of the last lagoon. Dispiritingly, we found that the wind had picked up and turned against us; the sail was of no use and paddling was doubly difficult. When finally we beached the canoe an hour later I was dizzy with exhaustion, scarcely able to haul my rucksack out of its black waterproof trash bag and onto my shoulders. I staggered after Fernando and Glenn down the path to the village until we came to a patch of marsh. To cross it I would have to remove my boots and socks and roll up my trousers. The effort required seemed suddenly beyond my reach, and I exploded in anger that no one had built a bridge or laid a network of logs to carry the path across the swamp. I threw my pack down and raved while Glenn and Fernando looked on with amazement that after so much exertion such an insignificant obstacle should elicit such fury. Their regard shamed me and I quietened down. They, after all, had done a great deal more paddling than I.

Lidaukra, one of the nine hamlets strung out along the shore that make up Big Sandy Bay, appeared idyllic. A scatter of wooden stilted huts, bleached silver by the sun, ran down to the lagoon edge and spread widely through groves of coconut palms and trees bearing mangoes, lemons and cashew nuts. Tucked between the bush and the beach, the village stood on an unlikely swathe of grassy meadow that a handful of cows and horses had cropped to a neatly tended lawn in front of each home.

The unannounced arrival in Big Sandy Bay of an Englishman unsteady on his feet and incoherent with exhaustion brought the village to a standstill. A crowd of small boys scampered around me, and adults joined the throng in ones and twos to guide me to one of the village elders, whose name I had been given.

When I found him, Chesley Rojas was very dubious indeed about my identity and purpose. From under the peak of his faded pink baseball cap his bright eyes questioned me sharply. He was not unfriendly but on guard against any trickery. I introduced myself only briefly before bringing out my letter from Brooklyn Rivera: this was his hometown, and I was confident that his authorisation would mean immediate acceptance here.

Chesley took the letter, scanned it and asked me politely to wait while he consulted his fellow villagers. I was shown to a hammock strung between two trees while twenty yards away a huddle of elders passed around Brooklyn's letter and muttered amongst themselves. They were clearly persuaded of my authenticity, and Chesley came back with apologies for having kept me waiting. He wanted to introduce me to someone, he said. I was very tired, I explained, and I wondered whether the meeting could perhaps wait. Well, he said, maybe I ought to have a shower first, anyway. The open-air bucket shower revived me a little, and a quick plate of rice and turtle lent firmness to my step as I was led to my audience with Lidaukra's first lady, Brooklyn Rivera's mum.

A delicate squirrel-faced old lady, Señora Rivera was clearly as unprepared for this meeting as I was, fussing

over a pot of beans on a wood fire in her kitchen while I
asked polite questions. She told me how her famous son,
a protégé of Senator Edward Kennedy, had been a diligent
little boy at school and how she had hoped he would become a teacher or an office clerk. She was, she said, "a
little sorry that he has gone and got himself involved in
politics, because you never know when someone might kill
him over some problem. Do you think you could carry a
letter to him if I write one before you leave from here?"

There was only one question that I really wanted to ask
Señora Rivera, and as I got up to leave at the end of our
conversation I put it to her. Why had she chosen to name
her son after a borough of New York City? Or had she
named him after the bridge?

She looked up at me blankly. New York? What did I
mean?

Brooklyn, I explained. Brooklyn, New York. Brooklyn
Rivera. Why?

Señora Rivera pulled herself up to her full height, the
bun on the back of her head quivering. She had obviously
scented an insult. " 'Brooklyn' is not New York," she told
me defiantly. " 'Brooklyn' is an old Miskito name."

I bowed before tradition, and went to get some sleep.

Two hundred years ago Big Sandy Bay had been the seat
of the Miskito throne, but aside from the fact that Brooklyn
Rivera sometimes seemed to regard himself as the new
king of the Miskitos there was little in the village to recall
its glorious past. The villagers' lives, though, were still
focussed on the animal that had enriched the Miskitos for
generations and been the crux of their relations with the
English: the turtle. The Miskitos' skill at harpooning turtle
had astounded the first Europeans to visit the coast, and

the traders' desire for tortoiseshell and turtle meat was easily matched by the indians' appetite for weapons, tools and rum. A bargain had been struck that would last, in one form or another, for 350 years.

The western Caribbean, offering extensive coral reefs as shelter and mile upon mile of seagrass meadows as food, is home to one of the world's largest herds of green turtle, the variety most prized for its meat. When Columbus discovered the Cayman Islands the beaches were so thickly carpeted with turtles that he named the cluster of islets *"Las Tortugas,"* and for centuries thereafter seamen who lost their latitude in hazy weather steered by the sound of homing turtles in order to reach the Caymans.

By the early nineteenth century, though, generations of seafarers, stocking their holds with salt turtle for the return journey to Europe, had wiped out the Caymans' turtle population, and the Cayman Islanders found themselves sailing further afield in search of their catch. The Miskito Cays, off Big Sandy Bay, proved the most profitable hunting ground.

Big Sandy Bay men tell a story about a magic rock that once sat on the sandbar at the mouth of Sandy Bay Lagoon. The rock was known as the "Turtle Mother," and when she pointed west, she was telling the fishermen that the turtles were in close to shore. When she pointed east, it meant they were out by the Cays. If turtle fishermen took more than they needed, the legend runs, the Turtle Mother would send the turtles far out to sea. No one in the village had ever seen the Turtle Mother, although one old lady said her aunt had seen it before the rock moved down to Turtle Bogue in Costa Rica. Why the Mother had moved was a mystery, but *"de turkle fahlah de muther. Gat to go dere. Wooden go nowhere else,"* Chesley Rojas told me. *"Aal de turkle was where de muther was, use to leave eggs right here on dis beach. Nowadays only de oxbill and de laaggerhead lay here, no green turkle no more."*

Hawksbill turtle flesh is neither delicate nor tender, and loggerhead is frankly inedible, but if the Turtle Mother abandoned Big Sandy Bay in disgust at the way its fishermen were catching more green turtle than they needed for their families and friends, she was well within her rights.

Once, the animal had been a key to coastal Miskitos' culture, its meat the major source of protein and at the same time a prized gift cementing social relations when a fisherman distributed it among friends. Then came the Europeans, tempting the Miskitos to catch more than they themselves needed, and then came the Cayman Island schooners, which not only fished but bought all the turtle that Miskitos in their little catboats could bring to them. Still the vast herds replenished themselves, migrating like clockwork in overlapping cycles of two or three years to the same beaches to mate and nest. The Miskitos, though, were drawn into a new style of business with foreigners: where once they had bartered, the establishment of rubber companies, lumber mills, goldmines and banana planta-tions turned the indians into wage labourers. Resources became commodities. Sacred, magic, mysterious turtles lost all meaning but weight, paid by the pound to feed the processing plant in Puerto Cabezas.

In just a few years in the early 1970s Nicaraguan fish-ermen almost annihilated the green turtle herds before the government stepped in to close the canning plant and ban commercial turtling. Today, individual fishermen are al-

lowed to sell their catch at market only, and the green
turtle is returning from the brink of extinction along the
Miskito coast.

We slipped across the bar at moonrise, taking advantage
of the tide that sucked and hissed around our bows, tugging
the sharp-nosed catboat into the swell of the open sea.

"Rise op de sail," Captain Zeledon called sharply from
the tiller, and the two boys up front who had been straining
at heavy oars shipped them and scrambled to hoist the
rough canvas mainsail that gleamed against the night sky
like a pewter dish as it picked up the wind and billowed.

Zeledon Webster, owner of the *Miss Aneeth,* reckoned
the idea of going turtling this late in the season was pretty
daft. But he had been thinking of taking his boat down to
Corn Island, towards the Costa Rican border, to catch lobster, and once I had persuaded him to take me with him
he was easily convinced to indulge me for a day or two.

Chesley Rojas had come along too—since I had sought
him out first on my arrival he felt responsible for my well-
being—and Zeledon had brought with him a couple of
crew: Cornejo, a lanky black youth with a simpering laugh
and muscles of steel, and Radley Bodden, whose name
sounded familiar to me. I thought about it as we clipped
steadily through the waves that night, and eventually realised why. In *Far Tortuga,* a book set on a Caymanian
turtle schooner on its last trip to the Miskito Cays, Peter
Matthiesen tells a story that I had always supposed to be
fictitious about a hurricane in 1932 that caught *The Majestic*
at Deadman Bar, and how Captain Steadman Bodden had
lost his life with his ship. There was indeed a turtle captain
named Steadman Bodden, Chesley told me the next morning, and before dying in that hurricane he had left a child

with a Miskita woman in Sandy Bay. Radley was Steadman's grandson, he told me, and he didn't understand at
all when I tried to explain how peculiar it felt to go turtling
with the descendant of someone I had always thought of
as an imaginary character.

The *Miss Aneeth* was a sturdy, wide-bellied skiff about
thirty-five feet long, gracefully worked to a point at both
prow and stern. The mast was removable, fixed through
an aperture in one of the cross benches that served as seats,
and the mainsail was attached to an enormously long pole
that was forked at one end to hook round the mast and
served as a boom. Tangled and cluttered in the bottom of
the boat were a dugout canoe, several sacks of mangoes,
a black plastic barrel of fresh water, a bed of turtle nets
heaped with white polystyrene floats, ropes coiled around
two boulders of grey brain coral to be used as anchors, a
bundle of jibsail, two ten-foot planks, sundry sticks of
wood, a plastic shopping bag full of cooked beans, a knotted tea towel packed with fried tortillas and a couple of
empty scuba-diving tanks.

I had already chosen the dugout as the most comfortable
spot to sleep, and was lying in it, half listening to Zeledon
twitching at the tiller rope and telling Chesley an endlessly
involved story about a giant who lived on the Coco River
and who had *"ribs de size of dis boat timbers and baals de
sizea yong coconots,"* when suddenly he broke off. *"Waatch
your body. Sqaall commin op,"* he shouted, and even as Cornejo pulled down the mainsail I felt the breeze freshen
and the waves cut up. Before I could get to my feet the
rain was driving down in cords and I found myself sharing
the dugout with Chesley, stretched out alongside me and
pulling a plastic sheet over our heads. The jibsail carried
us for a while until another fierce squall blew up behind

the thunderclouds that blotted out the moon, and Zeledon ordered that not just the sails but the mast too should be taken down. Rocking wildly, cramped in a tight dugout as the wind snatched at my plastic protection, I spent my first night at sea in an open boat.

At dawn we set off again. The wind blew steadily, the sea had settled, and the sun flattened the sky with its unremitting brilliance. For several hours we tacked across the crystal emptiness until two specks appeared on the horizon. "*Whiplin Key,*" Zeledon pointed them out. As we drew closer the specks transformed themselves not into islands but into huts, rising out of the water in the middle of the ocean like the fo'c'sle of a sunken ship. The waves washed around them a muddier brown, it seemed, than the turquoise clarity of the sea beyond, but that hardly explained the presence of what I could now see were two houses side by side made of sun-dried palm leaves thatched around a framework of sticks, standing alone above the vacant waves.

Once, Chesley told me mournfully, in the heyday of turtling, there had been a whole village of these huts, built on stilts driven into a sand-and-coral plateau a few feet beneath the surface that even at low tide never actually appeared. Turtlemen had brought out from the mainland the poles and twine and thatching materials with which to make simple tentlike shelters and had lived out here for weeks at a time during the season, when the Caymanian boats were buying everyone's catch. Now just a couple of huts were left standing alongside a turtle crawl—a makeshift cage of mangrove stakes woven into four rough walls planted on the seabed—sufficient to keep turtles coralled and alive until a fisherman returned home.

We were to spend the day here, until it was time to set the turtle nets in the evening, and the first task was to prepare a meal. My fears that we were going to live for the next week or so on the cold tortillas and beans that I had seen in the boat were quickly dispelled. In the middle of the shelter's platform sat a smoke-charred cutoff oil drum, full of damp packed ashes, over which Zeledon leaned as he piled up some of the sticks I handed him from the bottom of the *Miss Aneeth* to make a fire. Chesley, meanwhile, pulled a cotton bag of flour from a compartment at the prow, produced a smaller plastic bag of baking soda from his bundle of personal belongings and in an enamel dish began mixing the flour and leaven with water into a pasty dough that when fried would become jacks.

Warm beans and fried bread, I thought. Already a considerable improvement. I had reckoned, though, without Cornejo and Radley, who had been splashing around in the middle distance from the dugout that they had paddled off over the coral. By the time we had got the fire going and balanced a pot of seawater on it, the two boys had returned with triumphant grins on their faces and half a dozen fat lobsters scrabbling around the bottom of their canoe.

Pausing only to hack their heads off with his machete, Zeledon tossed them into the boiling water. When they were cooked he handed us each a steaming lobster by its tailfin; sitting on the floor with the lobster in a plastic bowl on my knees, I tried to cut through the carapace with my Swiss Army knife but succeeded only in scalding my fingers. The local etiquette in these circumstances, I discovered, was to lay your lobster on the floor, belly down, and to stamp hard on it with your bare foot. The technique worked perfectly, cracking the shell cleanly so that it could easily be peeled away to reveal the firm milk-white meat with its coral-pink veneer.

We lounged through the heat of the afternoon in the thatched shade, lulled into a doze by the wavelets lapping around the stilts, until it was time to set the nets we would be leaving out overnight. We set off for the turtles' sleeping grounds, Zeledon standing with his feet splayed on the gunwhales at the back of the boat, the tiller rope tied around his waist to keep course, his belly bulging from underneath the one button done up on his shirt. Under the frayed camouflage jungle hat that he wore glued to his head night and day, the setting sun shone golden on his round face and he shielded his eyes with both hands as he searched for the coral heads.

"Tousanda raacks heer, mon," he said as he peered into the distance. *"Any copt'n can tek you dis side, bot few enoff know where de turkle likes to tek a waalk."*

Within half an hour we had arrived at the chosen spot, a labyrinth of passages winding between green-sprouting coral outcrops ten or twelve feet above the white sandy seabed. Where the reef emerged above the water at this low tide, the swell surged back and forth across its broad expanse, giving the abrasive, pumicelike rocks the insubstantial appearance of tufts of marsh grass. Chesley loosed a rope, bringing the sail down, and laid out the simple strategy of turtle hunting.

"See dahn dere? Lotsa big white hoals, white spahts. Das where de turkle sleeps cos dats dere sleepin place. To get dere, turkle hasta pass troo channils; put de nets in de channils, has to pass troo dere, dass where he gets in de nets. Joss like ambushin a man." But, he said, *"in strong weather, an'udder way is*

y'has to know where dey feed, seagrass, an you set long nets in shaller water on de feedin grounds."

It all seemed absurdly and unfairly easy. No wonder the fishermen had nearly wiped out the entire green turtle population in just a few years. Cornejo took a machete, swiped off an antler of rich brown elkhorn coral and proceeded to hack it into smaller chunks that could be used to weight the nets so that they would hang like invisible curtains across the underwater channels. If we were hunting an endangered species, I supposed, we might as well destroy an irreplaceable coral garden while we were at it.

Soon after sunrise the next morning the faintest breeze carried us over a glassy sea back to what I was increasingly coming to think of as the scene of our crime. As we approached the first net, Zeledon sniffed. *"Nottin in it,"* he snorted when we were still twenty yards away. *"When turkle caught net get shaarter as him tangle op and him floatin. Only when you go to cotch him he go down."*

The other nets over the feeding grounds were also hanging just as we had left them twelve hours earlier: one by one we hauled them in, Cornejo at the prow with a four-pronged grappling iron to hook the net out of the water, the rest of us strung out down the side of the boat to take it in and fold it up. No one spoke as the water dripped down our forearms and onto our legs, but the absence of turtle had clearly put Zeledon in a bad mood. He snapped at Radley for folding a net clumsily and chewed angrily at his lower lip.

I had expected to feel relieved that we hadn't caught anything, that the turtles had been too clever for us, that they would continue to feed that morning despite our

worst efforts, and would migrate south soon and then
be back next year to mate and nest. I should have
been relieved, but I wasn't. I felt just as disappointed at
having wasted our time as Zeledon and his crew so obviously did. This, after all, was their livelihood, and my
eco-consciousnesswas easily swamped by their frustration.
It didn't help, I suspected, that having brought a stranger
out to admire their skills as turtle hunters, they had come
up with nothing to show me.

*"Too late in de season, mon, most gaan down to Turkle Bogue.
Dat Costa Rica gumment mind de turkle good,"* Zeledon said
eventually. I couldn't tell whether he was praising the Costa
Rican authorities for their well-known turtle conservation
programme or cursing them for tempting his quarry out
of reach.

We turned south, heading for Haulover. Zeledon had
agreed that on his way to Corn Island he would stop off
at a village or two along the coast that I was anxious to
visit. We had been sailing for less than an hour, though,
when Radley shouted excitedly and pointed at a trawler
he had spotted a few miles out to sea. The only boats of
that size working Nicaraguan waters were pirate lobster
boats out of Honduras, and their crews were likely as not
Nicaraguan Miskitos. The temptation to find out who was
aboard, and perhaps to dive for a little lobster in return
for sugar, instant coffee and beef, was more than Zeledon
could resist. He set a course for the beetle on the horizon,
and instantly the sullen gloom that had fallen over the *Miss
Aneeth* evaporated.

Sure enough the *Water's Edge III,* a squat, heavily built
Honduran vessel, not much more than a floating cold store
really, was there to steal Nicaraguan lobster, like all the
other little blue-and-white boats I had seen tied up at the

wharf in Ceiba, like the boat at anchor off Rio Platano
whose divers had kept the village store in business. Though
the captain was Honduran he was a Miskito, as was the
mechanic in charge of the compressor that kept the divers'
tanks full of air. Everyone else aboard was from Nicaragua.
Almost every diver and canoe boy, it turned out, was from
Big Sandy Bay, all cousins and nephews and neighbours
to Zeledon and his crew, and as we clambered aboard up
a rope ladder the deck became a ferment of agitated boys
squealing cries of recognition and shouting for news of
their families.

We lunched with the captain, perched on stools in the
wheelhouse as the *Water's Edge* rocked at anchor, and the
bowls of rice and stringy beef stew were obviously a special
treat. My timid enquiry as to whether there might be any
lobster on offer provoked a collective attack of incredulous
eyebrow arching. Lobster, it seemed, was a dish of last
resort. I shut up and ate my stew.

In some muttered negotiations after the meal, Zeledon
arranged an afternoon's lobster fishing for the *Water's Edge*,
and pulling Cornejo and Radley out of a crowd of their
friends, we dropped back into the catboat. We had been
tacking away from the Honduran boat for about five
minutes, making our way through the scatter of divers'
dugouts bobbing over the shallow reef, when I heard an
ominous rhythmic thudding. In the cloudless sky, two fast-
approaching silhouettes confirmed what I had thought.
Sandinista helicopters.

They came at us low and with terrifying speed over the
open water, Soviet MI-24s, elegantly designed to resemble
infuriated hornets, bristling with guns and rocketry. One
after the other they swooped over the *Water's Edge*, their
rotor blades threshing up the water as they turned for

another run. What were they doing? Simply scaring off this pirate captain who was fishing illegally in Nicaraguan waters? Or were they going to use their weapons to teach him a more serious lesson?

He wasn't waiting to find out. Leaving the divers down below and the dugout boys paddling in terror, the *Water's Edge* weighed anchor and steamed for international waters.

The helicopters circled the boat a couple of times to make sure their message had gotten through, and then spotted the *Miss Aneeth*. Together they banked sharply, aiming their threatening noses towards us as we stared up at them like rabbits in a headlight. They swooped over us deafeningly, their wind tearing at our sail and rocking the little boat violently, but no one moved to bring the sail down. All four of my companions were sitting hunched over, their heads in their laps and their hands over their ears, petrified that at any moment we would be raked by machine-gun fire. I alone was watching the helicopters, fascinated by this intrusion of screaming modern machinery into the wave-lapped lives of these turtle fishermen.

Chesley tugged at my arm and threw me a shirt. *"Cover op your white belly, mon,"* he shouted above the din. *"If dey see dat we finish."*

But we weren't. The pilots merely circled over us, contemptuously it seemed as we cowered in fear and awe, flicked their dragonfly tails around and hurtled off towards the mainland. Soon they were just a distant hum.

Badly shaken, and far from convinced by my feeling that the helicopters would not return, Zeledon chose to seek shelter amongst a cluster of mangrove islets a mile or so away to recover our composure. It was not long before we were joined by the boys who had been diving when their mother boat had abandoned them. They paddled in pair by pair, their canoes full of lobster and diving tanks. They gathered their dugouts in a fan around the hut, dived into our sack of mangoes and gabbled and shouted and laughed in an explosion of high spirits that bubbled with relief.

It turned out that more than half of the divers and their canoemates had been on board the *Water's Edge* when the helicopters descended, and every one of them was a Nicaraguan draft dodger. Their fear was not only that the helicopter would rocket them out of the water, but that it might somehow land and capture them. In their panic at such a prospect they had thrown their canoes, their paddles and themselves into the open sea, and here they were, some of them with sheets that could be used as sails. The fact that they were stranded on an uninhabited cay in the middle of the ocean was not of the least consequence to them. Borrowing our machete they plunged into the mangrove thickets and hacked themselves stakes to serve as masts and booms. They untwisted their canoes' short painter ropes to make better use of the three strands they could tie together. They tore up their sheets, and one by one the tiny dugouts raised their makeshift sails—of floral patterns, geometric shapes and pastel shades—and headed for the horizon in single file like a mad flotilla advertising a department store's linen collection. At the rear limped one boy who had not been given a sheet. In lieu of a mast and sail he had cut himself a particularly bushy branch of mangrove and was counting on it to catch the wind. Miraculously, he was making headway.

The next morning we loaded aboard the scores of lobsters the diveboys had left behind and resumed our passage south. The wind blew unfailingly, the sun shone faultlessly, and as we all stretched out Zeledon and Chesley put puzzled questions about the world I came from.

"Are dere tigers in Inglan? Lotsa taxis, yeh? Much turkle roun de coast dere? If Inglan an island, how com dey no have no reef aroun dem? How does televisions work? How does computers work? How does satellites work?"

All these high-tech devices, I discovered, went in the Miskito language under the common denominator *"mirackil works,"* and I lost considerable face when I was found to be just as ignorant of the inner workings of a computer as everyone else aboard the *Miss Aneeth.* Especially since Chesley and Zeledon had no difficulty in answering any of my questions about turtling, sailing, the weather or the price of lobster.

Chesley had been adopted as a boy by a Caymanian turtle captain, and having spent his youth in the Cayman Islands he was a little too worldly wise for Zeledon's taste. The captain generally waited until Chesley was dozing before putting his most important questions.

"Dis beach, mon," he said to me that evening, gesturing towards the smudge of land to starboard, *"dis beach go all de way to Tampa?"*

I said that it did. That if you followed the coast north to Cape Gracias a Dios and then west along the Honduran shore, retraced the steps I had taken and then swept round the Gulf of Mexico, then you would reach Florida.

"At Tampa it stop, yeh?"

No, I said. Maybe you couldn't walk the shore the whole way, but after going up the side of America and Canada this sandy beach that we could see, fringed with palm trees, turned into the Arctic.

Zeledon pondered this for a while, and then simply pursed his lips. *"Sonnovabitchmon."*

A little later he tried me out on another subject. *"You ever hear of a state call Mississippi River?"* he asked.

"Yes."

"You ever hear of sirenas?"

"Yes," I said. *"Sirena"* is the Spanish word for mermaid. I wondered what the connection might be.

"You believe in sirenas?"

I told him that I did, but Zeledon clearly detected a note of uncertainty in my voice, because he paused for a moment, debating whether or not to continue this conversation with a probable unbeliever.

"Well is it true dey cotching sirenas *in Mississippi River?"* he asked, and when I told him that I had never heard of any mermaid hunters in Mississippi he brushed aside my ignorance. *"I want to cotch one in a net,"* he said confidently. *"Dey say dey cotchin em in Mississippi River."*

Maps of the Miskito shore mark a score of "Haulovers," for the name signifies a spot where the finger of land dividing the sea from a lagoon is narrow enough to make hauling a boat over it possible. Today they are simply place names. At one such site, though, a few wooden huts lining a broad grassy promenade mark a village. We put in to this Haulover, anxious for some breakfast after spending an uncomfortable night wrapped in sailcloth at the bottom of the *Miss Aneeth.*

I was sitting on a porch drinking a darkly bitter infusion of some sort of burnt tuber—Haulover had not seen coffee in years—when a stately old lady in a flowing pink cotton shift pulled herself up the steps to the verandah and addressed me imperiously in Miskito. A gnomelike man with his head permanently cocked followed in her wake and translated.

"She waan to know dis; inna kingtime, well de inglish who rule dis coas bot she wanta fine out why now she doan hear Inglan name at aal in de ear."

I tried a halting explanation of Great Britain's changing strategic interests over the past 150 years, a blustering apology for the way London had abandoned the coast at the end of the nineteenth century, but the old lady cut me short. She had not witnessed the betrayal herself for she was only eighty-eight, but she had heard all about it from her mother. The day that the *"Spainyard"* had taken Blue-fields in 1894 had been the saddest day in Miskito history.

"De laas time de king went to Bluefils, aal de crew dat was in Bluefils and Pearl Lagoon dey were cryin an mournin, well mournin fah de coas, fah de town, especially when dey see de flag how it was commin down an de Spanish flag goin op, dey were cryin. An aal was sorry, bot well dey coodn do anyting, dey coodn go against de king aarders. An in dat said minute de king was dronk dronk, didden know what he was doin."

This seemed rather unfair to young Robert Henry Clarence, who commanded no troops that might have offered any resistance to President Zelaya's invading Nicaraguan forces, but I didn't interrupt. The old lady had introduced herself as Olga Molina Joseph and sat down beside me, rocking her body gently to and fro as she recounted in a singsong voice her mother's memories. She paused patiently for the man who was translating, her wrinkled, freckled face smiling indulgently at him as he struggled sometimes to capture her meaning, and told me about the last moments of the Miskito kingdom.

"When dey were heistin daan de Miskita flag was a creole man who had de Miskita flag holdin, and a Spainyard had de Nicaragua flag. So when dere Miskita flag were commin daan slow de Nicaragua flag was goin op slow. Aafter it get

to de middle de creole man say 'Com daan you six stripe, won-
adays you fine happy,' bot meanin to say dat some aaf dese days
de Miskita flag will be op again."

Miss Olga closed her eyes and repeated dreamily the
foreign words she had held in her mind since childhood.
"Com daan you six stripe, wonadays you fine happy." Reaching
behind her neck she unknotted her headscarf, smoothing
it on her lap. Then she folded it ceremoniously and lowered
her voice in theatrical sadness.

"Aafter de flag get down, well dey fole it op. English man o'
war was out, a gennleman came down from dat, came to Bluefils,
fole op de flag put it in a lil valise and tek it out back aan de
boat. An dat is de en aaf de king history in de coas."

Miss Olga ended her story with an emphatic nod, turning
to look at me as if I had been personally responsible for
the whole affair. But as her memories faded away she gave
me a beatific smile, took my arm and offered to show me
around the village.

We went slowly down the grassy strip that constituted
Haulover's only street, Miss Olga shuffling along beside
me and leaning heavily on my arm, treating me like a
solicitous grandson. What she wanted to show me, she
explained, was the church. She wanted to take me there
because the church was built not of wood and thatch but
of plastered breezeblocks and corrugated iron whose so-
lidity Miss Olga clearly saw as an emblem of Haulover's
piety. She also wanted to show me the bullet-scarred walls,
the ugly pockmarks in the plasterwork a reminder of a
firefight a year or so earlier when YATAMA troops had
attacked a billet of Sandinista soldiers. *"Dis de trobble place,*
mon. Dis de trobble place."

Perched on the roof of the squat little church was a
belfry, but the bell itself sat on the concrete porch just

where it had fallen and cracked six months earlier, Miss Olga explained. In its place dangled a bright yellow diver's air tank that jerked like a suspended corpse when I tugged on its rope, knocked clumsily against a makeshift hammer and sounded a thin, muffled chime.

The original brass bell was embellished with angels' heads and florid curlicues, and around its girth a phrase was embossed in German, "*Ehre sei gott in der Hoehe.*" Glory be to God in the highest. The bell had been cast in 1889 and doubtless brought to Haulover by the Moravian missionaries who had spread throughout the coast in the mid-nineteenth century preaching the Lutheran doctrine that their church had developed in the Prussian heartlands.

The first Prussians arrived on the coast in 1846 when Prince Charles of Prussia sponsored a colonisation bid, a dispirited shipload who arrived in Bluefields with no clear idea of where in Central America they were meant to settle, nor of what they would do when they got there. The resident British representative in Bluefields fed them and put them up in the courthouse and the schoolroom, but they ignored his advice not to eat unripe guavas or to work in the midday sun, and many died. Those that survived established a small German community on the edge of Bluefields, and it was to minister to this community that the first Moravian missionaries arrived in 1849. As the settlers gradually dispersed the pastors turned their attentions to the indians.

The remains of several preachers and their families lay in a small sandy plot beside Haulover Church, protected by a picket fence in need of a new coat of whitewash and planted with a cluster of delicate white flowering shrubs. Anna Theodora Ziock, who had been born in 1850 in the town of Herrnhut, had departed this life only thirty years

later in Haulover, victim to some tropical disease un-
dreamed of on the plains of Prussia. She had probably not
even had time to learn Miskito.

If Anna Ziock had settled a little further south, Miskito
would have done her little good. As I jumped from the
prow of the *Miss Aneeth* onto the sandy beach at Rio
Grande Bar I was ready to call out the standard Miskito
salutation—*"Maarnin"*—to the knot of men gathered
there, and to receive the standard Miskito response in
return—*"Pine."* But the faces on the beach were darker,
the haircuts woollier, and something about the men's
loose-limbed, open posture told me that they were not
indians. I was out of Miskito territory, it seemed, and now
among creoles, as blacks were known on the coast. I recalled the creole greeting. *"Wha'appen."*

"Ry here mun," came the answer.

The night had been squally, and the early morning sun
shone in piercing luminous shafts through chinks in the
rain clouds. The light had an unreal quality to it, as if cast
by theatrical spots, and the emerald green of the dripping
jungle backdrop behind the village looked equally artificial.
Rio Grande Bar was a random scattering of huts set alongside the river in a broad clearing of lush meadow grass and
low scrub. Two bristly black pigs were rooting around in
the undergrowth. At seven o'clock on this damp morning
wisps of smoke rose from a few of the kitchen huts adjacent
to each house, and the men who had sauntered down to
the beach to watch our arrival were passing a bottle of rum
amongst themselves. That appeared to be the full extent
of village activity.

Chesley asked where we might find a cup of coffee, and
a toothless old man with a nicotine-stained toothbrush

moustache stepped towards us. *"Dis village in poor condition, mon, very poor condition. No caafee, no sugar no nuttin here now."* But when Chesley told him that we could provide some sugar his eyes brightened and he gave us a sly smile. He thought that perhaps he might have just a few beans of coffee left in his kitchen. *"I fix someting for drink. I hat the waater."*

Dan Moses was eighty-five and England meant only one thing to him. *"You from Queen Victoria home,"* he told me, in a tone of voice that suggested I myself was too young to know that fact. Fixing me with his rheumy eyes as we drank our coffee he told me of Rio Grande's glory days, beginning when Victoria was still on the throne.

"I din baarn as yet when de cumpny come from out and had a cannin factory in Pearl Lagoon, cannin fishes, fruit. Den some more com in bringin in saamill, plantin banana. I work for Atlantic Cumpny and den aafterward a bigger cumpny com, steamship, den aafterward a bigger cumpny com, Cuyamel. Dem were big cumpnies, mon. Cumpny useta have hundreds and hundreds of men, four barges carry fifteen tousand stems each out to de ships at de cay. Dis river bin shippin two times a week sixty tousand stems when I have twenty-five, tirty years.

"Cuyamel, dats wot built op dis place. At one time dere was twenty-eight Chinee stores, wholesale an retail. Dat was when dey put light here, every fifty yaard dey have a light post, and Cuyamel onliest won to put school in, dat why we caant read an write in Spanish only English—my daddy got teachers from Jamaica and Yunai States."

He pulled himself out of his low wooden chair, hitched up the baggy blue pair of flared trousers he was wearing and walked me over to the window.

"Dat was aal houses dere." He pointed towards the jungle edge a couple of hundred yards away through the rain that

had begun to fall again in blustery drifts. *"I remember when de back street stretch aal de way to de end. Mebbe tree faar hundred families here, aal dis was plenty dwellin house and rent house. Houses are rotten daan an aal like dat now. De onliest remnant is where dey useta keep de oil—de cement where de tank useta stand is right dere. Dat you gaat for remembrance."*

Four concrete posts, mossy with neglect, protruded above the long grass like the masts of a shipwreck. Rio Grande's single memorial to its history, a history Dan Moses remembered purely in terms of the foreign companies that had come and gone.

Up and down the coast they had been legion until the Great Depression, cultivating bananas, pressing copra oil from coconuts, mining gold, canning lobster and cutting timber. The Nicaraguan treasury earned forty percent of its tax revenue from the coast, and there were jobs for thousands, laying railways through the jungle for John D. Emery's lumber firm, manning river barges for Standard Fruit, humping stores in company warehouses, digging gold in the mines at Bonanza.

For forty years or so, it seemed that the dreams of those eighteenth-century English historians who had sung the coast's praises were coming to pass. But by the time the Second World War and U-boats brought trade in the Caribbean to a halt, the coast had relapsed again. Standard Fruit decided that the soil was richer in Honduras. The goldminers found that their rewards scarcely justified the effort of keeping the shafts pumped dry anymore. Timber was no longer in such heavy demand. A land that had fleetingly prospered from lobster, gold and mahogany fell back into its rut of cassava, plantain and fish.

Dan Moses slumped back into his chair and took a gulp

of coffee from a half-pint enamel mug. *"Faarty odd year now since de laas cumpny left out, said a disease is in de banana, and since de cumpny left dis side no work, no work at aal. We livin fraam cassava an plantain. De men fish turkle an aal like dat, fish, shrimp, but not pay so good. You mek a payday joss by de season. An I caant work now. I old, I fulla pain and sickness, I laid op. Joss turnin aroun you have to say. Joss turnin aroun."*

Somewhere a cock crowed, a cow mooched past the door impervious to the rain, and on the beach behind Dan's kitchen a captive turtle lay motionless on her back, breathing desperate, wheezing gasps and weeping gummy tears.

South of Rio Grande the wind died on us and we wallowed. We were making scarcely enough headway for Cornejo to steer a course, and like the rest of us he dozed in the morning sun, waking only to whistle quietly, trying to call up a wind. Zeledon had planned to reach Pearl Lagoon by midday, but it was soon clear that we were not going to arrive before nightfall. That meant that we would have to wait until the next morning in order to find our way across the bar. When I ventured a mildly frustrated remark about our slow progress Chesley sniffed at my impatience. *"It's like Jim Reeves said,"* he told me, tipping his baseball cap further back on his head. *"Whatever will be, will be."*

As dusk fell we anchored a mile or two off Pearl Lagoon Bar and I curled up in the bow, every bone protruding and rubbing raw against the boat's frame. During bouts of fitful sleep I dreamt of a bed.

Even though the wind had freshened in the morning, the tide was running out so hard at the bar that we could make no progress. Cornejo jumped overboard into the thigh-deep water, took hold of a rope he had fixed to the prow, and pulled the *Miss Aneeth* around the point and into the lagoon. An hour later, in deeper water where the currents were less fierce, we were able to tack laboriously towards the town half hidden behind the voluminous mango trees and clusters of palms that overhung the shore.

Zeledon hove to at the wooden jetty just long enough for me to jump out; he was anxious to get back across the bar before the tide turned and blocked his exit to the sea, and he was looking forward to earning some dollars by diving for lobster around Corn Island. I scarcely stayed longer at the dock, for just as I arrived a launch was putting out for Orinoco, across the lagoon. I jumped aboard.

In the early 1880s, when John D. Emery moved from Boston to Bluefields to set up a tropical lumber company, he found recruiting a workforce locally in the Mosquito Reservation unexpectedly difficult. The Miskitos themselves had no tradition of working in the timber trade, and the Jamaicans who were moving to the coast in increasing numbers were mostly townspeople, not jungle labourers. Emery turned to a group whose men were famed as loggers in Honduras and Belize, the Garifunas.

A hundred years later, the village of Orinoco resembled a planet that had lost touch with its solar system. The cultural radio waves from the past were growing fainter, the echoes of meaning more confused, and in the space of another generation the Garifunas around Pearl Lagoon will doubtless regard themselves simply as black, like their creole neighbours.

The first Garifuna to settle a lagoonside clearing was John Sambola from Sangrelaya, a forbear of the man who had let me into the fort at Trujillo. But why had he chosen the name Orinoco?

"Older people dem know dose tings but dem done die out now.

We's de younger set," said one woman close to seventy. "*Hardly any Garifuna here now, all mixed. None of dem children speak Garifuna. It's our fault we didn't teach dem; I speak it with Garifuna people like myself but right in my house I don't speak.*"

Some women still made cassava bread, but it was fifteen years since the last man who remembered how to weave a *ruguma* had died, fifteen years that they had been squeezing the toxins out of the cassava root by hand.

John Sambola's great niece was the only person in the village who could remember why her ancestor had chosen the name with which he had baptised his new home. In an isolated house twenty minutes' walk away through the mangroves, surrounded by rusted half-buried pieces of machinery, Miss Petrona kept the flame of Garifuna memory flickering. Wearing a tattered dress, her three teeth protruding from her lower gum, her eyes clouded with the pale blue mist of age, she explained haltingly.

"*Dat name Orinoco commin from out, where dem is in dem days—de ole time people, where dey livin den,*" she said. "*Ole time people come from St. Vincent, dem speak dere language bot dem not want to live dere no more so dem mek dere home Honduras.*

"*My ole time people,*" she sighed reflectively, and grunted. She sounded as if she thought they would have been better off to have stayed on St. Vincent.

ELEVEN

Since the time I once arrived in Bluefields drunk and under fire in the police chief's personal speedboat, listening to a Russian recite Shakespeare, the town has held a special place in my heart.

I had reached Rama, where the road from Managua stops and the river to Bluefields starts, to find that the contras had attacked Bluefields the day before and that the authorities had sealed the town off by cancelling the daily riverboat. At the wharf, however, a group of tall, well-dressed white men were unloading camera equipment from a jeep. Although I didn't recognise them they were clearly fellow journalists and I introduced myself. How were they going to get to Bluefields? I asked. They were from Soviet television, Viktor the producer explained, and as comrade allies of the Sandinista revolution, they had been promised a ride with the chief of police, who was hurrying home to deal with the aftereffects of the fighting.

I had been denied permission to go downriver, I complained. Viktor looked sympathetic. "In the name of journalistic solidarity," he announced, "I appoint you temporary soundman for Soviet television. Come with me."

So I heaved an ancient tape recorder aboard the policeman's speedboat, and off we roared down the sluggish
glassy river, hurtling round the meandering bends as two
young black militiamen, gripping their AK-47s nervously,
scanned the jungled banks for contras. As we came into a
wide, flat open stretch of the river a group of hidden gun-
men ambushed us. As the bullets sprayed above us I dived
instantly for the bottom of the boat, sheltered by the dubious protection of a fifty-gallon drum full of petrol. Our
militiamen fired back, and the shooting stopped as suddenly as it had started. I raised my head and saw Viktor
rummaging in his grip bag. Grinning, he pulled out a bottle.

For reasons best known to himself, Viktor was carrying
two bottles of sweet red martini with him to Bluefields.
We ended up draining both of them, and in the process,
to the police chief's huge amusement, abandoned all pre-
tence that I was a Russian. Viktor and I were speaking
Spanish to each other and improvising our way through
gaps in our vocabulary, but I stumbled in an attempt to
explain "dew." Absentmindedly, I spoke the word aloud
in English, as if that might help, and Viktor echoed me
questioningly, as if he was straining to remember something. Then it came to him. "The dew of yon high eastern
hill," he announced.

"Yerwot?"

" 'But look, the morn in russet mantle clad, walks o'er
the dew of yon high eastern hill,' " he recited fluently.
"Hamlet, the part at the beginning where the sentries have
just told Horatio about seeing the ghost. Dew, you see. I
know the word."

As we wove our way through the jungle, alone on the
empty river, Viktor stood at the prow waving his martini

bottle and declaiming his favourite passages from Shakespeare. The militiamen, their trigger fingers tense, stared
into the forest. The police chief, uncomprehending,
laughed. I leaned back against the drum of petrol and
reflected on how odd a place the Miskito coast had turned
out to be.

I was fairly seriously wasted when I arrived in Bluefields
this time too. The ferry from Pearl Lagoon had transformed
itself into a floating party.

The trip had begun predictably enough. The *Maria Bella*,
a squat wooden cargo vessel with peeling blue paint and
an alarming list, had set out in the early morning from the
mango-shaded wharf at Pearl Lagoon with only a handful
of passengers, and I had made myself a comfortable nest
in a coil of rope on the foredeck. Lulled by the steady
clatter of the propeller shaft as we limped down the Mon-
cada Canal through the mangroves, I slept.

I was woken by a clamour of excited voices, and opened
my eyes to find a wall of struggling men and boys about
to leap aboard from the jetty at which we were tying up.
They swarmed over the railings in a shouting, flailing tidal
wave, and instantly I was jammed up into a foetal squat
amongst a hundred or so new passengers, each cradling a
hessian sack of personal belongings. The *Maria Bella*'s list
grew steeper.

The new arrivals were workers on a nearby palm-oil
plantation, and after a fortnight in the back country they
were going home for the weekend. This called for celebration. Out of each hessian sack came a bottle of the
cheapest white rum on sale; harsh, crudely distilled spirit
that scalded my tongue and stung my nose when I drank
from the bottle my neighbour had thrust in front of me.

As I spluttered my thanks I suddenly found myself in a snakepit, the men around me squirming together into a collective writhe. Someone had put the music on.

They were wriggling to the simple, joyful, rocked-up nursery rhyme tunes that Bluefields lives by. *"Gimme back mi shillin wi de lion on it, de lion on it, de lion on it. Gimme back mi shillin wi de lion on it, girl you mussa tek mi fah a fool.*

"Laanch turn over laanch turn over, laanch turn over, over yonder.

"Aaaaal de nation like bana-ana, aal de nation like banaana."

The endlessly repeated lyrics were not the point. Most of them seemed to be snatches of old sea shanties or lullabies to which no one remembered all the words anymore. But they were set to a gleeful, jumping beat that slewed heedlessly through a chaos of Caribbean styles from the syncopated snap of *soca* to the driving lilt of reggae, from a hopping calypso to the rich horns of the rumba. In the confines of the foredeck of the *Maria Bella* we could do no more than twitch our rum-loosened limbs and clap our hands, but the drink and the noon heat exhausted the party anyhow. One by one the bottles emptied and shouts of laughter turned to drunken snores. The boat chugged on through the flat, hot afternoon.

We arrived in Bluefields a little before dusk, the town a low, untidy spread along the water's edge, punctuated by the sharp, clay-red spire of a Moravian church. As I walked the puddled streets in search of a hotel, I could feel the buildings around me decaying, steamed to the point of collapse by the tropical sun and rain. It was as if the town was held together physically only by the vibrancy and energy of its people, a collective act of faith defying decades of neglect. Each night, with the generators out of action, Bluefields dissolved into the damp velvet blackness. But the *Blufileños* came to the rescue. Flashing their torches on and off so as to save on batteries they crowded the streets, promenading past the carts where large women fried bananas and pork scraps by the light of their kerosene lamps. In noisy bars, men drank beers around guttering candles.

Blufileños call themselves individualists, but outsiders could be forgiven for finding them argumentative for the sake of being bloodyminded. As one black woman explained to me, "*creole people is haard people, creole system is not de same as indian system.*" I asked her what she meant.

"*Indian people when dey travellin in de lagoons, dey say, well we all gonna paass tru dis channil, and dey all pass tru. Bot de creole people would want to know de sense of de story. Why dey paass tru dat channil and not de udder channil? Why dey not use dis channil?*"

No authorities had ever found this approach to life more troublesome than the Sandinistas. Elsewhere in the country the revolution could be imposed when it was unpopular, but not in Bluefields. In Bluefields parents rose up and threw out the internationalist Cuban teachers (much to the detriment of the school system, it has to be said). Fishermen refused point-blank to become employees of the state fisheries company, and simply sold their lobsters to foreign pirates until the government caved in and paid them dollars for their catch. In Bluefields the government had to wheedle and cajole and see how they could make the revolution fit. Statuesque young creole women in the army had been shoehorned into their olive drab fatigues, but full uniform was too much to ask. From the ankle down they were freestyle soldiers. On parade, brightly embroidered Chinese cotton slippers stood alongside black patent-leather stiletto heels and there was nothing their heavy-booted commanding officer from Managua could do about it.

The Sandinistas' main man in town was doing his best to spice up the revolution with a dash of creole style. Lumberto Campbell looked like a *Playgirl* magazine centrefold, exaggeratedly muscled, lantern-jawed and master of a frank, engaging smile amongst other charms sufficient to have once tempted Bianca Jagger into visiting Bluefields. He himself had honed his uniform down to the informality of a khaki T-shirt and a pair of sharply creased camouflage trousers. The reggae music pumping down the street was as likely to be coming from his open windows as any others. But he knew that even his blackness, his deliberate informality and his Bluefields family background could not disguise the fact that he was President Daniel Ortega's personal representative in the town, a symbol of central government, a symbol of the Spaniard. And the *Blufileno*'s resentment of central government has been festering since President Zelaya's troops sailed into town in February 1894.

Bluefields looks over its shoulder, grudgingly, up the muddy Hidden River that is its only link with the rest of Nicaragua. But the town has always welcomed, with open arms and a reassuringly sheltered lagoon, any vessel bringing people, goods or influences from abroad. The port developed from its origins as a buccaneers' haven, named after the Dutch pirate Abraham Blauveldt, who made it his base. Blauveldt also worked as a guide and agent for the company that Puritans had established on Providence Island in 1631; it was his familiarity with the coast that opened the area up to English traders and paved the way for nearly 300 years of English domination.

Until the end of the eighteenth century, Belize and Honduras—The Bay and The Shore—had attracted most English interest, but over the next hundred years attention turned further south. When Britain pulled its settlers out in 1786, descendants of Robert Hodgson, the first superintendent of Black River, stayed on the coast swearing loyalty to Spain, and they moved to Bluefields. Importing slaves from the West Indies and begetting children by their women, the Hodgson family quickly creolised itself. A hundred years after Lieutenant Robert Hodgson married Isabel Pitt in Black River, the British consul general in Bluefields complained of their great grandson Alexander Hodgson that "his appearance is quite that of an African— he can sign his name but can write nothing else." By the end of the nineteenth century Hodgsons of one sort or another made up most of the Miskito Council, supposedly a conclave of indian elders gathered around the chief but in fact mainly a group of creoles taking orders from the British Consul. And the Hodgson hegemony proved durable: when I visited Bluefields the Sandinista mayor was a young member of the Hodgson clan named Johnny.

From the first Hodgsons to the last, and especially a hundred years ago, when Bluefields was shipping more bananas than any other two ports in the world put together, the town has preferred "de out." I met an old creole lady, Miss Rosalyn Allen, who had been brought to Bluefields as a girl in 1909 and whose greatest delight was to recall the days when "Bluefields was in her beauty in stores and houses." Sitting frail and papery in an upright chair, grumbling about how "our life here now is not so excellent," her eyes lit up when she recited a list of the goods that the traders had once brought in to town.

"Goods I cannot tell about, fine tings fraam Germany fine tings fraam United States, Englan, India. Ribbon was juss fifteen cents a yard, gingham was juss twenny cents a yard, good stuff. Sold catfish, mackeril, saltbeef, ham, bacon aal kine a good stuff, condense milk tomatoes in tin, rice onion grapes apple, nuts candies of aal kine, dollies—when dey com fraam Germany dey were pretty babies—pianos, tread were juss five cents for de baall, embroidery tread were juss fifteen cents. Sugar were five cents a pound, US sugar, an in Bluefields dere were an ice factory."

The Sandinista authorities were doing their best to emulate those days of consumer glory, and if that meant setting aside a few revolutionary principles, then so be it. The main street was lined with folding tables piled high with Colombian cigarettes, Costa Rican toiletries and other smuggled goods, and the government itself had set up a "dollar shop," accepting only hard currency and selling imported luxuries that would tempt the fishermen to part with the dollars they had been paid for their catch.

Amongst the advertisements carried in the *Bluefields Messenger* in 1894 was one for a fortnightly passenger service to New Orleans. Hamstrung by a US trade blockade against Nicaragua, Dexter Hooker, a Bluefields trader, could hardly expect to reestablish ties as close as that, but he was the first to admit that some things hadn't changed in a hundred years. It was still much more time-consuming and expensive to go to Managua than to go to New Orleans for anything that Bluefields needed, and if New Orleans was closed to him then Dexter Hooker would look in Jamaica, Colombia, Panama and Costa Rica.

Some strange driftwood from *de out* had remained long

after the tide had receded. The walls of the "Pearl Lagoon" beer hall, a concrete-floored barn with all the atmosphere of an empty packing crate, were bare of decoration save for a pair of elaborately framed prints, side by side. In one of them stood "Their Most Gracious Majesties King George V and Queen Mary, portrayed in the State Room at Buckingham Palace." The other tableau was a massive colour lithograph representing, according to its worm-punctured caption, "The Coronation of His Majesty King Edward VII And Queen Alexandra in Westminster Abbey August 9th 1902." An explanatory note added that "The Ceremony was postponed from June 26th 1902 on account of the serious illness of His Majesty the King, which necessitated his undergoing a dangerous operation, through which he was mercifully preserved."

I found more recent arrivals from *de out* in the public library, which in the days of the banana companies had been the headquarters of Tropical Radio. On the shelves now were some unlikely volumes: a privately published edition of short stories by Philip Roth signed by the author, for example, next to a book by Ngaio Marsh donated by Silvia Bodden—a member of the famous Caymanian turtling family and distant relative of Radley's. A Sandinista solidarity group somewhere in the Anglo-Saxon world was presumably responsible for the transcription of the Watergate tapes and the copy of *Women, Race and Class* by Angela Davis, but would even the Soviet embassy have off-loaded *Steel and Slag* on the unsuspecting Bluefields librarian? (Vladimir Popov won the Stalin prize for literature in 1948 with that one.)

Past and present influences blended neatly, if incongruously, in a substantial whitewashed concrete building protected by wrought-iron railings around its balcony. This

was now home to the dozen or so Cuban doctors who
staffed the town's new hospital, but an oval plaque beside
the front door announced the building's original use. Emblazoned in red and blue and gold were a lion and a unicorn flanking the English royal coat of arms, for this had
once been the British Vice-Consulate. The plaque shone
brightly among the surrounding scruffiness, the only thing
in Bluefields to have been given a coat of paint in the last
ten years. The Cubans were taking proprietorial care of
this relic of colonialism, bringing in enamel paint specially
from Havana to touch it up as needed. After a visit to
Bluefields once, in his dispatch to London, a British diplomat had mentioned the Cubans' curious solicitude. He
was astounded to receive a reply from the Foreign Office
to the effect that this plaque remained Her Majesty's Government's property, and that he should take steps to re-
possess it forthwith. The cable was discreetly mislaid.

It was in Bluefields in 1984 that I had first come across
the tribe of Rama indians. Five hundred of them, almost
their entire number, had fled their ancestral island in the
lagoon after a contra attack, and the Sandinistas had herded
them into the Moravian church hall while deciding what
to do about them. Sitting in the gloom, huddled over the
few possessions they had managed to snatch up in their
flight, the sullen and frightened refugees were unwilling
to answer my questions. I went outside to take some
photographs.

As I fiddled with a lens setting an old man followed me
into the tangle of weeds that had once been a garden and
sidled up.

"You English?" he asked in a whisper, looking theatri-
cally over his shoulder.

"Yes," I told him. "I'm from England."

"You gaat help os, mon," he said. *"Dat contra attack not like dem Sandinista say. After we gaan fram de island San-dinista plane trow bombs on de church. We in a sanwich, mon, tween de contra and de Sandinista. You gaat help os."*

I would go to visit the church, I told the old man, but I didn't see what more I could do to help.

"You English, right? You goin home to England when you leave out from here. Den when you get dere, tell de queen what happenin here. If de queen know, she do sumtin. Juss dat she doan know how tings is here. An we English, too, mon."

I had been so bewildered to find the elder of a dying tribe of indians in revolutionary Nicaragua claiming to be English that it did not strike me until later that the queen he hoped I would petition was Queen Victoria.

By the time I arrived in Bluefields the Ramas had long since returned to their tiny cay in the middle of Bluefields Lagoon, little more than a grassy knoll rising from the water in a froth of palm trees. Even back home, though, they were struggling to survive, living in ragged mudfloor huts, sleeping on rough boards covered only with hessian, eating spoonfuls of undersized shellfish that they scraped from the floor of the lagoon.

"I remember foss time o'days me in Bluefields get evryting free," Amos Solomon sighed, sitting on an upturned log and shaking sand out of the cut-off wellington boots that all the men wore as shoes. *"Dat was dollars time, dere you find raiment, dere you find shoe, evryting to buy. Now when you go to buy have high price bot when you go to sell, one sack o'carbon one hundred Cordobas dey no waant to pay."*

Turned in on themselves and their island, decimated once by Miskito slave raids and then by cultural assimi-lation and now numbering just a few hundred, the Ramas had little enough to hang onto as reminders of who they were. As far as Amos was concerned *"Aal de Rama people dead. Only youngest people commin up now an we no use de Rama language cos dey never laarn us. We spik broken creole."* In fact, the Ramas lost their language in the middle of the last century, when they meekly handed it over to Moravian missionaries.

In 1858 a Moravian missionary from Denmark, Jens Paul Jurgenssen, arrived in Rama Cay and set himself up as a religious dictator. Finding the men often drunk and lounging around in hammocks while the women worked, he banned alchohol on the island, forbade traditional mystic healers from practising, allowed no one to leave the cay without his permission or to visit it without a good reason, and announced that henceforth no boats would put to sea on the Sabbath. He also decided that it was hardly worth his while to learn the Rama language to save only a few hundred souls and that he would teach the gospel and the schoolchildren in his broken English. Soon he had converted everybody on the Cay, and over the years, encouraged by Jurgenssen's German successors, the Ramas came to use English rather than their own language even amongst themselves.

But the missionaries didn't simply force the Rama language into oblivion and fill their converts' mouths with a foreign tongue. They taught them badly spoken English, a thin and awkward version that the pastors themselves had had to learn as a foreign language in order to proselytise, and what Amos called *"broken creole"* is full of German words and phraseology.

A handful of old people, though, still remembered some Rama, and the Sandinista government was encouraging them to help teach the children at school. *"Dis year, laast year dey try to mek aal de childen spik Rama cos dey no waant de language for lost,"* Miss Nora explained to me, sitting in the sand by the door of her hut, shucking tiny mussels and throwing their gleaming shells into a silver-violet heap beside her.

"I not know for read, you know, but I tell dem what I hab to tell dem, words for animals and tings. I tell childen how chicken name, how pig name, how daag name. I tell em about eat laugh vex sleep wake baath."

Miss Nora was very old, but she was reasonably intelligible, which was one of the reasons she had been asked to help at the school. But the Rama language had almost disappeared, and those who did remember, one American researcher found, were unable to pronounce it properly because they had lost all their teeth. A woman with a practical bent, she spent the first installment of her research grant on providing her subjects with dentures.

The Moravian missionaries left a heritage not only of garbled language, but of garbled gospel. Once upon a time the Ramas had believed in a prophetic tiger, but the Reverend Jurgenssen saw him off quickly enough. Today the Ramas trace their origins back to the *"foss time people"* who were brought in from *de out* by the great leader, Adam. His sister Eve married a snake and became a snake goddess, while Adam's son, Jesus, had a wife called Mary. When the end of the world arrives a great flood will cover the earth, and the bigger of the two rock piles at Monkey Point, just south of Bluefields, will be transformed into Adam's boat. The smaller one will become Jesus' dory, and Adam and Jesus will then sail up the Miskito coast saving all the good people from the flood. If any sinners try to climb aboard, however, Jesus will hit them over the head with his oar and they will sink, turned into turtle or tarpon.

The boatman who ferried me in his launch back across the lagoon from Rama Cay said that with a friend who had a sturdier speedboat he would be delighted to carry me down the coast to San Juan del Norte, and then into Costa Rica. We agreed to meet that night, and to discuss a price with the owner of the boat.

I would have liked to walk to the frontier, but soon found that this was a thoroughly impractical and foolhardy idea. The journey would have taken a week or more, and I was told that nobody lived anywhere on the whole stretch of beach, which had been evacuated by the Sandinistas on account of contra guerrilla attacks. The coast was also bisected by a number of rivers, and with nobody living at their mouths any longer I would find no one to ferry me across them. Aside from which the area was reputed to be crawling with contras and I was growing homesick. I decided to go by boat.

Comandante Guerrillero Lumberto Campbell, true to the informality of his image, was happy to sign a letter of authorisation allowing me to break all the rules, ordering Immigration officials and everyone else to let me leave Bluefields by boat and cross into Costa Rica, even though the frontier was closed and there was no border post. San Juan del Norte itself, he thought, was a contra encampment and he did not advise me to stop there, but so long as I was doing this at my own risk he had no objections.

Contra camp or not, I was determined to find San Juan del Norte. For much of the nineteenth century it had been one of the most important towns on the coast; a busy port and commercial hub. Now it had faded to extinction.

Christopher Columbus anchored off the mouth of the San Juan River in 1502, but never realised that he was as close as he would ever get to a passage through the landmass that would lead him to the "coreland" of India. Twenty-five years later, exploring from the source of the river in Lake Granada, the Spaniards discovered that the river and the lake between them formed a waterway that all but cut Central America in two, leaving only a ten-mile corridor of land on the Pacific coast. Throughout the seventeenth century the Spaniards laboriously plied the route, which was shoaled with rapids, to ship indigo and cochineal, sugar, hides and silver from Guatemala to Cartagena on Colombia's Caribbean coast.

The river's value to military planners was as great as its use to traders, and when Spain declared war on England in 1779 the English chose San Juan as their first target. A large contingent of Miskito warriors, led by King George II and a party of settlers who had sailed down from Black River, were gathered under the command of Captain Horatio Nelson and sent upriver to capture the Spaniards' Fort Inmaculada. They succeeded, but it did them little good. The incessant rain wore down the soldiers' morale and encouraged all manner of disease—Nelson himself almost died of dysentery before being removed to Jamaica—while the Miskitos simply melted into the forest.

San Juan was nothing more than a strategically located hamlet when the Nicaraguan government decided to assert its rights to the Miskito coast in 1840 and sent a commandant to the river-mouth settlement. By this time the English had filtered back into the region, and the superintendent of Belize decided that it was time to mark a more formal presence. Taking King Robert Charles Frederick with him as political camouflage, and flying the Mosquito flag alongside the Union Jack, the superintendent sailed into San Juan Harbour, kidnapped the Nicaraguan *comandante* and sailed away again.

This brusque little incident caught the attention of the Americans, who had already turned their eyes to the Miskito coast because of their interest in a canal across the Central American isthmus. Preemptively, London declared the Mosquitia a fully fledged protectorate, and then in 1846 extended it to include San Juan. When the Nicaraguans again disputed control of the port, the British resident in Bluefields not only installed English officials in the town, but for good measure gave it a new name. Henceforth, he announced, the port would be known as Greytown, in honour of the governor of Jamaica, Sir Charles Grey.

The Americans were now seriously worried about British intentions, and their misgivings only deepened when the 1849 gold rush transformed Greytown into a thriving staging post on the way to California. Cornelius Vanderbilt's Accessory Transit Company was soon carrying over 20,000 fortune seekers a year by ship from the American east coast to Greytown, by giant "bongo" dugout up the San Juan River and across the lake, by carriage, down the ten-mile rutted road to the Pacific and then by boat up to San Francisco. Greytown, though, was a bottleneck on this journey, and travellers forced to stay there while they waited for transport upriver fuelled a boom. New streets were built along the shore and were extended back into what had once been forest. Soon they were lined by frame houses with verandahs that might have been plucked from a New Orleans suburb, and by billiard parlours, gambling halls and whorehouses.

The English municipal authorities soon complained that

they needed a police force to cope with the transient gold diggers, but they had no money with which to create one so they introduced docking fees. When Vanderbilt refused to pay them, the town council appealed to an English warship that happened to be in harbour. To back up the council the HMS *Express* opened fire on one of Vanderbilt's boats, sparking an international diplomatic incident. In Greytown, Vanderbilt shifted his whole operation to a spit of sand opposite the town that he made self-sufficient. Travellers disembarked there, stayed there and bought what they needed there. Greytown's shopkeepers were left without customers, and feelings were thus running high when the US minister to Nicaragua, passing through Greytown, offered his protection to an American riverboat captain accused of murder.

An angry crowd barracked the frightened envoy and somebody threw a broken bottle at him before he could make his way aboard the steamer to New York. When he reached home and reported the incident, the US government dispatched Commander Hollins aboard the warship *Cyane* to exact reparations. Arriving in the bay on 11 July 1854, Hollins sent a message threatening to bombard Greytown unless "the 'authorities' (so called)" provided satisfaction for their "gross outrages" within twenty-four hours. They didn't, and Hollins opened fire. He also sent a party ashore to ransack and put to the flame any building that had survived the shelling, and by the afternoon Greytown was a smouldering wasteland by the beach, its inhabitants cowering in the jungle a mile or so away.

William Walker's invasion of Nicaragua in 1856 put paid to the settlement for good by closing the interoceanic route. By then a train was running reliably across Panama, and Greytown fell into a decline from which it would never recover, left idle also by the waters of the San Juan, which diverted themselves into a nearby river after dramatic floods altered the lay of the land. Soon, silting made the harbour unuseable. Many of the town's residents left, the schools and churches closed, and grass grew in the streets. By 1865 Greytown's rotting timbers stood on the edge of a marshy lagoon rather than on a riverbank or seashore.

The town's mortal decay continued quietly for another two decades before the region was thrown into spasms of unexpected activity. The San Juan River's potential as a canal had never been forgotten, and in 1889 a private American company began to dig. *The New York Times* was on hand to witness the dawn of the enterprise, and if jingoist enthusiasm could have substituted for engineering the canal would have been built in months.

> Amid the booming of cannon, cheering of crowds of all nationalities, the clinking of wineglasses, speeches and handshakings, dinners and receptions, services in the churches and the jollity natural to a general holiday, at a given word one hundred American picks were driven into Nicaraguan soil, one hundred American shovels followed suit, and then the trundling of American wheelbarrows told that the soil was at least broken in the work upon the Nicaraguan Canal.

But the venture failed. The foul climate, the pestilential swamps and unexpectedly rocky ridges defeated the engineers, and in 1893 the company collapsed for lack of funds. The workers dispersed, the channels they had dug filled with water and weeds, the town they had lived in fell prey to the termites. Greytown expired.

———

Antonio, the boatman who had brought me back from
Rama Cay, introduced me that evening to his colleague
Pedro, owner of a seagoing speedboat and said to be knowl-
edgeable about the coast. Pedro and I circled each other
in a ritual bargaining session, but he proved an obstinate
negotiator. The longer we talked the surer I grew that his
inflexibility was based on second thoughts about whether
he wanted to make the trip. Before he could decide against
it I agreed to pay his price. We were to leave at dawn the
next morning, which Pedro said would give us time to reach
San Juan in the afternoon and explore the remains, and
perhaps to reach Colorado by nightfall.

Before going to sleep that night I laid out my maps on
the hotel bed and studied them by torchlight. Colorado
was just a day's boatride down a coastal waterway from the
port of Limon, and there I could pick up a road again for
the first time since the track had petered out in the Honduran town of Limon two months earlier. In Honduras, I
recalled, I had felt ashamed at having resorted to such a
mundane form of transport as a bus; the 700 intervening
miles by boat and foot had taught me a new respect for
buses, and I certainly wasn't going to turn down the one
that linked Limon with the Panamanian border. From there
it would be a hop to the banana port of Almirante, where
I could surely find a vessel coasting down to my final destination at the mouth of the Panama Canal: Colon. After
so many difficulties and complications, this final stage
looked simple.

Before leaving Bluefields we had to complete the paperwork in the port offices at The Bluff, the harbour tucked
into a long spit of land that protects Bluefields Lagoon
from storms. When we pulled up at The Bluff, a sorry

looking row of dilapidated government buildings, we
found that the immigration officials had not yet come to
work. And at the naval headquarters, the Sub-Lieutenant
in charge of signing the form authorising us to leave had
heard nothing about us. My blanket permission from *Comandante* Lumberto Campbell to do anything I liked did not
impress Sub-Lieutenant Treminio, secure behind his perfectly groomed black moustache and arrogant eyes that he
had the power to ruin all my plans unless I grovelled.

Realising that I would have to grovel at some stage, but
not ready to do so just yet, I left Pedro to get on with the
bureaucratic process and went to help Antonio load fuel.
By the time we had located the man in charge of the huge
tanks that fed the Bluefields fishing fleet, discovered the
pressure was too low to pump the fuel, filled our fifty-
gallon drums from the tap, looked for the man with a cart
to carry the drums the 400 yards from the tanks to the
wharf, been told he had not come to work today and rolled
the drums ourselves down the potholed track, it was noon,
a storm had burst, and I was soaked to the skin and furiously frustrated at all the delays.

We eventually set off in the midafternoon, the powerful
speedboat low in the water under the weight of a spare
outboard motor and two drums of gasoline. Clearly we
would not reach San Juan that evening, but Pedro suggested that we reconnoitre Monkey Point, a sheltered bay
some two hours south, and spend the night there so long
as there were no contras camped in the vicinity. When we
rounded the point into the bay, a Colombian shrimping
boat lay at anchor, and as we pulled alongside the sailors
reassured us that the area was *tranquilo*. From an industrial-
sized red plastic laundry basket they heaped us with fish,

too, and beaching the speedboat on the gently shelving sand we went ashore in search of firewood.

The early evening sun bathed the forest a luminous gold; in the still air the thick-leaved trees that swept down to the beach radiated the day's accumulated warmth, and the silence was broken only by the tails of lizards disappearing into the bush. Machete in hand, I threshed my way inland through the shoulder-high grasses, relishing the rhythmic ease with which I was carving my path. Inexplicably, my blade struck suddenly against a metallic obstacle, jarring my wrist with a clang that started a cloud of small birds from the trees around. When I had recovered some feeling in my hand I cleared the bush away. Half buried by the undergrowth lay a cast-iron chassis of some sort, its four wheels long rusted into immobility but still bearing the raised imprint of their origin, "Berwick Pa." Pennsylvania to Monkey Point? What was this?

Doubtless summoned by the noise, a nearby voice called out to me. Monkey Point was meant to be deserted and Pedro and Antonio had stayed on the boat, fiddling with the engine. I froze, but my whereabouts were obvious enough. Sure enough, crashing through the foliage the voice grew closer, hailing me curiously, and as I crouched on the ground a pair of enormous hands burst through the curtain of grass, parting the way for their bearlike owner.

Breathing heavily he stared down at me as I raised my eyes from his cracked and calloused feet (no boots, I noticed with relief, so he couldn't be a contra), up past a pair of trousers tied roughly at the waist, to a mighty chest and muscled arms swinging loosely at his side. As I rose to my feet to explain myself, however, I saw that he had a droopy moustache and a small tuft of hair beneath his lower lip, which combined with his aquiline nose gave him the comic air of a beefy black Frank Zappa. Jammed down tightly over his beetling eyebrows he wore a toy American GI's helmet. His eyes were full of astonishment as he offered me his hand. "Alphonse," he introduced himself. "Alphonse Presida."

Encouraged by the recent ceasefire, Alphonse had ventured home after four years away to find his hamlet swallowed up by the bush. Clearing a couple of patches, he and his brother had built their families a pair of precarious huts, planted some corn, and planned to reconstruct their village. He also explained the chassis I was sitting on. At least, he explained it to his own satisfaction. *"Dat my grandaddy,"* he announced proudly.

What he meant was that his grandfather, a Frenchman, had been an engineer on an ambitious scheme launched by a mad Englishman around the time of the First World War to force a railway through the jungle from Monkey Point. He enjoyed no more success than the American company that tried to dig a canal from Greytown, but one memorial to his effort still stood—a small concrete blockhouse that had once housed a boiler. Alphonse had gone to the trouble of clearing the undergrowth from around it, he explained, because his grandfather had built it with his own hands.

Deeper into the forest, Alphonse claimed, an even more remarkable relic lay hidden. On a stretch of railway track that had never been torn up sat not just a trainlength of wagons still coupled together, but their locomotive too, tangled with creepers. I was never able to explore it for myself. Dusk was falling and we went looking for fresh water.

Alphonse walked me through the woods, taking me to

the creek that weaved among jungle roots down the hillside. At a certain point the natural stream had been funnelled into a metal pipe that fed the water into a concrete tank set in stone walls. *"De Cubians put dis here,"* Alphonse explained to me. The *"Cubians"* who were here with the Sandinistas? I asked. *"No, mon, de Cubians dat here tirty year aback."*

Thirty years back, according to Alphonse, there had been work for everyone at Monkey Point. Some Cubans had showed up paying good wages to anybody who would help clear the land for an airstrip, build barracks or run them up the coast to Bluefields in their speedboats every now and again. For nine months they had stayed, Alphonse recalled, hanging out, doing physical jerks and occasionally some target practice, before one day they all just left. They never came back, said Alphonse, and he had no idea where they had gone. He was sorry when I told him that it sounded to me as if most of them had been killed or captured when they landed at the Bay of Pigs. They had been a friendly lot of fellows as he remembered them, they had livened up Monkey Point no end, and no one had ever paid wages like that, before or since.

We set out early the next morning for San Juan del Norte, and Pedro decided that rather than hug the long, slow curve of the coastline we would save time and fuel by cutting across the bay, heading due south for the San Juan bar. The weather was blowy, but Pedro said his boat could handle it, and I had no objections. We were about an hour out of Monkey Point and had lost sight of the land to our right some time ago, when the wind began gusting fiercely, sweeping rainclouds across the sky that blotted out the sun in an instant and then soaked us in sudden driving sheets.

The sea, which only minutes earlier had been a choppy, brisk pale green, turned an ugly purple and developed a long and menacing roll. The wind gathered force, whipping shreds of foam from the top of the waves, and I shouted over my shoulder that we should head towards land.

But we couldn't. For a few minutes we tried, but the weight of our extra fuel held the rear of the boat so low in the water that the waves rolling in towards the unseen shore broke continuously over our stern. Antonio and I baled furiously with a couple of old oil cans, but it was soon clear that the only way to keep the boat out of trouble was to hold her nose into the wind and the waves while running the motor as slowly as possible. It worked—until the motor choked, recovered, choked again and died.

The first wave that caught us pulled the boat broadsides to the next one, which tipped us up and swept us along in a slewing drunken lurch. I grabbed a paddle and tried to bring the boat into the wind again, while Pedro and Antonio, water streaming down their faces, each using one hand to hang onto the boat, bent over the outboard motor. When I looked back to see what progress they were making, Pedro was leaning overboard retching and Antonio was huddled in the bottom of the boat whimpering with fear. Suddenly I felt extremely sick.

In snatches of shouted conversation I discovered that neither Pedro nor Antonio had ever taken this boat out of Bluefields Lagoon before, and that neither had been down the coast since their boyhood. This was their first time as adults in the open sea, our engine had failed, we had lost our bearings and the storm was threatening to swamp us. Suddenly I *was* sick, vomiting in great heaving spasms of terror.

As I kept paddling, Pedro went back to the motor, but

he didn't tinker with it. For an endless half hour he pulled repeatedly on the starter cord in angry, futile jerks that wrung out nothing more than a splutter. And then, as if the outboard had finally cracked in its battle of wills with Pedro's mulish obstinacy, it caught and roared alive. We leapt to our feet with yelps of delight. The wind and rain had slackened by now, and though the clouds hung low it seemed as if the worst of the storm had blown over. Pedro turned the boat around and opened up the engine.

"Where are we going?" I shouted.

"I'm heading for land," he yelled back. "When we see it we'll turn south."

This seemed a practical enough idea, but I wondered how he knew which way was landward. We had already established that there was no compass aboard, and the sea had spun us around like a top. Only one way would take us back quickly to land. Wouldn't it be more sensible to wait until the sun came out, so that we could judge directions?

But Pedro would not be persuaded. The storm had thrown him into a sort of controlled hysteria. He had decided which way was home and he was headed there. For twenty minutes we ploughed headlong across the waves, smacking from crest to trough, until we glimpsed a pale watery sun filtering through a break in the clouds. It was half past eight in the morning and we were heading towards the sun. We were going east, I screamed at Pedro, grabbing his arm and pointing to the sun. We were heading straight out to sea.

Eventually, when I had calmed down enough to convince Antonio that we were going in the wrong direction, we both tackled Pedro. Finally he seemed to have got a better grip on reality and realised that we were heading towards

Spain. He turned the boat around, and with the sun on our backs and our clothes laid out to dry, we made for land.

Before long it appeared, a low grey smudge against the horizon, and because the motor was continuing to give us trouble, cutting out from time to time for no apparent reason, we agreed to go right in to the beach and to turn only when we were a few hundred yards offshore—a distance that could be paddled in another emergency.

Where we were I had no idea, but Antonio was confident that he remembered the coast from his days as a teenage worker on the coconut-palm plantation that stretched some thirty miles above the San Juan River. A distant hillock that we could just make out, he said, rose behind the lagoon where Greytown had stood. Close in to the shore we skimmed along, the empty strand littered with bleached driftwood and dried coconut husks that had fallen from the endless stands of palms. I remembered reading somewhere that a Swede named Emil Brautigam had planted these trees for their copra forty years ago. Now their fruit fell unharvested.

When we drew level with the hillock an hour and a half later Antonio decided that he had been mistaken—San Juan in fact lay a little further to the south, now that he thought about it. Certainly there was no rivermouth by which to enter any lagoon that might lie hidden behind the palms. Each time I looked at him questioningly, Antonio insisted that we had "just a little way more to go," but his answers grew less confident. We had been at sea now for nearly five hours, and even allowing for the time we had lost in the storm it was clear that we should have long since reached the San Juan. We passed two river bars, but Antonio was sure that neither was the one we were looking for. Nor was there any sign of life on the beach, no one to tell us where we were. We were truly lost, but all we could do was follow the beach south.

It was soon clear, though, that Antonio no longer recognised anything we saw, and when we spotted a hut among the palm trees we agreed that we should go ashore even if it was a contra base. If we went much further south, for one thing, we would not have enough fuel to take us back to Bluefields. Pedro brought the boat around and headed towards the cabin. Standing in the prow I scanned the beach, but saw no movement.

We were a couple of hundred yards offshore when a burst of automatic gunfire crackled above the roar of our engine. I dropped to my knees and Pedro pulled the boat around sharply, aiming out to sea and accelerating fast. The gunman sprayed another, longer magazine load, and this time we could hear the bullets cracking above our heads. We were an easy target on the open sea; whoever was shooting at us did not seem to be aiming at the boat itself, nor trying to frighten us off. He must be forcing us to come in. I tore off my shirt and waved it as a makeshift white flag above the edge of the boat while Pedro slowed the motor and turned in towards the beach.

Holding my shirt aloft, I rose to my feet. A dozen uniformed men were emerging from the trees onto the beach, their guns levelled at us. The Sandinistas had pulled all their troops out of this area; these soldiers could only be contras, and this far south they would not be the Miskito YATAMA forces to whom I had letters of introduction. These would be an altogether nastier lot, ill-disposed towards foreign journalists generally and especially those with special travel permits from the Sandinista government.

Pedro and Antonio, I could see, were just as frightened as I was, Pedro babbling about not telling anyone where we had come from or who we were. As I looked towards the hut again a flag on its roof fluttered in a gust of wind and I was overcome with first relief, then fury. Its colours were the red, white and blue of Costa Rica. We weren't in Nicaragua at all; we had far overshot San Juan Bar, and the men on the beach were members of the Costa Rican Civil Guard.

The storm had cleared from the sky, but the swell it had built up was still crashing against the coastline. As the rollers thundered in, each breaker picked us up, hurled us forward, swung us round and then smashed down on top of us. As fast as we could bale, the boat filled up, and on the point of being swamped we all leapt out. In waist-high water we struggled vainly to pull the boat onto the beach as the soldiers looked on, their rifles still at the ready. When it was clear that we could not beach it alone two recruits were ordered into the surf to assist us. Together we heaved it clear of the sea.

Wiping the water from my face I dug in my waterproof valuables box for my passport and presented it to the sergeant in charge of the squad. Dripping from head to toe, shirtless and shoeless, I was aware that I did not cut a very authoritative figure, but I did my best to give the impression that I had come to Costa Rica by an unfortunate oversight, which I would be glad to rectify immediately, and that if the sergeant didn't mind I'd be off now, back where I came from.

The sergeant wasn't malleable. He was not going to release two passportless Nicaraguans and an English journalist trying to sneak past Costa Rican border controls in an open boat just because they promised to go back to

Nicaragua. As he studied the stamps in my passport I explained what we had been trying to do. As he plodded through the sand to the radio set in his hut I explained about Greytown and the storm. The sergeant was impervious, and the message to headquarters that I overheard him transmit made it clear that I was not to be allowed to see Greytown that afternoon, at any rate.

"Three suspicious elements, foreign, departed Nicaragua, detained in vessel evading control post. Over."

We were under arrest. The lieutenant in command of the Civil Guard post at the Colorado Bar would be coming up in the patrol boat to interrogate us. No one was to move. The interrogation was straightforward and polite and its outcome was clear from the moment the lieutenant arrived. I explained that I was a British journalist travelling from Belize to Panama in order to write a book on the coast and that I had hired Pedro and Antonio to carry me to San Juan del Norte and to leave me in Colorado. We had got lost, and here we were.

The young lieutenant lamented that whether or not he believed this story was immaterial; whatever our purpose or intentions had been, our arrival in the country was thoroughly irregular and warranted further investigation. In the meantime, we were to accompany him to his command post in Colorado, where we would be held pending a decision by higher authorities.

Compared with the fates that we had only narrowly escaped that morning—perishing in a storm and being shot out of the water—this sounded entirely acceptable. We heaved our boat on tree-trunk rollers back from the beach across a spit of sand to a tongue of placid lagoon and, with a soldier on board to keep an eye on us, set off in the patrol boat's wake down the lagoon to Colorado.

Imprisonment by the Costa Rican Civil Guard was akin to being detained by the Muppets. Antonio, Pedro and I were sat at the communal dining table and then fed on stewed beans and crackers while curious squaddies lounged in the doorway staring at us. When I wondered aloud what sort of a place Colorado Bar was, one of the soldiers volunteered to show me around. I was glad to escape Pedro and Antonio's enforced company for a while, to take a break from the argument about whose fault this all was.

Reasonably confident that as soon as I had a chance to explain myself to someone in authority I would be allowed to go on my way, all I could do in the meantime was to lambast Pedro and Antonio for having failed to find the San Juan Bar, for being useless seamen and for having screwed up my chances of finding Greytown with their greed and dishonesty. The way they saw things they were being held incommunicado by a foreign army for illegal entry into an enemy country without the proper papers, facing a jail sentence and confiscation of their boat, merely because they had allowed me to talk them into this ridiculous journey.

My guided tour of Colorado did not take long. Under a low grey sky a collection of decaying wooden cottages squatted in a swamp. By a crumbling tarmac airstrip stood one of the three hotels, done out in tropical-rustic, catering to American sport fishermen who came to hunt the snook and the tarpon. At this time of year they were all empty; through the mosquito screen windows the stuffed prize fish on the walls gathered dust while caretakers outside lethargically swung their machetes, keeping the jungle at bay on behalf of next season's visitors.

The lieutenant, meanwhile, had reported his catch by radio to his superiors in the capital and was awaiting instructions. He did not think they would come soon. Our unexpected appearance, he predicted, would create all sorts of problems in San Jose.

"They've never had to deal with anything like this before: all we're really up here for is to patrol the beach and look after the turtles' nests," he confided to me. While guerrilla wars raged all around them, Costa Rica's Civil Guardsmen were taking care of turtles' eggs. With such a sense of priorities, I thought to myself as I dialled a British diplomat friend in San Jose the next morning, no wonder the lieutenant had not only let me telephone my embassy but also lent me the money for the call.

In the end it took two days of sitting around the kitchen watching the rain fall and exchanging increasingly confusing radio messages with headquarters before the lieutenant came in to tell us that the commander in chief of the Civil Guard himself was flying out to Colorado to take personal charge of our case.

Costa Rica disbanded its army in 1948, and successive governments have been careful not to dose the few thousand guardsmen they maintain too heavily with military values or to allow them the degree of power that has poisoned other Central American armies. But the news that *el gran jefe* was on his way up galvanised the platoon into a panic of boot polishing, pot scrubbing and floor sweeping, while Pedro, Antonio and I were assigned to picking up litter in front of the barrack hut and raking the mudflat behind it.

The commissioner's investigation scarcely stretched his powers of deduction. While we three skulked in the kitchen he heard the lieutenant's version of events, and then he came in, shook our hands and heard my version of events. It did not take long, and he did not appear to doubt my word. When I had finished he launched into a headmasterly lecture. We had been extremely irrespon-sible for having undertaken our journey in such a delicate border zone without making detailed preparations. Our foolishness had caused a good deal of trouble. Even if we had arrived in Colorado with passports entitling us to cross international frontiers, even if the two Nicaraguans had been issued with the necessary visas, our entry into Costa Rica would have been invalid, unauthorised and illegal because there was no immigration post here. We stood in direct contravention of all the regulations.

He paused. I held my breath. Costa Ricans are not keen on contravention of the regulations, and the commission-er's little sermon was beginning to sound alarmingly like the preamble to an expulsion order. He continued.

"The British embassy, however, has vouched for your probity and I am satisfied that this episode is no more sinister than a series of foolish and unfortunate errors," he ruled, magnanimity plastered all over his face. "You will be taken to Limon in my aeroplane to comply with im-migration formalities and then brought back here. The two Nicaraguans without passports must return home imme-diately. You will be free to proceed as you see fit."

No longer prisoners but not yet legitimate visitors we were escorted by unarmed guard aboard the Cessna, flown down the coast and delivered by jeep to the Limon im-migration office. There I was duly admitted to the country, Pedro and Antonio eagerly filled out exit forms even be-fore their entry papers had been stamped, and we were returned to Colorado for a grateful handshake with the commissioner, who stayed just long enough to watch the Nicaraguans cross the river bar and turn north towards Bluefields.

I was by no means sorry to see them go, but their departure left me stranded a long way from San Juan del Norte with no apparent way of ever reaching it. The lieutenant, though, offered me one last chance. If I paid for the petrol, he would lend me a launch and two of his men to take me up the Colorado River to the point where it met the San Juan. There, on the opposite bank, was the Sandinistas' regional command post at a point known as Delta. If I could make my way across the river, he suggested, perhaps the Nicaraguans might be able to take me downstream to Greytown.

How I would then get back into Costa Rica was a problem that could be dealt with later. It seemed churlish to turn down such a gesture of goodwill, especially as he clearly felt guilty of having cut short my first attempt. The next morning I set off upriver in a tinny little snub-nosed dinghy.

It turned out to be a miserable and fruitless journey, which I spent hunched inside a US army poncho, cowering from incessant rain, as we puttered weakly up the wide, flat, muddy river between dripping forest and soaking cattle pasture to arrive at the juncture with the San Juan River and a bleak, impossible prospect.

Through the driving rain, three hundred yards away across the river, a steep and impenetrably wooded bank rose to a cluster of huts that my guides told me was the Sandinistas' border outpost. Attracting their attention, let alone explaining what I was about, was clearly out of the question. I could pole my way across the river, the guardsmen suggested, in a long, heavy dugout tied up by the Costa Rican outpost. I studied the speed of the rain-swollen current, weighed my skills as a canoe-poler and discarded that idea quickly, before my brain could focus on the image of me being swept downstream and then hurled into some nameless swamp.

I walked down to the water's edge, cupped my hands and bellowed into the wind. But I did not shout with any hope of being heard. I was bawling with frustration, to have been tempted so far by Greytown's mystery and to see it slip through my fingers. I was also cold and wet. We turned back.

"In Limon, people have a very merry, happy way to move along." The old man sitting on the church steps in the afternoon sun spoke with a Jamaican lilt, and the faded black-and-white photographs in his barbershop across the street were of Jamaican heroes, cricketers and trade union leaders— an austere gallery of witnesses to the days of a wider West Indian reach.

Limon is now the port that Greytown once aspired to be, a knot that ties the mainland to the nearby Caribbean islands in a way that no other town on the coast comes close to achieving. Many of its people are black and speak English, many draw their cultural identity from memories and myths of Barbados or Jamaica, but none of them doubt that they are Costa Ricans with a government in the capital, San Jose.

In Belize and Guatemala, through Honduras and Nicaragua, the coast is neither Central America nor the Caribbean. On some maps the coastline is off at the right-hand edge. On others it is shown at the bottom left-hand corner. Whenever it appears, the coast is always on the margin, never the centre of attention, stranded by history and geography between two worlds. In that limbo it has developed all manner of mutant life forms, an anthropological Galapagos where the patterns that shaped the islands to the east or the countries to the west do not mean anything.

But in Limon the coast becomes *both* the Caribbean *and* Central America, a mixture that thrives, rising above all the faded dreams and failed adventures of the past to blossom into a creative confusion of interwoven histories and promises, a town that denies no one, speaking Kingston creole and Costa Rican Spanish with the same facility and turning its eyes east and west with equal ease.

Limon is a nexus, a major port looking out to sea and to the world, and at the same time a railhead, linked inland by train to San Jose, a town born of that marriage and peopled by its children. English and Spanish, reggae and salsa, cricket and baseball, black and mestizo, land and sea, the two poles of the magnet that so often on the coast repel, in Limon have been reversed and persuaded to attract. Here, at last, the coast realizes itself.

EPILOGUE

From Limon I hurried down the coast to Panama, seeking a boat in the banana port of Almirante that would carry me as far as Colon at the mouth of the Panama Canal—the point I had fixed with an arbitrary stab at the map as my final destination.

I never made it, and I never found out why not. At the docks in Almirante, tucked between the massive bulk of container ships longer than city blocks and higher than houses, I had found a modest coastal steamer bound for Colon but awaiting the arrival of its cargo in a ship from Hamburg. She would be leaving in three or four days, the captain told me. If I came back then he would be happy to take me.

I was already long overdue at home; another week or so's delay would make little difference. But I wanted to let my wife know that I would not be back in Managua for a while, and Almirante was nothing but a baked expanse of railway shunting yards narrowing down to the dockyard gates. It offered nowhere to stay, nor any telephone from which to make an international call.

Back up the railway tracks lay Changuinola, a flyblown clump of breezeblock huts thrown up carelessly by men who had expected to one day build their families something better and who now lay drunk in the dust outside the bars, resigned to living out their days in temporary shelter.

But Changuinola boasted a hotel, a long, low prefabricated building without a name and without any guests, and on the cheap office desk that was the bare-walled lobby's only furniture sat a telephone. I signed in, paid for one night, left my rucksack in a room that had apparently never been used, and returned to the desk to make my call to Nicaragua. The man behind the desk dialled it for me, through the operator, without demur. No one answered in Managua, and I went to have supper, intending to ring again later.

When I came back an hour later a different man was on duty, leaning back with his feet on the desk and picking his nose as he read a *foto-novela*. He looked up briefly as I pushed open the plate-glass front door and went back to his reading even before I could ask him for my room key. Instead, I asked him if I could call Managua again. No, he told me. It was not possible to telephone Nicaragua from Changuinola. He must be mistaken, I thought. I had made a call earlier that evening and it had gone through. It was only possible from the telephone company office, which was closed now, he explained. Again I insisted that I had called earlier from this very phone in front of us, and without any problems. I would simply like to do it again. No, he said bluntly, "*no es posible*." He stared at me complacently and pushed my key across the desk. The conversation was over.

Very rarely have I ever lost my temper. For three months

on this journey I had put up with all manner of difficulties and unhelpfulness and been able to shrug it off for most of the time. But that simple push of a key unchained every frustration I had curbed since Belize, and I was swept up in a wave of fury. Uncontrollably I screamed a torrent of foul-mouthed abuse at the desk clerk. I ran out of Spanish obscenities and broke into English. I thought of an especially disgusting and insulting slur on his mother and fell back into Spanish to make sure he understood it. Alone in the empty hotel I hammered on the desk with my fist and ranted while the concierge simply gaped at me in disbelief. My outburst cannot have lasted very long, and I felt very foolish when it was spent. The man behind the desk was seething. I snatched up my key and stamped off to my room. He did not move.

I was still shaking with rage fifteen minutes later when a fist beat on my door and the police announced themselves. A middle-aged man in plain clothes with a pistol in his belt pushed past me into my room, snapped an ID card in my face and demanded to see my passport. I produced it for him and asked why he wanted to see it. He said nothing as he flicked through its pages, looked up and nodded towards the door. "You're coming with me."

"What for?" I asked. "What's this about?"

"It's nothing, don't worry," the policeman said, grabbing me sharply by the shoulder and pushing me into the corridor. "Outside."

By the front door the concierge was shifting from foot to foot with excitement as I walked past him. On his face was a triumphant sneer. It was he who had turned me in, obviously, but what for? Was I being held on suspicion for wanting to telephone Sandinista Nicaragua? Had he invented some allegation against me? Or was he simply an informer who had asked the police to do him a favour and arrest me in order to give him his revenge?

Outside in the darkness I was hustled into a military Jeep, jammed between the driver and the man who had arrested me, who was now cradling an Uzi submachine gun, caressing its stubby barrel in a peculiarly revolting manner. As we careered down the town's dirt roads trailing plumes of dust, our headlights blazing, I recalled stories of interrogation at the hands of General Manuel Noriega's Panama Defence Force, and tried to forget them. We pulled up at a pair of gates in a tall wire fence topped with coils of knifelike steel, and even before they had been fully opened the Jeep charged through into the barracks compound. I clambered out and was led at a fast march around the back of the building, across a courtyard, through a door marked *"Inteligencia"* and into a small, dimly lit office where a tall black man in military uniform was sitting behind a desk strumming a guitar. This, I gathered, was the chief of intelligence for Changuinola's batallion of the Defence Force, the expert in interrogation.

I asked him what I was doing there, and he replied with precisely the same question. I explained, as I had explained so many hundreds of times before, that I was travelling the coast from Belize to Panama in order to write a book about my journey. My interrogator looked bored and didn't even glance in my direction as he asked the plain-clothes officer if I had been brought in with my belongings. When he heard that my rucksack and bag were still at the hotel he ordered them brought to him, and ordered me taken out into the corridor while he waited.

Twenty minutes later a recruit appeared lugging my rucksack, and the man who had first arrested me followed with my shoulderbag. After five more minutes I was summoned back into the office to find the intelligence chief thumbing through one of my notebooks. He looked up as I came in, a forbidding glare on his face. What had he found, I wondered. Accounts of my interviews with Sandinista officials? Notes from the time I had spent with the contras? The story of how I had been detained by the Costa Rican border guards? My notebooks were full of suspicious material. How could I ever explain it to an interrogator? I held my breath.

"So you say you are writing a book," he sneered, almost gagging on his disbelief. "Tell me one thing. What's its title?"

Was this a trick question? Had this man been on a US Army intelligence training course that had taught him peculiarly cunning opening gambits for questioning suspects? It seemed a harmless enough enquiry. Why not tell the truth?

"I haven't thought of a title yet," I said breezily. "I probably won't choose one until I've finished writing the book."

"Take him away."

Clearly honesty had not been the best policy. As I was marched back down the corridor I reflected that probably as far as the intelligence officer was concerned a book could not be a book without a title, ergo if I could not provide a title when one was asked for I could not be writing a book.

On the other hand if I was not writing a book he did not seem terribly anxious to find out what I really was doing. I was deposited on a bench at the end of a short corridor, under the gaze of the duty sergeant who sat at the barracks entrance, and left there. When I stood up to stretch my legs the sergeant shouted at me to sit down.

PETER FORD

When I opened my mouth to ask him if he knew why I was being held here he shouted at me to shut up. I was not even allowed to lie on the bench to get some sleep, which I tried to do at about two o'clock in the morning when it became clear that no one had any idea what to do with me.

All night I sat on my bench beside a stem of bananas that someone had left there for safekeeping. I counted the number of hands on the stem. I counted the number of bananas on each hand. I counted the blotchy brown blemishes on each banana. For as long as I could I filled my mind with anything that would keep me from speculating on my future at the hands of the Panama Defence Force.

Since no one would talk to me, I could do nothing but wait for the commanding officer's arrival in the morning in the hope that he might at least give me a chance to explain myself again. Meanwhile every soldier who came into the barracks gazed at me as if I was an animal in a zoo. When a fat, middle-aged man with a bloated face and eyes more used to hiding behind mirrored shades peered down the corridor at me, I simply stared back at him. Only when he was about to withdraw did I notice the number of brass bars on his uniform epaulettes and recover myself enough to jump to my feet. This was the colonel.

Before I could even open my mouth he barked at me. "What the fuck are you doing here?"

"With all due respect, Colonel, I have no idea. I've been trying to find out for the past twelve hours."

He snorted and turned away without a word. I went back to my bench.

An hour later a lieutenant I had not seen before beckoned to me from the end of the corridor. He was carrying my belongings, which he handed to me as I approached. "Am I free to go now?" I asked him.

"You are free to go to the airport," he replied. "And from there you go to Panama City. Understood? And you don't come back to Changuinola."

I asked him why not, and he merely scowled as he pushed me into the same Jeep as had brought me to the barracks the night before. He obviously didn't know.

At the municipal airport the lieutenant escorted me to the check-in desk, watched as I bought a ticket to Panama City, and then went back outside to sit in his jeep until I had definitely left. As the plane banked over the carpark, I could see him looking up at us. He wanted to be in no doubt.

I arrived in Panama City just in time to catch a flight home to Managua. I took it.

BIBLIOGRAPHY

This is a list of books and documents that I found most helpful while doing the research for this book.

CIDCA (Centro de Investigacion y Documentacion de la Costa Atlantica). *Demográfia Costeña.* Managua, 1982.

Coelho, Roy. *Los Caribes Negros de Honduras.* Tegucigalpa: Editorial Guaymuras.

Conzemius, Edward. "Ethnographical Notes on the Black Carib." *American Anthropologist.*

Dampier, William. *A New Voyage Round the World.* London: James Knapton, 1697.

Davidson, William V. *Historical Geography of the Bay Islands, Honduras.* Southern University Press, 1979.

Dawson, Frank Griffith. *Gregor MacGregor.* London: The Banker, 1982.

Dawson, Frank Griffith. William Pitt's Settlement at Black River on the Mosquito Shore. *The Hispanic-American Historical Review.*

Dobson, Narda. *A History of Belize.* London: Longman Caribbean, 1973.

Dozier, Craig. *Nicaragua's Mosquito Shore: The Years of British and American Presence.* Tuscaloosa: The University of Alabama Press, 1985.

Esquemeling, Alexandre Olivier. *The Bucaniers of America.*

Baltimore: Penguin Books, 1969. (First edition published by Jan ten Hoorn, 1678.)

Floyd, Troy S. *The Anglo-Spanish Struggle for Mosquitia.* Albuquerque: University of New Mexico Press, 1967.

Foster, Byron. *Heart Drum: Spirit Possession in the Garifuna Communities of Belize* Belize: Cubola Productions, 1986.

Foster, Byron. *The Baymens' Legacy.* Belize: Cubola Productions, 1987.

Gonzalez, Nancie L. *Sojourners of the Caribbean.* Champaign: University of Illinois Press, 1988.

Helms, Mary W. "Of Kings and Contexts: Ethnohistorical Interpretations of Miskito Political Structure and Function." *American Ethnologist 13.*

Helms, Mary W. *Asang: Adaptations to Culture Contact on the Miskito Coast.* University of Florida Press, 1971.

Henderson, George. *An Account of the British Settlement of Honduras.* London: C. and R. Baldwin, 1809.

Holm, John. "The Creole English of the Nicaraguan Miskito Coast." Doctoral thesis, University of London, 1978.

Holm, John. "We Want Britain Back." *The Sunday Times.*

Long, Edward. *The History of Jamaica.* London: 1774.

M. W. (anonymous). *The Mosqueto Indian and his Golden River.* London: , 1699.

Manuel, Anne, ed. "The Sumus in Nicaragua and Honduras." *Americas Watch* (1987).

Newsom, Linda A. *Indian Survival in Colonial Nicaragua.* Norman: University of Oklahoma Press, 1987.

Nietschmann, Bernard. *Caribbean Edge.* Indianapolis: Bobbs-Merrill, 1979.

Olien, Michael D. "E. G. Squier and the Miskito: Anthropological Scholarship and Political Propaganda." *Ethnohistory* 32:2.

Olien, Michael D. "The Miskito Kings and the Line of Succession." *Journal of Anthropological Research* (1983)39:2.

Palmer, Paula. *What Happen*. San Jose: Rica: Ecodesarrollos, 1977.

Roberts, Orlando W. *Narrative of Excursions and Voyages on the East Coast and in the Interior of Central America*. University of Florida Press, 1965. (First edition published by Constable and Company, 1827.)

Strangeways, Thomas. *Sketch of the Mosquito Shore, Including the Territory of Poyais*. Edinburgh: William Blackwood, 1822.

Young, Thomas. *Narrative of a Residence on the Mosquito Shore*. London: Smith Elder and Co., 1842.

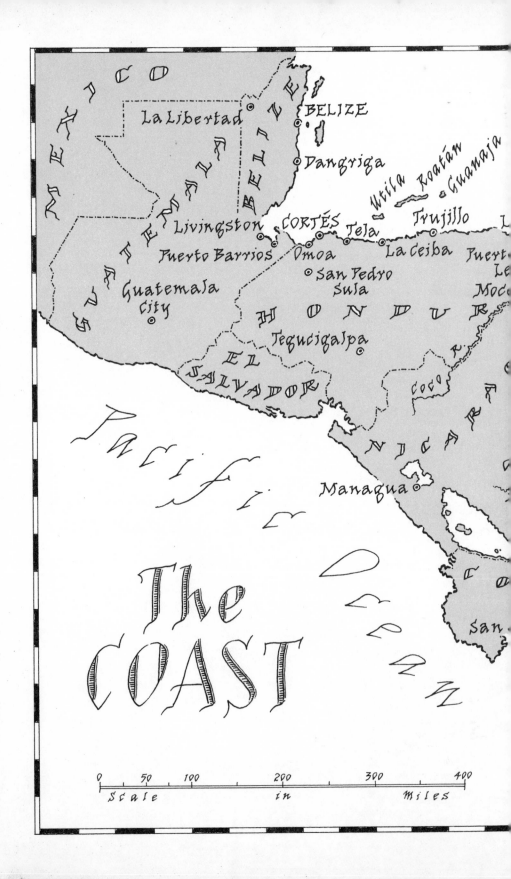